THE

MAITLANDS

OF

LAUDERDALE

A

Border

Family

that

Made

History

Rognvald A. Livingstone

Rognvald A. Livingstone

British Library Cataloguing in Publication Data

A catalogue record of this book is available in the British Library

All rights reserved.

ISBN: 978-0-9570931-2-6

ISBN-13-978-0-9570931-2-6

For

Rognvald Maitland Livingstone, son of the author.
Published on the occasion of his 80TH birthday
27th January 2015

In memory of:
Rognvald A. Livingstone
Anne Maitland Livingstone

Those of the Maitland Clan who have passed this way
before us

Rognvald A. Livingstone

The Maitland Motto:

Consilio Et Animis
By wisdom and courage

CONTENTS

Rognvald A. Livingstone

ACKNOWLEDGMENTS AND THANKS

Earl of Lauderdale, Ian Maitland

Editors:
Rognvald Maitland Livingstone
Frank Maitland
Rona Livingstone
Livingstone Family

Published and Typeset by:
Livingstone Media Limited

Additional Research:
Rona Livingstone
Earl of Lauderdale, Ian Maitland

Original manuscript typed and converted to digital
by Danielle Millar, Priority PA

Rognvald A. Livingstone

EDITORS NOTE:

This book is published exactly as Rognvald A.Livingstone proposed with the manuscript copy, typed and hand written, passing to his son R. Maitland Livingstone. This first edition is based on research and texts available at the time of writing (1960s and early 1970s).

A few minor additions to the text have been added where there has been an obvious omission or the text was unable to be deciphered from the original handwritten section. Otherwise we have remained true to the text and for this first edition have not re-edited the work, apart from updating in Chapter 31 the lineage of the Clan Chiefs. Consequently the reference to "the present day " in this edition refers to the early 1970s.

Since the time of writing and with the advent of the internet, research in this field has become much more accessible and a historical update particularly for Chapter 1 is proposed for future editions. However, in preparing to publish this first edition, specifically in memory of Rognvald A. Livingstone and to mark R. Maitland Livingstone's 80th Birthday in January 2015, we have made the deliberate editorial decision to publish the manuscript for the first time in 2015 as if it had been published in 1972. Distribution of this first edition is limited to the immediate family of R. Maitland Livingstone.

An updated second edition, reflecting current research/knowledge, will be published and released for wider circulation.

LIVINGSTONE FAMILY
JAN 2015

Rognvald A. Livingstone

THE

MAITLANDS

OF

LAUDERDALE

Rognvald A. Livingstone

1. FOREBEARS STOUT AND STOIC

Once upon a time …

> "William, sone to King Elfinus and brother to King Achaius,
> in pursuance of the league between his brother Achaius and
> Carclus Magnus, the Empror, went abroad with an armie of
> four thousand Scots to assist the Empror in his warres. He
> had a daughter, Trustwola, who married Charles, sone to the
> Vocompos, ane of the Urquart's progenitors,, whose mother,
> Advilena, was borne in Italy and was daughter of William
> Dowglas (decended of Sholto, that is his grandechidle) who
> went in companie of William, Achiaus, his brother, to these
> warres. Gilomachus, another sone to King Elfinus and brother
> to King Achaius, went abroad to the same warre and for his
> good service to Charles the Great he advanced him to the
> marriage of the Earl of Mediolanus (Milan) his daughter, of
> whom is descended a gentlemen, Robert Mediolanus, who in
> time of King Kenneth II (971 – 995) came to Scotland and
> married heer, being called Robert Mediolan. He was the
> progeneitor of all the Maitlands in Scotland."

Once upon a time – the beginning of every fairy story, of

1

every folk tale, of every legend, and the beginning of the story of the Maitlands, as set out in the Maitland Club Collection, which we have quoted.

In those times of old, the bards and harpers could repeat the whole list of the ancestors of their chiefs and kings, a list they had learned by rote from their fathers before them. When the chroniclers came to write their "histories" on parchment, it is not surprising that they contained a great deal of legend. For, after the fashion of old, far-off things, the real origins of noble and ancient families are shrouded in the musts of time, a splendid cloud screen behind which fancy may roam.

The courtly chroniclers who fashioned the pedigrees of their Lords and Kings vied with each other in their researches into the mists and did not hesitate to produce family trees reaching to heaven itself — or, at least to Valhalla. The Saxon Kings of Wessex, East Anglia, Kent, Essex, Sussed and Northumbria were all given decent from the Marriage of Wodin and Friga (Odin and Freya) by several sons of the divine pair. It is in the spirit of genealogies which stem form Rome, Athens and Troy – if not from the abode of the gods – that the ancestor "of all the Maitlands" was the grandson of a King Elfinus, who married the Earl of Milan with the blessing of Charlemagne, Emperor of the Franks.

No wonder that John Pelham Maitland, that expert in genealogical research, held such fable to be without foundation. Even so, the fact that such a story was thought up and written down my medieval chronicler gives the Maitlands a true claim to ancient ancestry, for it enables us to stand alongside the Celtic Chiefs and Saxon Kings for whom the chroniclers strove to contrive origins in Troy and Valhalla. A man is known by the company he keeps.

Mr John Pelham Maitland, a few years before his death in 1964, was kind enough to give the author the benefit of his research into the name of Maitland and it is some tribute to the memory of such an authority to give his remarks just as he wrote them:

> "Various ingenious, but more or less fanciful, etymologies have been put forward from time to time, none of which will stand up to serious historical critique, Reaney, in his 'Dictionary of English Names,' 1958, asserts that Maitland was originally a nickname and with this I am in accord. He translates the original form (so far as it is known) as a 'person with discourteous manners' but I would rather favour 'a provider of bad advice', to some degree comparable with the French 'Mauconseil' and the Italian 'Malatesta'.

> "Reaney also cites some evidence for the use of 'de' before the name, which would tend to indicate a place-name. but upon investigations it is found that the only locality quoted, 'Mautalant', near Pontorson, Departmente Nanche, Normandy, cannot be traced, and the other citations in favour of this presumption are far from conclusive as they stand. Until further and much more substantial evidence is forthcoming in its favour, the origin of the name as a place-name may therefore confidently be rejected.

> "One thing is certain, the name is definitely of Norman-French origin, and thus fits the ancient tradition, which, however, I have been unable to confirm from any other source, that the Maitlands came to England in the time of Henry II from the borders of Anjou and Maine. We may even possess

that rare distinction of being descended from contemporaries of such legendary figures as Cinderella or Puss-in Boots!"

Pelham Maitland's favour for "provider of bad advice" rather tends in the direction of the derivation given in "Family Names and their Story," where S. Baring-Gould says that the name of Maitland is derived from Mautalent, meaning "little-wit." This is a somewhat searing thought. It suggests that the Maitlands are descended from some wantwit who came North with William the Conqueror.

Harrison, in his "Surnames of the United Kingdom," plumps for a Scottish-English derivation meaning meadow land, from the Old English moed-land, which more directly means wormy-land, for throughout the centuries the Maitlands have always had a good eye for profitable agricultural land! If, we Pelham Maitland, we reject a place-name origin and with it the writing of the medieval "land" as "land", so abandoning the attractive simplicity of some for of "midland", the origin of the name remains an open question and we can indulge our fancies.

The Aberdeenshire pronunciation of Maitland is "Netlen," with the "e" given the characteristic long drawl in both syllables, so the first "e" is not "ai" and the second is not "a." This Maitland has a distinctly Flemish sound: and Fleming (In Aberdeenshire pronounced Fleemen) is a well recognised Scottish surname.

In some genealogical notes left by Mr Andrew Coventry Maitland-Makgill-Crichton, he writes that, "The local pronunciation is 'Mettlin'." This refers to the way the name is spoken in Lauderdale itself.

This suggests a new line of inquiry. Experts are in the

habit of finding all the old documents and studying the names as spelled by the writers and copyists, but it is more than likely that close argument on each letter used may take them wide of the truth, for the fanciful spellings of medieval – and of even more modern – scribes is notorious. Would it not be better to proceed from the general pronunciation of Mettlin, regarding the written Mautlants and Mautelands, and so on, as an effort by more educated writers to give a more "educated" sound to the name or to Latinise of Frenchify or Anglify the name, according to their individual ideas?

This approach would remove "land" and also "ant" and give us "lin", having the meaning of offspring or quality and Saxon in derivation. This leaves us with "mett" – and more mystery. For, if the origin be Saxon, the most general meaning of the word "met" is to measure or, as an extension of this meaning, to give judgement, to "meet out" sentence. Thus we could have a choice of one who measures out, land, most probably, or of a judge. The greatest objection to this result, on our own premise, is that there is no Scots word which sounds anything like Metlin which still exists and could be called upon as evidence.

We have to go back to John Pelham Maitland's preference for a Norman-French origin, but to his certainty on this point philologists of the Celtic school might retort by staying that there was nothing to prevent an ancient family from stubbornly preserving its Celtic name into the Norman-French period, when the Gaelic sound of Maithelinn could be written down in Norman-French, slightly latinised, as was the way of early medieval charter clerks, who were in most cases monks taught ecclesiastical Latin. Maithelinn unites "maithe", chieftains, rulers, heroes, and "linn", offspring, family. This gives a truly resounding greatness or origin. A family of chiefs and heroes! If only

5

we knew when the Gaelic was last spoken in the Borders!

Well, the whole question remains unresolved and we can either leave it comfortably concealed behind the haar of the Lammermoor Hills, standing in for the mists of antiquity, or have a lot of fun trying to work it out.

It is time to return to the Maitlands of whom we can be sure to a sufficiently reliable degree.

It may be that the first Maitland did "come over with the Conqueror" and that, despite the music-hall type jokes and prejudice of those who believe that the fair Saxon land of England was despoiled and oppressed by the Norman usurpers (having conveniently forgotten that the Saxons in their day were invaders), this family may justly claim that mark of ancient lineage. In the Roll of Battle Abbey there is recorded a Maitland who was a commander in the army of William the Conqueror when it invaded Scotland in Only the bare name is entered on the Roll.

As with many another ancient and noble house, the early family records are no longer available. The historian has to rely on scattered references found in documents which still exist and when these go back to early feudal society, in which the owning of land was all important, these are generally to be found in land charter
s.

The first Maitland whose signature can be traced in Scotland is Thomas de Matulent, who in 1227 witnessed a charter by John de Landelles to the monks of Melrose. It is possible that he may be the same Thomas Mautalent, designated as a Knight, in a charter by Sir Thomas de Alnete to the monks of the same Abbey. There is also mention of Gilbertus de Maltalent as a charter witness about 1215 but there appears to be no traceable connection.

Thomas de Matulent died in 1228.

Evidently he came to the Merse from Northumberland, where the early Maitlands seem to have settled near Alnwick round about the year 1190. At that time, during the reign of Alexander II as King of Scots and of Henry III as King of England, the Border between the two kingdoms had not been defined. In 1222 a commission consisting of six Scottish and six English Knights were empowered to settle the boundary but they could not agree and the matter was dropped.

The whole question of the Border bristled with difficulties. The attempt of the English King, Edward I, to conquer Scotland, the English defeat at Bannockburn and the final recognition of Robert the Bruce as King of Scotland by the English Court were all a century ahead. The idea of Scotland as a kingdom had scarcely begun to exist.

From Danish times the peoples of Northumbria, the Merse and the Lothians had close connections and when the Norman-French invaders spread northwards, the occupied lands without regard to any boundaries. Westminster was not yet a capital city in the modern sense and besides was too far away. Knights in Scotland owned land in Northumbria and those whom we would now call Englishmen owned land north of the Border. Alexander II himself owned lands in Tynedale and in Penrith, Cumberland. And in 1291, when the question of the succession to the Scottish kingdom first became the matter of dispute, both the major claimants, John Baliol and Robert Bruce, had large estates in England as well as in Scotland, It was not only a matter of politics between the two developing kingdoms, however. The Border was in dispute for a long period of history and after the Wars of

Independence, the encroaching ways of the English were a constant source of local warfare. Added, to this, of course, were the raiding activities of the rivers on both sides of the Border.

The next ancestor who can be traced is William Mautalent, who between the years 1220 and 1240 figures as a witness in various charters to the monks of Kelso. He is described as "*servientes abbatis.*" The relationship is not known but a good guess might be that he was a brother or son of the Abbot of Kelso. Some authorities argue that this William Mautalent was the father of the Sir Richard Maitland, the first of the Maitlands to occupy an authentic place in the history of Scotland.

2. AULD MAITLAND

This Sir Richard Maitland, whose life occupied the second half of the thirteenth century, firmly founded the family of Maitland at Thirlestane, in Lauderdale. There was no doubt about the side of the Border on which his loyalties lay. He was a formidable warrior, beholden to no man, and as one of the heroes of the Wars of Independence he occupies an imperishable place in the history of Scotland.

Modern historians have concentrated on William Wallace, Robert the Bruce and the good Lord James of Douglas, but the famous defence of Thirlestane Castle by Sir Richard Maitland against the English and the revenge of his three sons were celebrated in popular poetry during those centuries when the ballad held the place which books and newspapers now occupy.

The wide renown of this heroic Maitland can be measured by the fact that three centuries later, Bishop Gawin Douglas, a poet in the reign of May Queen of Scots, placed "Maitland with his auld beird grey" among popular heroes like Robin Hood and King Arthur, not to mention:

"Great Gowmacmorne, and Fin Mac Cowl, and how
they suld be goddis in Ireland, as they say."

Finn Mac being reputed to be the original Old King Cole.
The ballad of "Auld Maitland" was first printed in Sir
Walter Scott's "Minstrelsy of the Scottish Border."

Sir Walter received a copy from James Hogg, the Ettrick
Shepherd, who assisted him in his collection. Scott writes,
in his introduction to the poem:

> "This ballad ... has been preserved by tradition; and
> is, perhaps, the most authentic instance of a long and
> very old poem exclusively thus preserved. It is only
> known to a few old people upon the sequestered
> banks of the Ettrick; and is published as written
> down from the recitation of the mother of Mr James
> Hogg, who sings, or rather chants it, with great
> animation. She learned the ballad from a blind man,
> who died at the advanced age of ninety, and is said to
> have been possessed of much traditionary
> knowledge."

Mrs Hogg died in 1820. Thanks to her wonderful memory
and the work of Sir Walter Scott, "Auld Maitland" was
rescued from a past which, in Scott's day, was rapidly being
lost with the advance of industrialised society.

The ballad has all the drama of a folk tale. Here is how
it describes the ravaging English invaders being brought to
a halt before the house of Sir Richard Maitland.

> "As they fared up over Lammermore
> They burned both up and down
> Until they came to a darksome house,

Some call it Leader-town.
'Wha hauds this house?' young Edward cried,
'Or wha gi'est over to me?'
A grey-haired Knight set up his heid
And crakit right crousely:
'Of Scotland's King I haud my house,
He pays me meat and fee;
"And I will keep my guid auld house
While my house will keep me.'
They laid their sowies to the wall
Wi' many a heavy peal;
But he threw ower to them again
Baith pitch and tar barrel.
With springalds, stanes, gads o' airn
Amang them fast he threw;
Till mony of the Englishmen
About the wall he slew.
Full fifteen days that braid host lay
Sieging Auld Maitland keen;
Syne they have left him, hale and fier,
Within his strength of stane."

The word "sowies" used in the ballad refers to large rectangular stacks, probably covered with straw and ridged, to provide cover while the troops sapped the castle walls, but doubtless not proof against blazing pitch – especially when followed by the blazing barrel for good measure! As we would say to-day, Auld Maitland "let them have it." Oblong haystacks with ridged tops are still called "sows" in Berwickshire; "soos" in Aberdeenshire.

There is another tradition of how the mother of the Ettrick Shepherd came to know "Auld Maitland" so well, different from the story given by Scott of the convenient blind man of ninety with his traditionary knowledge. Mrs Hogg is reputed to have listened as a lassie with wide-eyed wonder as the poem was recited to her by "auld Babby Matlan", housekeeper to the last of the family of the Scotts of Tushielaw, in Ettrick, who in their time were renowned moss-troopers, reivers and freebooters, but who now as a family as extinct. They were a branch of the famous border family whose present Chief is the Duke of Buccleuch.

"Auld Babby Matlan" is said to have been related to Sir William Maitland of Lethington, Secretary of State to Mary Queen of Scots, but it may have been that she was only a member of his household before she went to keep house at Tushielaw. We have to remember that in the olden days, Lairds and chiefs kept a large body of retainers and followers, who lived in their strongholds and who customarily adopted the surnames of their masters, upon whom they were dependent throughout their lives. Surnames as such were an innovation of the time when the populace gradually broke away from the old allegiances and went to live in towns.

Sir Walter Scott writes: "The date of the ballad cannot be ascertained with any degree of accuracy." And he adds: "The inveterate hatred against the English, founded upon the usurpation of Edward I., glows in every line …" We can say with some accuracy that "Auld Maitland" is amongst the earliest productions of Scottish patriotic literature and the Maitland who first composed it, perhaps to grace a banquet of clansmen in the stone hall of Thirlestane Castle, was the progenitor of those poets and writers of the name of Maitland who have since embellished the pages of Scottish and English literature.

Scott quotes from the pages of the Maitland Manuscripts of consolation to Sir Will Maitland a poem of Lethington, which says (and I have Englished the old Scots wording):

> "Renowned Richard of your race record,
> Who praise and prowess cannot be expressed;
> More lusty lineage never had a Lord,
> For he begat the boldest bairns and best,
> Most manful men, and maidens most modest,
> That ever was since Pyramus on of Troy, …"

In another verse, the poet praises the forebears of Secretary of State Maitland, whose "hardy hearts, haughty and heroic" the "storms withstand with stomack stout and stoic."

Another poem in the Maitland MSS, in praise of the House of Lethington, says:

> "Of old Sir Richard, of that name,
> We have heard sing and say;
> Of his triumphant noble fame,
> And of his old beard grey,
> And of his noble sons three,
> Who that time had not make;
> Who made Scotland renowned be,
> And all England to quake.
>
> Whose loving praises, made truly,
> After that simple time,
> Are sung in many far country,
> Albeit in rural rhyme."

There seems no doubt that the Maitlands of Lauderdale had a heroic and poetical entry into history.

Sir Richard Maitland was married to Avicia, daughter and heiress of Thomas de Thirlestane, round about 1249. He thus inherited by marriage the lands and castle of

13

Thirlestane. This original Thirlestane was some two miles east of the Royal Burgh of Lauder and stood on the Leader Water, which rises in the Lammermuir Hills and flows due southwards to join the Tweed. The valley of the Leader is Lauderdale and the ancient burgh is set in the middle of the dale. It is in the county of Berwick.

All that remains of this ancestral home of the Maitlands is an ancient tower. It was vacated during the 16th century, when the head of the family built the present castle on the site described in Sibbald's MSS as "of old called Fort Lauder."

If the date, 1249, is right, Sir Richard must have been an old man (even allowing for teen-age marriage) when the Wars of Independence began in 1296 and merited the title, Auld Maitland. However old he was, he showed himself a bonnie fighter in the protection of his house.

Sir Richard's wife was also heiress to lands at Abertarff, in the county of Inverness. Research has not revealed so far whether this refers to estates in the burgh itself or to the site on which Abertarff House stands. It remains in excellent condition, one of the oldest 16th century houses in Scotland. It is now under the care of the National Trust for Scotland and let to An Commun Gaidealach as its Northern Headquarters. In any case, Abertarff seems to have disappeared early from the family history.

Sir Richard had three sons, who in the ballad take ample revenge upon King Edward and his nephew (who existence in the poem Scott rightly regards as "a poetical license") for their siege of Thirlestane. The poem dwells thirstily on the combat between the three sons and the English Knights, Piercy, Ethert Lunn and the young Edward. First, the Maitlands took exception to King Edward's standard, which

(Scot explains) showed the arms of Scotland quartered, and the eldest brother took natural action.

> "He stabbed the Knight the standard bore,
> He stabbed him cruellie;
> Then caught the standard by the neuk
> And fast away rode he."

> He clankit Piercy ower the head
> A deep wound and sair,
> Till the best blood of his body
> Came running down his hair."

Then, having "clankit" Ethert Lunn, the eldest Maitland deals with the King's nephew.

> "He pierced him through and through the heart,
> He mauled him cruellie;
> Then hung him ower the draw-bring,
> Beside the other three."

(Both sons and slain are slightly mixed in the ballad between three and four, but we need pay no attention of these arithmetical discrepancies, which detract nothing from the verve and valour of the story.)

The eldest of Auld Maitland's three sons was William and the names of the other two are not known. When William succeeded to Thirlestane, he was the sole surviving son.

All that is known about Sir William is the tradition that he was a staunch supporter of King Robert the Bruce. The date of his death is placed at 1315. He left two sons, the elder, Robert, succeeding to the family lands.

This was a stormy period of Scottish history. King Edward I of England was ruthlessly pursuing his plan to subjugate the whole country, from Cape Wrath to Land's End, to his sole rule. In 1286, Alexander III, King of Scots, died, leaving as his heir his three-year-old grand-daughter, Margaret, the Maid of Norway. For six unhappy years, Scotland was ruled by Guardians until Margaret's father, Eric, King of Norway, sought Edward I's help to secure the Scottish throne for his daughter. Edward agreed immediately, for he intended to seize the Princess on her arrival in Britain and marry her to his son. As fate would have it, Margaret died in Orkney on her way to Scotland.

Unfortunately, Edward I was asked to mediate between the claimants to the throne and he backed John Baliol as the man more amenable to his plans. As soon as Baliol was crowned, he was summoned to London, where he was bluntly told that Edward was Lord Paramount of Scotland, that he must return to Scotland to impose punitive taxes and raise levies of men for Edward's foreign wars and that he must allow a horde of English officials to travel north to act as supervisors of these measures. The Scots reacted with vehemence. They refused to accede to Edward's demands and negotiated a secret treaty with France for mutual aid against their common enemy.

Enraged at this defiance, Edward set out to humble the rebellious Scots. He captured Berwick, then the richest port in Scotland, and leaving a burning town to dispose of the massacred inhabitants, he ravaged his way northwards. At Scone, near Perth, he seized Scotland's Stone of Destiny, on which every King of Scots had to be ceremoniously seated in order to be effectively inaugurated as monarch, and deposed Baliol.

After raiding farther north, he returned to Berwick

Castle and there summoned earls, Lords, Knights, bishops, Laird, chiefs and clergy – 2,000 in all – to appear before him and on bended knees swear fealty and sign the "Ragman's Roll". This inglorious document is preserved in the Public Record Office. Its name is a contemptuous reference to the catalogue of signatures and seals attached; from it the word "rigmarole" derives. The penalty for non-appearance to do homage to Edward I was outlawry and the forfeiture of all lands and property. With the grim thought of what would happen to their families and retainers, the Scots sullenly obeyed – with the private reservation that a signature of oath made under duress were neither legal nor binding.

Amongst those who joined the slow process to Berwick Castle was Robert Maitland of Thirlestane.

There followed unhappy years for Scotland. But the Maitlands were among those who supported the cause of Robert the Bruce and emerged as one of the more powerful and rising families in the new kingdom of Scotland. Although there is no direct evidence of this, the fact that Sir Robert married a sister of Sir Robert Keith, the Earl Marischal of Scotland, who was one of Bruce's most active adherents and busy in all the events, military and diplomatic, of the Wars of Independence, is evidence that he, too, was intimate to the counsels of those who had the task of guiding the destinies of the war-torn nation. By his marriage, Sir Robert acquired the estates of Bolton and Lethington in East Lothian and so began a long family connection with Haddington.

According to available information, Sir Robert had four sons. The social standing and stability of the Maitlands now seemed assured, for two of those sons were the progenitors of the Maitlands of Aberdeenshire and the Maitlands of Dumfriesshire.

From now on the Maitlands were a truly Scottish family. From their estates in Lauderdale and the Lothian, they looked in to the Royal Court and to Edinburgh, developing as the Capital of Scotland, for their future. They were no longer merely a Border family, a content to live across the Tweed and quarrel with neighbouring clans. Auld Maitland had ably defended the "darksome house" of Thirlestane and it was still held by a doughty Maitland, for there seems little chance that Sir Roberts was not among the Knightly cavalry who charged at Bannockburn, in 1314, when the Scots broke Edward I's tyranny in one glorious, triumphant battle.

From now on the Maitlands were to play an important part in the history of Scotland – in diplomacy, in law, in the army, in literature. Any there were to "haud the house" as fiercely and tenaciously as their forebear, "auld Maitland keen."

The death of King Robert in 1329 was a sad misfortune to young Scotland, for his son David was only a child of five when he succeeded to the throne as David II and it was not until the 24th of November, 1331, that he was actually crowned at Scone. It is worth noting that David was the first King of Scots to be anointed. His father had made provision for this to be done by obtaining the Pope's sanction and the grant of the holy oil for the anointing of his heir.

With a child King, Scotland was plunged into internecine warfare, for John Baliol determined to win back the throne for himself. After initial victory, he had himself crowned at Scone. There were now two Kings and the struggle for supremacy intensified. The young King David was sent to France for safety. The renewed warfare, however, clarified one issue: it separated before the eyes of the people those who fought for what we would now call quislingism from those who strove for the freedom of their country. In the words of the famous Declaration of Arbroath of 1320:

> "We fight not for glory nor for wealth, nor honour, but for that freedom which no good man surrenders but with his life."

His support gradually dwindling away, Baliol was chased over the Border. David II hurried home from France to begin rule. His youthful mind was filled with chivalrous notions of winning fame and honour on the field of battle. Disregarding sound advice to be cautious, he insisted on raising an army and, starry-eyed, marched south to invade and conquer England. The result was the disaster of Neville's Cross, near Durham, where the English slaughtered some 15,000 Scots. David was wounded and captured. Among those who fell fighting for their monarch was Sir Robert Maitland of Thirlestane and a younger brother, whose Christian name is not known. The year was 1346.

3. LEADER BRIDGE

The heritage of that Maitland who had, tongue in cheek, pledged his fealty to Edward of England at Berwick and then had been killed at Neville's Cross, fell to his eldest son, John He married Agnes Dunbar, daughter of Sir Patrick Dunbar, who became Earl of Dunbar and March, and whose wife was Black Agnes, the heroine of the famous siege of Dunbar Castle by an English army under the Earl of Salisbury during the Wars of Independence.

The Dunbars were a powerful family, who, like the Maitlands, had originated in Northumberland from Norman-French stock. Patrick Dunbar was a cousin of King Robert the Bruce and had been one of the original claimants to the throne of Scotland, being a descendant of a daughter of William the Lion. The family could not forget their pretensions to the Crown and, like the Baliols, continued both intrigues and open warfare in the feudal manner against the Stewarts.

They were wide landowners and the eighth Earl of Dunbar, Patrick Black Beard, became Earl of March (or

Merse), an indication of the standing of the family in their day. Three centuries later, when John, the second Earl of Lauderdale, was created a Duke, he chose for his second title the Marquis of March, to mark his descent from the Dunbars.

John Maitland died in 1395 and was succeeded by his son Robert, who had won his Knighthood probably in Border fighting but more likely at the Battle of Otterburn in 1388. In this battle during the reign of Robert II, the Earls of Dunbar, Douglas and Moray led the Scots army to victory over the English under Henry Percy and his brother, sons of the Earl of Northumberland. Douglas lost his life, as did the younger Percy, while the older brother, whom the Scots had nicknamed Henry Hotspur, half in scorn and half in admiration of his forward spirit, was taken prisoner. In all likelihood, young Robert Maitland was one of Dunbar's captains. Afterwards, he became governor of Dunbar Castle, which was an important stronghold on the sea road from England to Edinburgh. His wife was Marion Abernethy.

His eldest son was another Robert Maitland. The fate of this young man is unknown. In 1406, King Robert III died and his heir, James, who was to become James I, the poet King, was then only twelve years of age. For safety he was to be sent to France, as was the usual way with kings who were minors, but on the way his ship was captured by English pirates and the young King was handed over to King Henry IV. James was imprisoned for twelve years and was not released until Henry VI sat on the throne as a minor and England was under the protectorship of his uncle the Duke of Gloucester. One of the hostages sent to England for the payment of 30,000 pounds of ransom money for the return of James was young Robert Maitland. He was held first at Knaresborough Castle, Yorkshire, and later at the Tower of London. Whether he died in the Tower or was persuaded to join the French wars of Henry VI against Joan of Arc and died in France will never be known.

His brother, William, came to the succession of Thirlestane and Lethington. Nothing is known of him except that he married a Margaret Wardlaw and that he died around 1471.

His successor was his eldest son, John, who is thought to have married one of the Dundas family. He must have died at a comparatively early age for it was his son and heir, another William, who succeeded his grandfather in possession of the family estates.

This William Maitland, who styled himself "of Lethington", seems to have been a minor on his father's death and at the time of his inheritance, for he had a curator named Duncan de Dundas, who was probably his maternal grandfather. He did not receive sasine of Thirlestane – that is, legal investiture in his estate – until 1477, in the reign of James III.

He married Martha (or Margaret), daughter of George, second Lord Seton, another magnate whose family history was similar to that of the Maitlands and Dundases. The great-grandmother of George Seton was Black Agnes of Dunbar, so that once again the families of Maitland and Dunbar inter-married.

Of the children of William Maitland and Martha Seton, Richard, born in 1496, lived to become heir; Robert, of whom nothing is to be learned, is only a name; and Janet married Hugh, the fifth Lord Somerville.

The Somervilles, also a Norman family, had a more romantic history than any of the Lothian and Border families. A brother of the first Somerville who came to Scotland with David I, after that King, who had been brought up in the English court, succeeded in 1124, was the squire who instituted the Dunmow Flitch – the gift of a flitch of bacon to husbands and wives who had lived together for a year and a day without any quarrel or disagreement.

A grandson of the William de Somerville who came to Scotland with King David won even more fame than Auld Maitland by slaying a monstrous animal who was devastating the countryside round Linton, in Roxburghshire. The tradition is that it was a serpent and as a reward for this exploit, Somerville received the lands of Linton from William the Lion. The family of this Border St George played their part in Scottish history under the Stewarts.

During this period of Maitland history, Lethington was the Chief residence of the family. Perhaps this is characteristic of them, for, as Sir Herbert Maxwell says in "The Story of the Tweed":

> "The Maitlands seem to have been a quiet law-abiding race, for their names do not appear, like those of every other border family, as frequent actors of victims in crimes of violence."

The head of the family was Maitland of Lethington. Although it was certain that the family still retained Thirlestane Castle and land in Lauderdale, there does not seem to have been a close connection with events in the dale.

The burgh of Lauder belonged to the Lauder family, but the head of the Lauders was also a Lothian Laird, being Lauder of Congalton and the Bass. The Bass, that great rocky islet in the Firth of Forth, was then a fortified place and of great importance. The Lauders were best known as Lauders of the bass and were clearly proud of this title.

It seems that the Maitlands and Lauders, unlike other Border clans, lived in peace together in spite of their lands and interests adjoining in the dale of the Leader Water. We find a charter of Sir Robert Lauder, granting lands in "his burgh" of Lauder, being witnessed by John de Mautelant (the husband of Agnes Dunbar) and his brother William.

It was Lauder's grandson, the Bishop of Glasgow, and builder of the steeple of Glasgow Cathedral, who went as an ambassador to the court of England to negotiate the release of James I, together with his brother, Sir Robert of the Bass, known as Robert with the borrowed whinger (sword). It was Elizabeth, the only daughter of Richard Lauder of Halton (Hatton) in Midlothian, whom Charles Maitland, third Earl of Lauderdale, married in 1652.

Scotland in the second half of the 15th century was beginning to be affected by the first signs of that revolutionary movement which we know as the Reformation. In 1474, William Caxton printed his first book. In 1492, Christopher Columbus discovered America. The world was preparing for a great change and feudalism, although it was still to continue for a long time, began to show the first stirrings of coming events.

The Maitlands were to be in the forefront of these events. The Stewart Kings, most of whom were brilliantly intellectual, were capable of recognising the Maitland qualities and in the turbulent times of the Reformation, they had not better statesmen in their service.

King James III, however, was in advance of his times and in his interest in learning and the arts, he foolishly drew around him men chosen from the third estate. As an attempt to emulate the brilliant courts of the Borgias and Medicis, if failed. At that time, amidst the plots and counter-plots of the "bands" or factions of Scottish nobles, men like Cochrane, the architect, and Rogers, the musician, stigmatised by the nobles at court as "the mason and the fiddler", were quite unable to inaugurate a Scottish Renaissance. Scotland was unable to produce a Michelangelo, a Dante and a Monteverdi.

A man like Cochrane was more concerned to build his own fortune that to dower Scotland with fine buildings. He was created Earl of Mar and entered into a band with the Humes, directed against the King's brothers, the Duke of Albany and Earl of Mar. Albany was arrested, but escaped to France. Mar was imprisoned and died in confinement in mysterious circumstances, a usual rather than a strange occurrence in medieval times. Later, Albany turned up in England and once again the old game was played, as it had been by every pretender to the throne of Scotland since the time of John Baliol. Albany agreed to become King of Scotland, with the help and protection of the English King.

In 1482, the Duke of Gloucester, who afterwards became King Richard III, led an army into Scotland, bringing Albany (now King Alexander IV) with him. The Scottish army, under Archibald Douglas, Earl of Angus, was joined by the King and the Cochrane faction.

At Lauder, the Scottish army halted. Angus called a meeting of those who resented and opposed the Cochrane party in the Kirk of Lauder. Faced with battle and with the pretensions of Cochrane, who no doubt saw himself, through his influence with King James, as the commander-in-chief who would place victory in the lap of his sovereign, it was time for the nobles to deal with their upstart rivals.

In all the angry discussion, Lord Gray girned that they were like the mice who could not find a mouse brave enough to bell the cat.

"I will bell the cat, " growled Angus, and was a good as his word.

When Cochrane entered the church, with the intention of asserting his rights in the council of captains, Angus strode up to him and tore the golden chain from his neck.

"A rope would fit you better, " he threatened.

"My Lords, is this mows or ernest?" cried Cochrane, who was a man of courage if of doubtful culture.

"Hard ernest," Angus told him, "And so you will find it."

Cochrane and the rest of his faction were seized and hanged over the parapet of Lauder Bridge. King James was made captive and the army was dispersed, the nobles taking their King back to Edinburgh and imprisoning him.

This affair, known to historians as the Conspiracy of Lauder, is familiar to every Scottish school child. Angus was of course nicknamed "Archibald Bell the Cat" and under that name has all the charisma of a fairy tale character.

It cannot be said that any Maitland took part in these events but as they took place on their doorstep, it would be strange if no member of the family was enrolled in the army of Bell the Cat, who had succeeded the exiled Albany in the important military command of Warden of the East Marches.

Although James III was afterwards liberated by his rebellious nobles, their discontent continued until they rallied a party round France. James, the heir to the throne, and open war broke out between them and James III. They met at Sauchieburn, near Stirling, and James, fleeing from the field, was thrown from his horse and taken to a nearby cottage, where he was murdered.

James IV proved to be a different kind of King, a valiant Knight who could lead his nobles. By his marriage to the youthful Princess Margaret, eldest daughter of King Henry VII of England, in 1503, it was hoped that peace might come between the two countries. But the thistle and the rose could ill agree. With the coming of the hot-blooded and imperious Prince Hal to the throne of England as Henry VIII, the scene was set for ructions. Both kings were quick tempered. Henry was a bully and sadist; James was apt to live in a rosy world of Knight errantry. The two kings were good friends at first, but fiery anger was aroused over various matters – the depredations of the sailor brothers, the Bartons, against English merchant ships, for examples – and it only required an appeal from the King of France – the French Fleet had been destroyed off Brest by the English and the French army defeated at the Battle of the Spurs – for James to prepare to invade England. Chivalry and loyalty to the auld Alliance played their part with the King, but the old Scottish fear of a powerful and aggressive English monarch was the important factor. The Scots feared that Henry, having defeated the French, would seek further aggrandisement by striking north of the Border and they were eager no doubt to clip his wings.

When the Royal Standard was raised at the Borestone, in the boroughmuir of Edinburgh, the flower of the nation's manhood mustered – earls, Lords, bishops, Knights, Lairds, gentlemen-at-arms and their followers, burghers and their apprentices – every youth who could handle a weapon – until the Scottish army reach some 30,000 men.

Readers of Sir Walter Scott will remember the lines from Marmion:

> "Highest and midmost, was descried
> The royal banner floating wide;
> The staff, a pine-tree, strong and straight,
> Pitch'd deeply in a massive stone
> Which still in memory is shown,
> Yet bent beneath the standard's weight
> When'er the western wind unroll'd
> With toil, the huge and cumbrous fold,
> And gave to view the dazzling field,
> Where, in proud Scotland's royal shield
> The ruddy lion ramped in gold."

In brave array (and despite some misgivings from wiser heads), King James's host marched south, crossed the Tweed and in a position of strength awaited the enemy at Flodden Hill, overlooking the River Till.

On the morning of the 9th September, 1513, the Earl of Surrey, "an auld crooked carle" but a cautious and experienced general, advanced his troops from the south-east. Swiftly he crossed the Till and deployed his 32,000 seasoned troops in positions to cut the Scottish army off from Scotland. If – and Flodden is another of the great "ifs" of history – if James had but attacked the English as they forded the river, he could have destroyed them and the whole course of future events might have been changed. But the advantage was missed.

In an effort to recover the initiative, James, who had the impetuous blood of the Stewarts in him in good measure, directed that the tents be fired and undercover of the smoke screen, he raced his men to Branxton Hill, a mile distant, to prevent Surrey from occupying this commanding position. So the two armies came face to face.

In the late afternoon the battle began. The Earls of Huntly and Home charged the English right wing and completely defeated it. On the Scottish right, the clansmen, goaded to fury by the heavy fire of the English archers, charged headlong into the fray and suffered disastrous casualties in the bloody conflict.

The fighting now centred round the main division of the Scottish army, led by the King. As night fell the ring of desperate Scots still fought on in unbroken rank, although already in their midst King James lay dead. A smore of rain covered the tragic field like a weeping of sorrow.

With the dawn, a grim-faced Surrey surveyed the scene of carnage and realised that, although he was nominally the victor, he had suffered such terrible losses that he could only, like the Scots, creep away and lick his wounds. Great pits had to be dug on the battlefield, in which were laid friends and foes together. Flodden Field lies now in a countryside of peaceful pastoral loveliness, hiding beneath the well-tilled ground all vestige of the surge and clash of history. The monument commemorating that September day in 1513 bears the simple tribute: "To the Brave of Both Nations."

Throughout the whole of Scotland there was scare a

family, from the highest to the lowest, that did not mourn a fallen father or son. In the long list of the honoured dead is recorded the name of William Maitland of Lethington.

Maitland relatives who died at Flodden were the third Lord Seton and Sir John Somerville; and three of the Lauder family also were killed.

This contents of long ago seems remote in our modern age and is sometimes dismissed as one of those history book battles. But the defeat at Flodden lingers in the national memory. No Scot can hear the name of Flodden without feeling a pang, not of shame, but of nostalgia for the courage and honour of those brave old days. A generation of proud Scots were lost.

> "I've heard them lilting, as the ewe-milking,
> Lasses a' lilting, before dawn o' day;
> But now they are moaning on ilka green loaning,
> The flowers of the forest are a' wede away."

4. THE BLIND POET

To the lady of Lethington the disastrous news of Flodden was brought by the fleeing remnants of the Scottish army that had so bravely marched out from the boroughmuir of Edinburgh. It was hard to believe, but when her own people confirmed the news that Sir Williams was dead, she bowed her head both in pride and in sadness, realising that she was now a widow along with thousands of others, from the Queen herself downwards. Her eldest son, Richard, heir to his father's estates, was a mere stripling.

In Scottish history and in the national sentiment, the defeat by the English at Flodden has been a focus for a great deal of discussion and nationalist feeling. But there were defeats before Flodden which were as overwhelming for Scottish arms – Halidon Hill, Neville's Cross and Homildon Hill – and there was another to come, at Pinkie, in the reign of Queen Mary. Although there may be indecision about which side really won a victory in that battle, the loss of life in the Scottish army was very great. Yet the Battle of Flodden remains a unique event in history, like the Battle Bannockburn.

Undoubtedly the reason for this is that, beneath the patriotism and stirrings of warlike glory, Bannockburn and Flodden marked the beginning and the end of the feudal period in Scottish history. In 1517, four years after Flodden, Martin Luther nailed his 95 Articles on the church door at Wittenberg and in doing so set a flame to medieval Europe. Nowhere in the world were the new ideas about religion and politics more eagerly received than in Scotland and within half a century, Presbyterianism became the law of the land.

It was of this new century of turmoil and revolutionary change that Flodden was the herald. At the same time, it rang down the curtain on the old chivalrous order. The King had died on that fatal slope by the river Till and his nobility had died with him. William Maitland of Lethington, a man of great courage and resolution, who had stood close to the King in life, stood close to him in death and died defending his sovereign's body in the last desperate stand that would not admit defeat.

Life had to go on and with a new King on the throne of Scotland, new men filled palace and Parliament hall and occupied their father's places at home. A month after Flodden, William's son was served heir to Lethington. He was a man moulded for the new times in which he lived. His ancestors had served the Stewarts with their swords. He served James V and Queen Mary with his intelligence and ability in affairs and lived to die at the age of ninety, not many months before his Queen was beheaded at Fotheringay.

He was a man whom some historians may describe as "a man of the renaissance." After a bury life at court, he became blind in 1560, the year in which the Confession of

Faith of John Knox was approved by the Estates of Parliament. He then became a poet, one of the last of the "markaris", as Professor Millar calls him in his Literary History. More, he showed himself to be a true man of his age, who, though he might regret the past in his poetry, was wise enough to hope to preserve that past. Not only did he leave a collection of poetry by Scottish poets, but also a history of the House of Seton, his wife's family, and the decisions of the Court of Session for a period of 15 years.

Born in 1496, in the reign of King James IV, Richard was seventeen when he succeeded his father. A student at St Andrews University, he completed his education in France studying law. On his return to Scotland, he found favour with King James V and was employed in various public commissions in the service of the King, who died at Falkland Palace in 1542, then in the service of the Regent Arran and when the infant Mary Queen of Scots was sent to France for safety after the battle of Pinkie in 1547, of the Queen Mother, Mary of Guise.

In March, 1551, he took his seat as an Extraordinary Lord of Session and soon after was Knighted. The Court of Session, founded in 1532, was a new arena in which the factious heads of families and landowners could settle their disputes by arguments before a judge concerned with the law instead of by the sword. It was to be a long time before the sword was to be laid aside for the deponement but in his day even the turbulent Border factions respected Maitland's judgement and trusted him.

At this time the Reformation was sweeping Scotland but the hot passions it aroused did not appear to have affected him to an extreme, although he was a Protestant. In October, 1560, before the return of Mary Queen of Scots from France, a great misfortune overtook him in that he lost his eyesight. This was a severe privation to a man of his character and tastes but he bore the affliction with cheerfulness and did not allow it to interfere with the way in which he carried out his public duties. About a year after he became blind, he was admitted an ordinary Lord of Session and took the title of Lord Lethington. He was appointed privy councillor and then Lord Privy Seal.

The political storms of the day perturbed his little and amidst the seething jealousies and tangled intrigues of State and Kirk, Lord Lethington, "ane worthy Knight, baith valiant, grave and wise," remained a faithful and steadfast councillor to the young Queen, insistent always that she must see that her laws were kept, otherwise she would find no obedience from her lieges.

Much of his time was of necessity spent in Edinburgh or where-ever the court might be but whenever possible he escaped to his favourite home at Lethington and there he found peace in his well-loved garden and in his literary work, in the collecting and transcribing of ancient Scottish poems. In 1567, he resigned the office of Lord Privy Seal in favour of his second son, John, Prior of Coldingham.

It was a stormy time in Scottish history. That same year the Queen abdicated and in 1570 the Regent Moray was assassinated. His successor, Lennox, was killed the following year and the Regent Mar held office until his death in 1572. Then Morton was elected as Regent but was unable to gather stability, so in 1578 the young King James VI took the throne into his own hands.

In 1584, with all the surge of national change and upheaval Sir Richard felt on account of his age that it was time to retire. For nearly seventy years he had given of his best in the public service. In the letter from King James VI to the Court of Session on his demitting office, the King wrote:

> "... hes dewlie and faithfully servit our grandshir, gud Sir, gud dam, muder, and ourself, being of tentymes employit in public charges, quhereof he dewtifullie and honestlie acquit himself, and being ane of you ordinar number this mony yeiris, hes deligentlie with all sincerity servit therein, and now being of werry greit age ... hes willinglie demittit... "

And so to Lethington the elder statesman went to pass the twilight years of his life.

Sir Richard was married about the year 1521 to Mary, the daughter of Sir Thomas Cranstoun of Crosby, who survived him, only to die tragically on his funeral day. He had by the marriage four daughters and three sons, the eldest of whom, William, became the famous Mr Secretary Lethington of Queen Mary's reign; the second son, John, rose to be Lord High Chancellor of Scotland, while the third of these remarkable boys, Thomas, is remembered mainly as one of the brilliant controversialists in Buchanan's celebrated symposium, "De Jure Regniapud Scotos" (George Buchanan, Scottish humanist and historian, 1506-1582). The daughters all married into noble Border families and one, Mary, acted as her father's amanuensis for many years. It is a pleasant picture to think of the blind poet sitting at the window of the Great Hall, with his daughter beside him writing in her beautiful hand to his dictation or transcribing the collections of verse. She eventually married the son and heir of Sir William Lauder of Hatton and there is an interesting old charter giving confirmation of Alexander Lauder and Mary Maitland, daughter of Sir Richard Maitland of Lethington, his future spouse, of the lands and town of Cringletie, of old called Wester

Wormestoun, with towers, fortalice and manor, and the lands of Nether Kidstown, Wormestoun and Stewartown (there all lie half-way between Peebles and Eddleston).

Besides being an eminent lawyer, Sir Richard was a voluminous writer and preserved in the "Advocater Decisions of the Court of Session" (1550-1565). His principal performance however was the "Cronicle and Historie of the house and Sirname of Seaton". As he says himself in the Preface, "I am unable to occupy myself as in times past. But to avoid idleness of mind, and because in these days I think it perilous to 'mell' with matters of great importance, I have among other labours gathered and collected the things set forth in this little volume." He was the dochter's son" of the noble House of Seaton, his mother being a daughter of George, second Lord Seton, so it was with keen enjoyment he "gaderit, and set furth" the records of that gallant race. The History was first printed in 1829 by the Maitland Club, named in his honour.

But the occupation which absorbed his leisure was the collecting of verse, and it is due to his assiduousness that much has been preserved of the early poetry of Scotland which otherwise would have been irretrievably lost. His Collection of Early Scottish Poetry, in two volumes, is a treasured possession in the Pepysian Library at Magdalene College, Cambridge.

It is as a poet in his own right, however, that Sir Richard is best remembered. Most of his work was written after his sixtieth year and the verses reflect the things he had most deeply at heart. They throw a light upon what was passing through his mind, the mind of a wise, but shrewd Scotsman, disturbed at the impact of change, distracted and distressed by the upheaval of the great events of the day, who lamented that things would never be the same again.

> "Amend your livis ane and all,
> And bewar of ane sudden fall,
> And pray to God that made us all
> To send us joy that lestis ay. (lasts)
> And lat us nocht to sin be thrall …
> Bot put all vice and wrang away!"

This verse is from his "Blyithness that has been", a wise and modest poem, in which is seen his love for ordered life, but expressing the sorrow at the sadness latent in it.

The mood changes, and in "Thocht I be Auld", the old gentleman shows his relief at not having to play football!

> "Quhen young men cummis fra the green,
> Playand at the futeball had been,
> With broken spauld; (shoulder-blade)
> I thank my god I want my een,
> I am sa auld."

Again he muses upon the dilemma of old age in his "The Blind Baronis Comfort". His estates by Blythe in Lauderdale had been harried and spoiled by English raiders under the command of Rollent Foster, Captain of Wark. Sir Richard would dearly have loved revenge on the ravagers but is conscious that such a thought is inconsistent with his Christian principles.

> "Blind man, be blyith, thocht that thou be wrangit,
> Thocht Blyith be herryit, tak no melancholy …
> ………
> Bot thou art blyith that thou eternally
> Shall ring with God in eternal blyithness." (reign)

In all, Sir Richard is a much neglected poet.   His

37

lamentations are perhaps a trifle tedious, his complaint against the feuds and discontents of the people irksome to appreciate, but there is much humanity and sincerity and good deal of homely honesty in his writing. He could never be classed as brilliant but there is a "couthiness" which endears him to those who persevere with his poems. Beneath all lies the deep wisdom of the true Scot. His collections of Poems were printed for the first time in 1830 for the Maitland Club.

Sir Richard died on the 20th March 1586 at the age of ninety.

5. MR. SECRETARY LETHINGTON

William Maitland was born at Lethington, East Lothian, about the year 1525, the eldest son of Sir Richard Maitland of Lethington, and Mary, the daughter of Sir Thomas Cranstoun of Crosbie. The age in which he lived was one of the most exciting and troubles some in Scottish history. For years, the armies of Henry VIII had ravaged the country, but the Scots refused to be subjected, and fought back. Crops were burned, villages and towns laid waste, and their Scottish army routed at Solway Moss, but Scotland still remained unconquered. Then Henry made one last desperate bid to master the unruly land: he would marry his baby prince Edward to the infant Queen Mary. The plan was rejected, and the thrown Scots were hammered to defeat at the battle of Pinkie in 1547, the bloodiest and last of Scotland's disasters in her contest for national existence. A few days after the battle, the victor Somerset declared his Royal Master's determination "to forward the godly purpose of marriage by force, if other methods failed". The threat fell on deaf ears. A band of loyal nobles escorted the child Queen to France and to safety.

In the aftermath of defeat Scotland found herself in serious plight. Civil strife was rife. By religious differences, for mediaeval Catholicism was struggling for existence against the upsurge of the Reformation. The great Lords, each with his armed following, contended with one another in the struggle for power, made more bitter. And into the cauldron of conflict came the young Laird of Lethington. One wonders how he would have fared if he had buckled on broadsword and clattered into the Capital with a band of Lauderdale lads at his back! For the times were such that it was only a sharp blade that settled disputes, and won a place in the world.

But the brilliant son of Sir Richard was cast in different mould. Little is known of his early boyhood except that following the fashion of the day he was educated at St. Andrews, and received the polish of maturity at the Sorbonne. Unlike his contemporaries, he did not favour the usual spirits and pastimes, but found more stimulus in the study of human nature and the art of statecraft. It was in Paris too, that he may have caught glimpses of Mary, Queen of Scots, and she had opportunity of observing her future Minister.

His father's advice, "not to seek prematurely for advancement, and not to be over-confident in a changeable world", he took to heart, and for the first few years in Government service after his return from France, he walked warily, attentive in his duties and taking note while biding his time.

In 1553 he married Janet, the daughter of William Menteith of Kerse, and thereafter began gradually to enter public life. For in the Capital great things were stirring. In England, Mary Tudor's persecution of her Protestant subjects had sent many of them as refugees over the Border, and one and all were zealous for change in Church and State. In John Knox, fresh back from Geneva, they found a willing champion. Like many of his compatriots, Maitland attended the private preaching of the Reformer, and while impressed by the doctrine he was alarmed at the inflammatory oratory, and the outright denunciation of the *Mass as idolatrous.* To the Roman Catholic autocracy this was rank heresy, and could lead to the savagery of a religious war. If the movement was to succeed, such utterances would have to be controlled. He had no illusions therefore when he accepted the invitation to the Laird of Duns' supper-party, at which were convened "John Knox, David Forress, Robert Lockhart, John Willock and William Maitland, younger, a man of good learning, and of a sharp wit and reasoning." In the debate that followed he spoke his mind, arguing that while a change in the form of worship was necessary, it must be approached realistically, with moderation, and conciliation shown by both Catholic and Protestant. But the passionate dogmatism of Knox would have none of it. The Mass must go: so supremely confident was he in his own infallibility. Friction between the two was inevitable, but as events proved, Maitland was right.

Busy with diplomatic correspondence, and more and more entrusted with state work, Maitland gradually attained a recognised and assured position at Court. He was sent as an envoy to London and Paris, and conducted himself in such a manner that won him fame as a diplomat. On home affairs he kept a watching brief, finding support and friendship with the younger men of wider culture and liberal outlook, who were adherents of the Reformation, but were not willing to be caught up in the hysteria of the movement.

There was need for caution, for in 1554 Mary of Lorraine became the Queen-Regent, and increased the strength of what was known as "the French Party". High posts of office were filled with Frenchmen and French levies were imported for the Queen-Regent's bodyguard. There was an angry public reaction; the nobles were sullen and the people resentful. Up and down the country Knox spread the new doctrine of Reform, but so violently that, as Maitland had foreseen, there was danger for his life. The Catholics determined to get rid of the heretic, and it was only due to Maitland and his friends that he was hustled out of the country in the summer of 1556. His work had not been in vain, for by the following year a party of the nobility openly identified themselves with the Protestant movement as "Lords of the Congregation". A Reformed Church was set up at Dundee, and emboldened by success the Lords demanded the liberty of public worship according to the reformed ritual. But their efforts received a check by the important events in 1558.

In France, Mary, Queen of Scots, married the Dauphin of France, heir to the French throne. This encouraged her mother, the Queen-Regent, to resist the overtures of the Lords. From England came the news of Mary Tudor's death. Amid general rejoicing, the Protestant Elizabeth was proclaimed Queen and there was immediate revulsion against the Catholic Church.

As the close of the year the Queen-Regent played a trump card. She appointed William Maitland to be the Secretary of State for Scotland and a member of the Privy Council. It caused dismay to the Lords of the Congregation, and satisfaction to the Romish Party that the most able statesman in Scotland as now under the control of the Queen-Regent.

The new Secretary came to his task with a profound sense of the magnitude and complexity of the issues before him. He was not deceived by the subtlety of the appointment; a Protestant with known adherence to the Lords and at the same time Prime Minister to a Catholic Queen-Regent, he would be suspect by both factions. There was only one way out of the dilemma, to conform rigidly to his own policy of moderation and common-sense.

In his first contacts with Mary of Lorraine, he found that despite the rancour which her Catholic rule had engendered, she appeared to be a reasonable woman whose political views were in harmony with his own. Her Court, he observed, was a model of decorum. What did disturb him was the close-knit circle of French advisers who were hostile and anti-Protestant. His relations with the Lords was strained, for they regarded him with suspicion.

The burden of high office was not eased by the news in July 1559 of the death of Henri II and the accession of Francis, which made Mary, Queen of Scots, now the Queen of France. In an ill-advised moment she quartered the Arms of England on her own Coat-of-Arms, thereby publicly flaunting her claim to the throne of England. For this, Elizabeth never forgave her, and the episode rankled for years.

The Spring of the year brought Knox back from Geneva, virulent and fanatical as ever. His recklessness alienated many of the more prudent and gave the Catholics the chance they were waiting for. "This man," they complained to the Queen-Regent, "fomenteth a revolution, not a reformation", and against her better inclination she found herself forced to take strong measures. Assured of help from France, the Romish Party became bolder. A delegation of learned doctors brought from Paris tried to convert Maitland to the Roman faith. But as one writer records: "As matters stood, a company or two of soldiers would have proved a stronger argument.". The delegation retired discomfited, for the Secretary had a sharp tongue. The Bishop of Amiens, one of the instigators, then declared, "more effectual means will have to be taken for his conversion". From that moment, Maitland's life was in danger.

It was a critical situation. It was quite clear that if the Reformers were left to themselves, the country would be plunged into a destructive religious war. If the sympathies of the English Queen could be enlisted, Scotland might be saved. For if Elizabeth did not marry, or died childless then Mary, Queen of Scots, was the obvious heir to the English throne. A Protestant England, supporting a Scotland fighting to overthrow a Roman Catholic regime, might lead in time to a union of the two countries with a Scottish monarch on the throne. The dream of every patriotic Scot.

To all these problems Maitland gave agonising thought. The Queen-Regent was now a sick woman and rapidly losing control of affairs. Hedged in by hostility, the Secretary was anxious to regain liberty of action to promote his far-seeing schemes for the national benefit. Rather than wait for French swords to be thrust through his body, he made a swift political decision. He decided to throw in his lot with the Lords of the Congregation. Slipping away from the Court he sought refuge with William Kirkcaldy of Grange, reputed bravest and most skilful soldier of his time, and one of the Lords of the Congregation. He was well received, and the whole range of events discussed. Acting with urgency, the Lords entrusted him with the delicate mission of going to the English Court, to lay the position before Elizabeth. Maitland accepted with alacrity, although he knew it was a difficult task.

To his surprise he was well received, for Elizabeth was known to be unpredictable. But the English Queen had a quick eye for merit and she found respect for this cultured ambassador from Scotland. "The flower of the wits of Scotland" she dubbed him, and throughout the vicissitudes of her reign had no reason to change her opinion. He stated his case with sincerity and conciseness and won approval. Elizabeth would consider Mary's claim to accession: meantime military aid would be forthcoming. It was a triumph for his diplomatic skill. There was no other man in Scotland at the time who could have achieved it.

The incision into the religious life of the nation had been too swift, The statesman in Maitland foresaw difficulties. The Lord James Stuart he had revised the Confession of Faith before it was ratified, modified the language and cut out large sections. He was aware of the larger issues at stake of which Knox was contemptuous. If there was to be peace and union between England and Scotland, then the new religion must be in accord with the thought of English Protestantism. He wrote to Elizabeth's Minister, Cecil, "that it is not too late to amend any article that the Queen might hold to be amiss". It was essential, he felt, that at the first opportunity the two Queens should meet, when understandings could be reached on priority problems. This could be more easily effected in an atmosphere of religious agreement.

Then the unexpected happened. The feeble Francis was dead. Maitland saw that there was now only one course, the return of Mary to Scotland, but on certain specific conditions: if she could be induced to prefer the friendship of England to that of France and if she would adopt a lenient attitude towards the Reformed Kirk. His own position was one of difficulty. Politically, he had deserted her mother and sided with the Lords of the Congregation. He had negotiated with Elizabeth and Cecil, and piloted a new religion through the Three Estates in her absence. His fears however were proved to be groundless. On the eve of her departure from France, Mary wrote him a letter stating that she would trust him entirely for she had always appreciated his wisdom and sagacity. She had no doubt of his goodwill, and anything he had done in the past was forgiven. She would judge her Minister in future by his actions, his zeal and faithfulness to her person. It lifted a weight of doubt from Maitland's mind. But his high hopes were dashed when with shameless caprice Elizabeth demanded that Mary should renounce her claim to the English throne and refused a safe-conduct through England. An English fleet was sent to intercept her, under the plausible excuse that it was to clear pirates from the area. It wrecked Maitland's plan for a royal meeting, and he wrote tersely to Cecil of, "so great a discourtesy at your Queen's account". Mary, however, matched this political blunder with wisdom. She turned a deaf ear to the Earl of Huntly, who pressed her to land at Aberdeen, where he would raise the Gordons and march to Edinburgh, and there proclaim her a Catholic Queen of Scots.

"Now I am determined," she wrote, "to adventure the matter, whatever come of it." Appointed to meet her were the two most able men in Scotland, her half-brother, Lord James Stuart, and William Maitland.

The haar came in cold and dank on that morning of the 19th August 1561, as the pilot brought the royal ship safely to harbour at Leith. A fleeting shaft of sunlight seemed like an omen of more peaceful times to come, if …. That "if" loomed large in the mind of William Maitland as he watch the prow emerge from the mist. "Her coming could not fail to raise wonderful tragedies, "He wrote. Mr. Secretary

Lethington was more of a prophet than he knew.

He went back to Edinburgh with a feeling that the clouds were lifting. In February 1560 he travelled to Berwick to negotiate the Convention with the Duke of Norfolk, whereby the English took Scotland, her liberties and rights, under English protection. The ink had hardly dried on the signatures before an English army struck camp and were marching on Edinburgh, and an English fleet was sailing into the Firth of Forth. The Queen-Regent, seriously ill, sought safety in the Castle, while, fighting for the first time together, English and Scots laid siege to the beleaguered French garrison in Leith Fort. The foreign levies had not much heart for the fray and after the death of the Queen-Regent on the 11th June, they capitulated. A Treaty was signed on 6th July, the French troops sailed for home, and in August the English army was marching south. The Auld Alliance was severed, the cause of the Roman Catholics was shattered and Protestantism was assured.

Then began the argie-bargie. Their absentee Queen was also the Queen of France and no Scot would have a Queen of France as their Sovereign. The news from Paris was disturbing, for the weakly young Francis was ailing, with no great expectation of life. What was to happen meantime? To the heated arguments, Maitland, taking the whole burden of government on himself, counselled the setting up of a provisional government in Mary's name, pending her return at some future date, and advocated that Parliament should formulate proposals concerning the religion of the country. Accordingly he summoned the Three Estates and they met in quarrelsome mood. The Catholic Earl of Huntly absented himself and in his place Maitland was elected the "harangue-maker", as the Speaker was called. He faced a crowded chamber, with the nobles, clergy and burgesses seated on their own separate benches. "Silence being commanded, the Lord of Lethington began his oration." It was modest and restrained. He gave a review of the recent events, called for peace and unity, and appealed for common-sense by all men as opposed to dreams and visions. It had a calming effect on all, except Knox, "the Prophet of the Lord", who was rarin' to go. In record time, he and his committee had drawn up and presented "The Confession of Faith", embodying the Protestant beliefs, and with only a few dissentient voices, the Three Estates passed it on 17th August. A week later, three Acts destroyed the Roman Catholic Church in Scotland, abolished the authority of the Pope, annulled all practices not in conformity with the Confession, reduced the sacraments to those of baptism and the Lord's Supper, and prohibited the celebration of, or attendance at, the mass, with the direst penalties for infringement.

By the turn of the year, the First Book of Discipline was presented to Three Estates. It set forth the organisation of the new Kirk, a Kirk that dominate and organise the whole nation in accordance with the Will of God. The Presbyterian Kirk, as it was called, was to be governed by the General Assembly, consisting of ministers and elders. Each congregation was to choose its own minister and the elders, elected from the congregation, were to form a Kirk Session to help him with his work.

Maitland was no theologian, though where civil rights or interests were affected, he fought strenuously to protect them, but in the matter of the Mass his tolerance was overruled, and the death penalty was retained.

6 . THE HEARTBREAK YEARS

"I was the Queen o' bonnie France,
Where happy I ha'e been;"

Mary, Queen of Scotts, Queen Dowager of France, and in the eyes of every Roman Catholic the rightful heir to the throne of England, returned from France and landed at Leith on the 19th August 1561.

She was barely nineteen, a tall graceful woman, with a certain beauty, of exquisite charm and manner, accomplished, and with a physical strength that seemed incapable of fatigue. She tended to be passionate and self-willed, a trait inherited from her grandfather, James IV, which was set off by her frankness, generosity and warmth of feeling towards others.

In her new Secretary of State she found much to give her confidence. He was grave and cultured, spoke to her in scholarly French, was firm, but treated her with respect and consideration. With a woman's instinct she sensed that he had given her his whole-hearted allegiance. She was right. The cool, wary diplomat found her fascinating, and his loyalty to her, though often sorely tried, was staunch to the end.

As virtual Prime Minister to the Queen, Maitland at the time was the most conspicuous figure at the Scottish Court. He was widely known and generally respected as an able statesman. Two men only opposed him, Knox and Elizabeth's Minister, Cecil, against whom he had to wage a constant battle of wits.

His policies were simple and wise to secure a stable government and peace in the country, to promote a union between Scotland and England, with succession to a Scottish Prince, and to establish a religious freedom on reasonable conditions. But in everything he was thwarted by events.

The experience of the first few weeks of Mary's reign gave evidence of the difficulties which had to be overcome. She refused, as a devout Catholic, to ratify the legislation passed by the Three Estates setting out the new religion of Presbyterianism. Maitland had expected this, for beyond the capital the impact of the Reformation had not been fully felt. There was still adherence in the rural areas and especially the highlands to the old faith. It would take a few years to determine what impress the new religion would have on the nation as a whole. Deftly he won Mary's signature to a Royal Proclamation dated the 25th August 1561 providing that the form of religion "public and universally standing" should in the meantime continue, to the contentment of the nation.

It was a concession to both sides, allowing passion and prejudice to cool off. It checked the extremists and irreconcilables, and gave time to work out a final settlement. Mary saw the adroitness of it, for as Maitland pointed out,

Scottish Presbyterianism should be established on a basis which would be in accord with English Protestantism, as a pre-requisite to any talks between the Heads of State regarding union.

Mary was in agreement with her Secretary's policy for alliance with England, but the stumbling block was the clause in the Treaty of Edinburgh signed at the capitulation of the French forces in 1560. This provided that Mary (then in France) "in all times coming" should renounce her right to the English throne. This she had rejected and refused to ratify. On patriotic grounds Maitland agreed with her, but, to create a more favourable atmosphere, he pressed her to advocate for a revision of the terms so that negotiations could be opened on the wider issue of the union between the two Kingdoms.

Again Mary saw the sagacity of this move, and armed with authority Maitland paid a courtesy call at the English Court to present a message of greeting and goodwill from his Royal Mistress to Elizabeth. His diplomatic talks covered a wide range, religion, Mary's claim to the succession, union and the possibility of Mary's marriage, if a suitor could be found acceptable to Elizabeth, which would bind the alliance. In all Elizabeth was evasive, hinting and vaguely promising, sheltering in excuses. Cecil was no better. Maitland was too astute not to sense that behind the veneer of the friendship there was a bitter animosity to Mary and all she stood for.

He was disappointed but hid the frustration he felt and left with an assurance that the talks could be continued.

On his return to Edinburgh he found the place in a steer.

In his absence Mary had attended private mass in the

Royal Chapel. The news had leaked out, Protestant fanatics had stormed to the Palace and were only prevented from breaking in to kill the "idolatrous priest" by the intervention of Lord James Stuart, the Queen's half brother. Up the high Street in St. Giles, Knox thundered menaces "that one mass was more fearful to him than ten thousand armed enemies landed in any part of the realm".

A sermon by Knox was not infrequently a great political event and the packed congregation gulped down his words of emotion and fervour. "Who guides the Queen and the Court? Who but the Protestants? O horrible slanderers of God and His Holy Gospel!" "Maitland", he went on "is the father of all mischief" and continued by pouring ridicule against "him that has the honour to be the Queen's brother".

Such outbursts rejoiced his followers but greatly disturbed his friends. Maitland sought audience of the Queen and pointed out that her action was interpreted as a secret promotion of her own religion. Mary was dignified and calm. Her plea was for liberty of conscience for herself and her household, the same liberty of conscience she had accorded her subjects. Maitland appreciated the logic of the argument, but realised that a compromise must be reached and advised that it would be a tactful act if Mary would meet Knox and reach an understanding.

So to the Palace Knox was summoned. The interview was spirited and the theological disputation was on a high level, but Knox was unyielding. The matter for the moment was left.

There were other pressing matters needing the attention of the Privy Council. Watching the trend of events with ambitious eye was George Gordon, the 4th Earl of Huntly, the Chief of the "Gey Gordons", well named for they were a wild, fast lot, ready for any ploy. The Earl had earned the nickname of "Cock o' the North" for of all the nobles he was the most powerful, having amassed wealth and lands during the turbulent period of the Queen Mother's regency. Against Lord James Stuart maintained an inveterate animosity. "Let the Queen command me," he boasted, "and I will set up the mass in three counties". To which the Lord James had replied, "It is past your power, and so you will find out, if you try".

The hostility turned to implacable hate when the Queen bestowed the title and estates of Moray, previously held by Huntly, on her half-brother Lord James Stuart, who now became known as the Earl of Moray. It was an award for services, for Mary was generous to her friends. Maitland had received a grant of the abbey lands at Haddington. Lord James had crushed the plot instigated by the Guises in an attempt to restore the Roman Catholic power to Scotland, whereby Huntly's son, Sir John Gordon, should marry the Queen.

The enraged Huntly, ripe for rebellion, was faced with a new dilemma. There was a bitter feud between the Gordons and the Ogilvys. In June that year (1562) Sir John clashed with Lord Ogilvy in the streets of Edinburgh, swords, flashed and Ogilvy fell severely wounded. Sir John was arrested and imprisoned, but managed to escape. He was put to the horn, a fugitive from justice.

When tidings of this encounter and its results reached Maitland at the Palace he realised the gravity of the incident. It was imperative for the success of future policy that the Queen's authority should be recognised. He advised a Royal Progress throughout the northern counties to establish the Queen's Peace, and to bring the Gordons to heel.

Mary accepted with eagerness, glad to get away from the Calvinistic atmosphere of Edinburgh. She was never happier than when in the saddle travelling the country, with the clatter and jingle of her bodyguard around her. She enjoyed meeting and dining with the burgh burgesses, and for the ordinary folk she had a winning smile and cheery word.

By August the progress had reached Aberdeen, where we are told the accommodation was so scare that Maitland was forced to share the same bed as Sir Thomas Randolph, the English envoy attached to the Court.

An invitation had been received from the Earl of Huntly to stay at Strathbogie, but on the way there the Royal Party was met by the Earl, who made a passionate plea for mercy for his son. Mary, however, was inexorable, having already rejected an appeal by the Countess of Aberdeen. Sir John must give himself up and the law maintained.

Maitland became suspicious and with Moray advised the Queen to alter the itinerary and proceed direct to Inverness. It was fortunate that they did, for they evaded the plot Huntly had hatched. At Inverness the Queen was refused admission to the Castle by the deputy governor who was a Huntly dependent. The Queen sent out a call to arms, invested the Castle, which shortly capitulated, and the deputy Governor was hanged. Information revealed that Huntly was on the march and planned to ambush the Queen in the woods on the banks of the River Spey. With skilful scouting, the royal party crossed the river unmolested an rode swiftly back to Aberdeen. A proclamation was issued calling all loyal citizens to arms.

The die was cast. Huntly marched south hand camped a Cullerlie, about a dozen miles west of Aberdeen, where he was joined by Sir John Gordon with his own armed following. Lord Moray at the head of the Queen's forces came out to meet him. The Gordons retreated to the hill o' Fare and formed a defensive line overlooking the Corrichie Burn. The day was 28th October.

Before the engagement Maitland addressed the troops, exhorting every man to call upon God, to remember his duty and not to fear the enemy. He concluded with the following prayer.

"O Lord, thou that ruleth the heaven and the earth, look upon thy servants whose blood this day is sought, and to man's judgment is sold and betrayed. Our refuge is now unto Thee, and our hope is in Thee. Judge then, O Lord, this day betwixt us and the Earl of Huntly. If ever we have sought unjustly his or their destruction and blood, let us fall on the edge of the word. If we be innocent, maintain and preserve us, for thy great mercy's sake".

With the Queen he took up a stance on a big rock on the hillside, traditionally known as the Queen's Chair.

The Gordons, as always, fought desperately, but against Moray's cool and prudent leadership and the deployment of his superior forces they had little chance. The battle soon became a rout, Huntly was killed and Sir John was captured. A small cairn, on the B977, commemorates the victory. Because he had conspired for the hand of the Queen, Sir John Gordon was taken back to Aberdeen and executed. Huntly Castle was plundered. The power of the Gordons, for the moment, was crushed, but the whole episode left a bitter taste. Far from settling anything, the futile struggle was only the prelude to more terrible events.

A poem about the battle succinctly sums up the feelings at the time,

> "I wis our Quine had bett er friends,
> I wis our countie better piece,
> I wis our Lords wid n discord,
> I wis our weirs at hame may cease."

Politically, Maitland felt that Mary's cause had benefitted by the show of strength. He was anxious to know what the effects would be at the English Court. Accordingly Randolph wrote to Cecil, "It is now resolved that the Lord of Ledington shall visit the Queen's Majesty".

The visit was unproductive. Elizabeth was facing a crisis with her own Parliament, who were passing measures of a new severity against the Catholics. As a makeshift she offered her own favourite, the Earl of Leicester, as a candidate for Mary's hand, and then retracted her proposals. Travelling on to Paris, Maitland heard of marriage proposals from Austria and Spain, but they were too dangerous even to contemplate.

Home in Edinburgh the fractious Lords had plotted against him in his absence but the sharp tongue of the Secretary soon settled the misunderstandings. He found Knox to be as bitter and as vehement as ever, for the Queen's growing popularity with the people was anathema to the fiery prophet of the Reformation. An accidental outburst by some of his more fanatical followers in the Abbey Church brought two of the rioters within the arms of the law. Knox promptly called his faction to arms and to attend the trial in strength, in an attempt to overawe the judge.

Such a move could not be permitted, and Moray urged Knox to withdraw the obnoxious circular of a call to arms. The reformer was summoned to appear before the Council, for this action was treason. Maitland was certain in his own mind that the verdict would be guilty and he advised the Queen that he had no doubt. He conducted the examination, coldly, coolly and with full apprehension. But there had been collusion among the Lords, who both feared an adverse verdict might lead to a riot on a scale they could not control and wished to see Maitland defeated. Knox was acquitted. Stunned by the result, Maitland left the Chamber to summon the Queen, who had withdrawn for the voting. In her presence he demanded a re-cast of the votes. The Lords were incensed. "What!" they cried, "Shall the Laird of Lethington have power to command us?" and immediately repeated their vote absolving Knox of the charge. Mortified and humiliated, the Queen swept from the Council Chamber, leaving Maitland to bear the same.

The finger of fate and pointed. From that day on Mary flung prudence to the winds and steer her own destiny.

The following months were anxious ones for the already over-burdened Secretary. In June, 1564 there was a conference with the leading members of the General Assembly, and in exhausting debates he strove to iron out the differences on various points of the reformed doctrine regarding them ode of prayer for the sovereign and on obedience to authority. He handled the matter in a masterly way, stressing that there must be understanding between the Crown and State, and that the present surge of invective practised by the preachers must be curbed. It was a just settlement, not anarchy that was needed. But Knox was unbending. Common-sense was a word he had never heard.

There were other matters concerning the court which brought furrowed lines to Maitland's brow. He was uneasy at the growing influence being brought to bear on the Queen by those who were admitted to her circle. One was David Rizzio, an Italian, first a musician to the Queen, then promoted to be her private secretary, with much correspondence to France. Another, gradually becoming a more frequent caller, was James Hepburn, the Earl of Bothwell, who had met the Queen in Paris, and whose brash ways Mary seemed to enjoy. His worries were not diminished by the fact that the Earl looked with greedy eyes on the abbey lands which the Queen had rewarded him with and which he openly claimed to belong to the Hepburns.

His domestic life also was not running smoothly. A widower now, he had been attracted from the first sight of her, by Mary Fleming, daughter of Malcolm 3rd Lord Fleming, and Mistress of the household, one of the "Four Maries" and close friend and confidant of the Queen. At first the Queen had watched the love match of her dearest friend with affection, but later relations had become tinged with jealousy and she refused permission for Fleming to resign her post to be married. Maitland's position was awkward in the extreme and he was stretch on a tight-rope of nerves.

Then the denouement happened.

Mary met the tall and personable Henry, Lord Darnley, who was able to talk to her in French, sing love-songs and dance galliards to perfection. A quick flirtation swept her off her feet and she announced that she was going to marry him.

She had borne the cares of State with discretion for too long. She desired some compensation by way of domestic joy and natural affection.

The Lords of the Congregation awoke with a start. They accused Darnley of being arrogant, lacking in morals and with an inflated idea of his own self-importance. But their protests were swept aside.

The news caused Elizabeth dismay, for Darnley's father, the exiled Earl of Lennox, with his strong Catholic sympathies, would now be restored to favour, a move that could prove dangerous. It was nothing to the alarm that Moray experienced, for together Mary and Darnley would command the chief power in the Kingdom. All that he and Maitland had so assiduously worked for would be lost. He left the Court peremptorily to round up what Protestant support he could find.

As her first Minister, Maitland aided and abetted by the slim, auburn-haired Mary Fleming, besought the Queen to re-considered her hasty decision, but he was rebuked.

On the 29th July 1565 the infatuated Mary married according to the rites of the Roman Church the man of her choice. Inevitably the marriage brought the Earl of Morton, the Douglas connection, the Lords Lindsay and Ruthven and all the Catholic faction into the Royal circle. It was some time before Mary realised the full implication of the hornet's nest into which the marriage had landed her. Only Maitland understood the danger. It was the same pattern of events which had brought the downfall of the Queen-Regent.

Moray meantime had taken to arms and refused a summons to appear before the Council. Mary accepted the challenge. With a husband at her side, she personally led her troops, and chased the insurgents from place to place and finally over the Border, in what became known as the Run-About Raid.

Elated, she returned to Edinburgh Castle, feeling very much a Queen.

Ill-at-ease, Maitland remained at his post, but he was debarred from the confidence he had previously enjoyed. All too soon it became obvious that the marriage had been a fiasco. Prudently the Council had refused the Crown Matrimonial to Darnley, a decision which hurt his pride. Thwarted from obtaining the recognition he craved, he drank heavily and quarrelled with the Queen. In the autumn the Queen became ill "with a grievous pain in her side" a recurrence of her ulcer complaint, but Darnley went off to Fife with his drinking companions.

At the Palace the atmosphere became tense. Rizzio was always with the Queen on confidential business, whenever he was not accepting bribes from the nobles to obtain favours or working hard to discredit Maitland. The masterful Bothwell openly flirted with Mary, and the crafty Morton influenced the thought and opinion of the Court. The quarrels between Darley and Mary became more frequent and bitter, and the Kings consort accused Mary of taking her Italian secretary as her lover.

Watching the way things were going, the restless Scottish Lords, planned a *coup d'etat*. It was an age when murder was justified as a political necessity. Rizzio was to be the victim. His murder would not only implicate Darnley, it would also spread abroad that the hated Italian was plotting for a Catholic revival and so would win the Protestants to their side. Moray was to be brought back, provided he acknowledged Darnley as 'King', and to this bargain Elizabeth's support would be assured. Knox could be relied upon to stir up trouble. The Queen would be seized and Maitland hustled out of the way to marry Mary Fleming.

In the twilight of a winter's evening two hundred armed men in the livery of Morton and Lindsay surrounded the Palace. Entry was effected and ruthlessly and tragically in the presence of the outraged Queen. Rizzio was done to death, his inert body dragged from the chamber and cast into a ditch outside. The prostrate Queen was eventually persuaded to retire to her bed-chamber. Sentries were posted.

It took Mary forty-eight hours to recover her composure. She acted quickly. The sentries were replaced with Darnley's men. After midnight Mary accompanied by Darnley slipped out of the Palace to a side gate, where by arrangement the faithful Arthur Erskine, the Queen's equerry and brother-in-law of Mary Livingstone, was waiting. Mounting, the party fled into the night. At Seton house they changed horses and rode non-stop to Dunbar, where on resourceful man could be found, capable of dealing the situation ... the Earl of Bothwell.

At the head of a powerful force Mary was brought back to an Edinburgh from which the conspirators had fled.

Darnley was in a paralysis of fear at having betrayed the conspirators. He even swore that Maitland was implicated, but on being taxed by Mary, confessed that the accusation was false. It appeared that Athol, Huntly and Maitland had been embroiled in the yard with Morton's troops and that Ruthven, who had butchered Rizzio, intervened and after consulting Darnley had allowed them to leave the Palace.

Athol certainly was not of the plot and being married to a Fleming he shared Maitland's confidence. However the Secretary deemed it safer to keep a wise distance from Holyrood House.

As uneasy tension dominated the Court and observers were baffled, for Mary did not seek revenge, but rather appeared eager to forgive and forget. The tragic event of that dark 9th March had imperilled the Queen's health, and there was general relief when on 19th June she gave birth to a son, James VI of Scotland, later to be James I of England.

The happy event brought a lull to animosities but Mary regretted the absence of her most able adviser. It was not until the early autumn, after an abusive scene between Moray and Bothwell, with the latter storming out of her presence, that she asked her Secretary to return to his post.

On the 7th October the Queen left for Melrose and then proceeded to Jedburgh for the Circuit Court, staying in what is known now as "Queen Mary's House", a strongly fortified building in the quiet surroundings of lawns and trees. News had been received that in an encounter with a Border freebooter, John Elliot, the Earl of Bothwell had been wounded and was lying seriously ill at his remote stronghold of Hermitage Castle in Liddesdale. Mary decided to visit him. It was an arduous and dangerous journey at the best of times, but in her exhausted state of ill-health it was folly to undertake it. But strong passions were working in her heart and she would not listen to caution. With a few attendants she set out, taking the more circuitous, but safer route to Hawick, a distance there and back of some sixty miles.

The Castle of Hermitage strongly situated, stands on a bluff, overlooking a strip of level ground on the north bank of the Hermitage Water, with all around the frowning hills and moorlands of Liddesdale. The structure is massive and dominating. What transpired between the Queen, Bothwell and his recently wed wife, Lady Jane Gordon, Catholic sister of the Earl of Huntly, will never be known. But the impetuous venture nearly cost Mary her life. The white frost of the morning turned to rain and the return journey was an nightmare of wet, cold and darkness. The relics preserved in "Queen Mary's House" recall the hazards; the watch found in boggy ground near Hawick, the horse-shoe in a bog known as "The Queen's Mire", the thimble case in the same region where the royal party stopped to allow Mary to repair her dress after a mishap. It was an exhausted Queen that was helped to her room. Within a week she was dangerously ill, running a high fever with acute pain and vomiting blood. All the signs of a severe gastric ulcer, with internal haemorrhage. Her life hung in the balance, but the strenuous efforts of her French physician literally forced her back to recovery.

During all this anxious time, Maitland was kept in close touch with the royal patient's progress through the devoted Mary Fleming. In his private talks with her he came to the conclusion that the Queen's illness, once the crisis had passed, was more mental than physical, attributable to the behaviour of Darnley. As he wrote in a letter:

> "Scho hes done him sa great honour without the advyse of her friends, and contrary to the advyse of her subjects, and he on the tother part hes recompensit her with sik ingratitude, and misusis himself sa far toward her, that it is ane heartbreak for her to think that he sould be hir husband, and how to be free of him scho sees na outgait."

Darnley had come to Jedburgh, but finding no suitable

accommodation, rode out of the town. Bothwell, on the other hand was brought by litter from Hermitage to the Queen's House, ostensibly to receive medical attention from the royal physician.

The weeks of convalesce passed, then the Court moved to Mary's favourite residence outside Edinburgh, Craigmillar Castle, which stood on a low ridge fringed with trees with an extensive view of the sea. Her entourage was housed nearby at what had become known as "Little France". The next move was to Stirling for the baptism of the young Prince. Darnley put in a reluctant appearance, but when he heard that the English envoy was not to pay homage to him as 'King' he took umbrage, retired to his room and avoided the guests. The Queen in gracious mood granted an amnesty to all who had taken part in the Rizzio affair. In a panic the frightened Darnley fled to Glasgow, followed by the jeers of the nobles, who now openly showed their enemy. The Court moved once again to the peaceful surroundings of Craigmillar Castle. Here, Argyll, Moray, Maitland, Huntly and Bothwell went into secret conclave, and agreement being found, they sought audience of the Queen.

As spokesman, Maitland outlined the position. It could not longer be disguised that Darnley's actions and behaviour were becoming a potential danger to the safety of the realm. At any moment he might provoke an incident, for which it might well be impossible to find a remedy. Would Her Majesty consider a divorce?

The silence was acute. Eventually the Queen spoke. Yes, she was prepared to consider her Ministers' advice, provided nothing would prejudice her son's rights and nothing was done to her hurt of displeasure.

"Madame", replied Maitland briskly "let us guide the matter among us and your Grace shall see nothing but what is good and lawful, and approved by Parliament."

This meeting was in early December. Before the month ended the faithful Mary Fleming had been relieved of her duties as maid of honour. She had pleaded with her royal mistress to cease the reckless flirtation with Bothwell in the present taut situation. Mary covered a guilty conscience by a show of anger. It was time, she declared, that Fleming was married and the postponed wedding could take place. In spiteful mood, she refused the promised gift of a silver gown, similar to those given to Livingstone and Beaton.

So, in the Royal Chapel of Stirling Castle on the 6th January 1567, William Maitland of Lethington was married to Mary Fleming, and as man and wife they went out into the winter sunshine. But all around the ominous storm clouds were gathering, waiting for the final deluge.

7. THE FINAL PHASE

Many of burghers of the city of Edinburgh, who gathered at the Tron Kirk on Hogmanay, awaiting the arrival of the new year 1567, must have wondered what the future held in store. For the times were troublous. There had been some strange capers at the Palace, down at the end of the Canongate. It was a matter of rejoicing that there was a young Prince who might some day, God willing, be the King of England as well as of the Scots. But his mother, the Queen, should have known better than marry a feckless cratur like Darnley, and they did say that James Hepburn was making eyes at her which boded no good for anyone. And so, with doubts in their mind they watched the old year ebb away.

On 6th January William Maitland, Mr Secretary Lethington was married to Mary Fleming, the Queen's Maid of honour.

It was either just before or shortly after his wedding that Maitland was asked to go with Bothwell to Whittinghame to help him to find accord with the Earl of Morton, who was staying there with is kinsman, Archibald Douglas. Maitland had been instrumental in obtaining Morton's pardon for his part in the Rizzio murder, but the wily Bothwell had other ideas besides friendship. According to Morton's confession, taken before he was beheaded in 1581,

> "the erle of Bothuel and I met in the yaird of Whittingham, and he proponed to me the purpose of the kingis murther, recuyring what wald be my pairt thairinto, seeing it was the queinis mynd that the King sould be tayne away".

Tradition places the secret meeting, from which Maitland was excluded, as being held under the ancient yew which still stands in what according to an old map was then the courtyard. The two conspirators were joined by Douglas, and eventually Morton agreed to the scheme on certain conditions.

> "The erle of Bothuel bring to me the quenis handwrite to me of the matter, for a warrand, and then I sould give him an ansuer ... and thairfoir, seeing the erle of Bothuel neuer reported ony warrand of the queine, I medlie never farther with it."

It appears clear therefore that Maitland was not cognizant of the plot til ill the King. In the beginning of February, Mary asked him to visit Elizabeth, but he excused himself as being still on his honeymoon.

Meantime Darnley had fallen ill of "the small-pos". With natural solicitude Mary arranged for the King to be brought from Glasgow to Edinburgh, where he was lodged at the Kirk o' Field, a lonely house on the outskirts of the city. The crisis of illness brought a reconciliation and Mary was attentive in her ministrations. On the night of the 9th February she left as usual to return to Holyrood to attend a dance at the wedding of one of her retainers. In the early hours of the morning a tremendous explosion shook the town. Sent out to investigate, the frightened watch reported the demolition of the Kirk o' Field by gunpowder and the finding of the strangled bodies of the King and his page lying in the garden.

The news spread like wild-fire. The Earl of Lennox, the father of Darnley, renounced the murder at the work of Bothwell, and demanded he be brought to trial. With a formidable force, Bothwell rode into Edinburgh and so terrorised everyone that none dared appear for the prosecution. The cowed jury, on direction from the judge, returned a verdict of not guilty. Not using his advantage Bothwell, closely guarded by is swashbuckling riders, forced the nobles to sign a bond, declaring him innocent of the murder, and that they approved him as a worthy husband for the Queen. Only Maitland refused.

The Court moved to Stirling, and towards the end of April Mary returned to Edinburgh. As the royal party approached Almond Bridge they were surrounded by Bothwell's men in overwhelming force, the Queen abducted and the remainder taken prisoners.

"What I have done", boasted Bothwell "is by the Queen's consent, and neither resistance or punishment need be feared".

By-passing the capital, the party went to Dunbar Castle, where Bothwell's will was law. Here his hate of Maitland boiled over, for the Secretary was the obstinate impediment to his plan to marry Mary. As long as Maitland refused to sign the bond, Mary would not willingly yield to him. In frustrated anger, he and Huntly threatened violence, and it was Mary's intervention that saved Maitland's life.

Whatever Mary's faults may have been, she was loyal to her friends.

Shaken by the narrow escape, Maitland realised that nothing now that he could do would prevent a marriage of which he disapproved and resigned himself to the role of passive prisoner. A day or two later, to ease the tension, a shoot was arranged in the grounds. Although guarded, Maitland took his chance, and spurring his horse, dodged between the marks and rode for the open country. Bothwell checked the pursuers. Free, Maitland would not upset his plans, but held a prisoner, he constituted an embarrassment. Time enough to deal with him, once Mary was led to the altar.

There was need for haste. Bothwell broke down Mary's resistance at last, and on 15th May, having obtained his divorce, been publically pardoned and created Duke of Orkney, he married Mary. The Catholics were shocked, the Protestants furious, and the nobles stunned.

The government of the country had to go on, but the tension was too great. One by one the nobles absented themselves from the Council. Maitland was the last to go. The savage ruthlessness of Bothwell finally exhausted his patience; moreover, his life was in constant danger. Intellectually and emotionally he was in despair. In a stormy scene in the Queen's chamber, Bothwell drew his sword against Maitland but once again Mary intervened, Maitland lost no time and rode hard and fast to Athol, who quietly had been mustering his forces.

Morton, who had fallen out with Bothwell also gathered his troops, and tongue in cheek had written a proclamation

"That James Hepburn, Earl of Bothwell, having on

the 24th April, put violent hands on our Sovereign
Lady's most noble Person, and having since then
detained her in captivity the Lords have risen to
deliver her from prison".

William Kirkcaldy of Grange, the most capable soldier in
Scotland, assumed command of the joint forces to liberate
the Queen, and prepared to march on Edinburgh.

Having no desire to be hemmed in the Capital, Bothwell
took Mary on a "honeymoon" to Borthwick Castle, which
lay close to his own Crichton stronghold.

But he reckoned without the Confederate Lords. They
seized the capital and made a swift night march the twelve
miles or so to Borthwick. Bothwell, always lucky, escaped
through a postern and left Mary to her fate. But she
managed to get away disguised as a man, and was picked up
by Bothwell the next morning wandering round the
country. One of his men foraged a rough gown and kirtle
for her and bemused with fatigue she joined Bothwell as he
advanced to meet Kirkcaldy's army. The two sides came
face to face at Carberry Hill, near Musselburgh. The day
was lost before it was begun. Many of Bothwell's men
deserted. Kirkcaldy rode forward to parley, but on hearing
the terms, Bothwell wheeled his horse and fled.

It was the most bitter day in Mary's life. Racked with
pain from her gastric ulcer, near fainting, dishevelled and
emotionally exhausted, the humiliated Queen was escorted
to her capital to meet the cursing frenzy of the crowd,
whipped to white heat by Knox and his ministers.

Morton took no chances and imprisoned her in the
Provost's Mansion, known as the Black Turnpike, now
commemorated by a plaque at the junction of Cockburn

Street and the High Street. The Lords met to consider what was to be done. It was then that the fraud was revealed. The Morton faction clamoured for the Queen's death, and for making Moray, on his return, the Regent. Knox wanted "the idolatrous woman" hewn to pieces. Athol, Argyll, Maitland and Kirkcaldy were astounded and their anger was only mollified by the production of a letter purporting to come from the Queen, couched in living terms and addressed to Bothwell, in which she refused to abandon him. Maitland was not convinced, although his faith in the Queen was shaken. He was eventually allowed to see her, but was bewildered at the outburst of accusations. He withdrew baffled and could only think that Mary was in a shocked condition and temporarily unhinged. The series of events had swept them all into a net of indictment, the responsibility for which it was difficult to evade. One thing was certain, the Queen must be given time to recover her health, for only through her could the goal of union between England and Scotland be achieved. He threw all his will power and strength of argument into the discussion to convince the Lords to take only action which would not impair the right of succession to the English throne. The weary hours of debate ended with compromise. The Lords accepted Maitland's advice. During the hours of darkness the Queen was taken to Loch Leven Castle to be held under close arrest.

A breathing space had been won. When Moray returned from France, Maitland felt sure that he would find support for the return of Mary and his policy of union.

From London came the English envoy, Throckmorton, despatched by Elizabeth to ascertain what had happened. He was met by Maitland at Fast Castle in Berwickshire. He brought a message "to comfort the Queen of Scots in this her calamity". But the Secretary was suspicious of

Elizabeth's motives and as the envoy went on to enlarge on the Queen's good faith, he merely smiled and shook his head. "It were better for us you would let us alone", he said "If you will do us no good, do us no harm, and we will provide for ourselves".

The envoy arrived in Edinburgh, but Morton refused to see him and eventually gave an evasive answer. On the 24th July the Lords agreed to an abdication and resolved that the young Prince should be crowned King.

Maitland at once went to meet Moray at Whittinghame and urged him to be lenient with Mary, placing all the facts before him. Although Moray gravely promised, underneath his cold, lofty manner burned a fierce ambition, and he had not the slightest intention of saving his half-sister. At the interview he reduced Mary to bitter tears.

The abdication was signed. Five days later the infant Prince was crowned James VI King of Scots and Moray was proclaimed Regent.

There was now a distinct coldness between Moray and Maitland, although the speech Maitland made on behalf of the Regent at the opening of the Three Estates was a skilful effort which met the needs of the moment. Although forced to appear friendly, Maitland could not forgive Moray for the way he had broken is promise. As for Moray, it irked him to be dependent on his former friend for ministerial advice, yet he could find no way to get rid of him. He had to suffer him as "the necessary evil".

Meantime Kirkcaldy of Grange had chased Bothwell out of the Orkneys. To escape his pursuers the Earl had fled to Norway, where he was arrested and imprisoned by the King of Denmark. He died in 1578, insane.

Under Moray's Regency Scotland had begun to settle down, when a fresh crisis broke on the 2nd May 1568 with the escape of Mary from Loch Leven. Moray was in Glasgow when the news reached him and he at once sent out a call to arms.

Maitland was deeply moved. To him the escape of his Royal mistress was premature and could only lead to disaster. He hastened to Moray, in the hope that he might be allowed to mediate, but the Regent was adamant. With a powerful army he met Mary's smaller force at Langside. The engagement was short, severe and decisive. As she saw her hopes crumble Mary lost heart and allowed herself to be led from the field of Langside by her few devoted friends, the Lords Livingstone, Fleming and Seton. Weary and dispirited, the hunted party made their way South until at eventide on 15th May they came to the Abbey of Dundrennan. Here she held her last Council, and with some of her former dignity and grace made the decision to surrender to Elizabeth. The next morning she crossed the Solway to England. It was one of the poignant moments in Scottish history.

Her coming embarrassed Elizabeth. She had either to support Mary or let her go free. Each course was fraught with danger, so she contrived with her usual cunning to do neither.

In Scotland Moray and the Lords were in a dilemma. They had de-throned their sovereign, put her in prison and threatened her with death. Mary, her health improved, was now in a position to make her voice heard. Somehow or other the Lords had to save face. By fair means or foul she had to be discredited. The answer came in the famous "Casket Letters". These were some letters and sonnets attributed to Mary and addressed to Bothwell, which if genuine, proved her complicity in the murder of Darnley. Morton professed to have found them in a silver casket, now to be seen at Lennoxlove, which he stated had been taken from a Bothwell retainer, a George Dalgleish, who had been promptly executed. The authenticity therefore of the controversial letters is open to challenge, for the whole affair is wrapped in mystery.

Elizabeth made the first move by calling a conference at York to adjust the differences between Mary and her subjects. This took place in September, and Moray insisted that Maitland attend, for he was frightened at what might happen if the Secretary was left behind to his own devices. But Maitland refused to have anything to do with what he called "the odious accusations". He only spoke once and that was on the opening day, when the Duke of Norfolk called on the Regent to make homage in the King's name to the Crown of England. Forestalling the furious Moray, he gave such a tart answer that the matter was never raised again.

Elizabeth's duplicity became evident. Her Minister, Cecil, wanted an alliance with the Protestant nations in Europe, a war against Alva in the Low Countries, and Mary returned to Scotland. The Duke of Norfolk, representing the Catholics, dreaded a continental war, which would ruin the Flemish trade upon which so much of England's prosperity rested. He desired that Mary's right of succession should be recognised. Moray made his point that nothing would meet his case unless Mary was brought to trial. Vacillating, Elizabeth first declared the Casket Letters to be forgeries, then commanded that the originals should be produced. She hinted that Moray drop the charges, and that Mary should get her freedom, provided Moray be left as Regent. Neither Mary nor Moray would listen to such terms. So Elizabeth sent financial aid to the Low Countries and rejected Mary's claim of succession.

While these shifting negotiations were in progress, Maitland spent his time with the Duke of Norfolk. For a solution he pressed the scheme that Mary should re-marry and favoured the idea that Norfolk would be a suitable husband. Sussex and Throckmorton were consulted and agreed that the proposal had merit. Moray, when approached, approved, subject to the proviso that it would be for the Scottish Courts to declare the Bothwell marriage invalid. But once he returned to Edinburgh, he sabotaged the plan. The Lords met and the question of a divorce was ruled out. Furious at being tricked, Maitland made a sarcastic speech congratulating the Lords and the Regent on their new found seal for Bothwell's domestic happiness. Abruptly he left the Chamber and wisely put a mountain pass between himself and Moray, for the breech between them was now too great for reconciliation.

Part of the agreement had been that once the divorce was sanctioned, Maitland should see Elizabeth and obtain her consent. As it turned out, the English Queen heard of the proposal through gossip at the same time as new leaked of a projected rising of her Catholic Lords. She responded swiftly by placing Norfolk in the Tower and sending her envoy Drury to bring Moray and Maitland to heel. The Regent was penitent and apologetic. Maitland however was completely unrepentant and when asked to accuse Norfolk of conspiracy, refused on the ground that it was not his habit to betray a man who trusted in his honour. It was on the evidence of Moray only, therefore that Norfolk eventually went to the block. Another fugitive, Northumberland, sought Border hospitality but Moray outraged the Border Lords by having him arrested. Plotting with Morton, the Regent schemed to exchange

Northumberland for Mary, and once in Morton's power, she was to be given short shrift. To prepare for this coup, it was essential to get rid of Maitland. The trap was set by calling a Council meeting at Stirling and, all unsuspecting, Maitland attended. At an opportune moment Captain Thomas Crawford, one of the Lennox faction, entered the Chamber and declared that he was arresting William Maitland as an accessory to the murder of Darnley. Bail being refused, Maitland was hustled out by the armed escort, taken to Edinburgh and lodged in a house close by the Castle belonging to David Forrester.

The news that the "Secretar had been taen" spread like wildfire, for the public had a high regard for their able statesman. Morton became uneasy and decided to transfer him to Tantallon Castle, where few prisoners in the dungeons ever again saw the light of day.

Commanding the Castle at Edinburgh, however, was William Kirkcaldy of Grange, who was not prepared to stand idly by and see an old friend ill-used. With the nightfall he swooped down and whisked Maitland into the safe precincts of the Castle. Moray was bitterly mortified at the turn of events and the outspoken expression of public satisfaction was even more galling to his pride. Morton however forced his hand by fixing a date for trial. Into the Capital came armed bands of Lowland and Border nobles, determined to see fair play. The Regent professed to be shocked at the show of force, while Kirkcaldy promised to produce Maitland provided there was anyone ready to accuse him. Then John Maitland, his younger brother, rose to point out that there was no prosecutor, and William Maitland should accordingly be discharged unconditionally. White with anger Moray declared the Court had been intimidated and the trial was postponed. This was the end of November. In January, Moray fell to an assassin bullet in the streets of Linlithgow.

Thereafter the Lords met in Council, and Maitland appeared at the Bar of the Chamber to answer the charge of treason. As the record puts it:

> "After his coming, he made one perfect oration, in sic sort and manner, that all the Lords, yes, his very enemies, judgit him to be innocent thereof".

Maitland now became the acknowledge leader of the Queen's Party, as he held the view that there could be no peace until the country's lawful Sovereign was restored. He made his headquarters in Meal Market Street, and the local wits dubbed him and the meeting place as 'The School and the Schoolmaster'. From his abode in the High Street, the unscrupulous and much feared Morton formed the King's Party, for to him the Queen was an impediment to power and a personage to be got rid of as quickly as possible. The next two Regents, Lennox and Mar, were puppets in his hands.

Anxious to bring accord and peace to the nation, Maitland opened negotiations with Elizabeth to obtain a Treaty whereby all differences could be honourably settled. While lending an ear to such proposals, Elizabeth instructed her envoys in Scotland to sow the seeds of further discord and backed this policy with cash.

Maitland's efforts failed, as Elizabeth intended them to fail. Lennox reported that without military assistance he was himself unable to contain the Queen's Party. With his waiting army the Earl of Sussex at once crossed the Border. "I am come", he said "to chastise her Majesty's rebels" and thereupon laid waste with fire and sword until, shamed at the wanton destruction, he ordered the army home.

Maitland speeded his departure with a 'flea in his lug', a letter of such searing sarcasm that even the Earl, tough as he was, was sorely disconcerted. But the Secretary was a sick man. The years of endless crisis, responsibility and overwork had taken their toll and he appears to have suffered a minor stroke which had left a paralysis in his legs. Mentally and physically, he was worn out. Leaving the Capital, he sought quiet in Atholl. But his active mind would not rest as long as there was work to be done. From the peace of the Highland hills, he conducted a voluminous correspondence. He still clung to his policy, summed up when he wrote

> "such an accord might be made between the Queen of Scots and her people as might stand with the honour of the Queen of England, the surety of the whole nobility of Scotland, and the continuance of the amity betwixt both realms, so that thus no foreign prince should have occasion to meddle in any matter concerning the Isle".

The futile struggle for power went on. Lennon summoned the Three Estates and on Maitland's refusal to stand trial, at Morton's instigation, he deprived him of the office of Secretary of State, declared him a rebel and sent troops to ravage his lands as well as those of his father, Sir Richard Maitland, the elder statesman.

The news of this act of vandalism appears to have brought on another stroke for in April, on sailing from Aberdeen to Leith, we read that Maitland had to be carried up to Edinburgh Castle in a litter and,

> "Mr Robert Maitland haulding up his head, and when they got him to the Castle yet (gate) ilka ane of the workmen gat three shillings, which they received

grudgingly, hoping to have gotten mair for their labours".

The clergyman, Robert Maitland, seems to have been connected to the Secretary for he was Dean of Aberdeen and had been made an Ordinary Lord of Session in 1564 and as one of the Commissaries of Edinburgh on the 29th April 1567 pronounced sentence of divorce at the instance of Jane Gordon, Countess of Bothwell, against her husband.

With his friend safely within the Castle, Kirkcaldy held a Parliament in the Queen's name and determined on retaliatory action, unfolded a plan to seize Stirling. The execution of this scheme was however bungled and in the skirmish Lennox was shot. In his place Mar was elected as Regent, but Morton remained the effective power.

Spurred on by Morton, the new Regent lost no time. He declared Maitland and his two brothers, John and Thomas as traitors, and laid siege to Edinburgh Castle, for as long as this stronghold held out, Mary's cause was not doomed. The winter of 1572 was exceptionally severe, the snow lying into the following April. In desperation Kirkcaldy foraged wood from some of the timber houses, as the owners had moved to the country to find better living conditions. In the city food and fuel were at famine prices.

With the coming of a more seasonable weather, a truce was called to the fighting. The spring sunshine brought no comfort to Maitland, who was growing weaker and weaker. He saw that the truce was a mistake but was too depressed to resist. The returning citizens were enraged at the loss of and damage to their houses and Morton was quick to exploit the situation. Elizabeth's agents, on being informed, unloosed the purse-strings. The news of the Massacre on St. Bartholomew's Day of the French Huguenots and the persecution which had continued was now being told in detail and curdled the blood of every Protestant. Knox, on his death-bed, lashed the populace to white-heat and they shouted vengeance on grange and Maitland as representing the Catholic Queen and all she stood for. A last effort was made by Maitland to come to a settlement and understanding, but the Regent Mar was dying and sent an ungracious reply. Elizabeth's army was on the move, and soon the heavy cannon were in position and the walls of the Castle being battered. Stubborn to the last, Kirkcaldy of Grange held on but eventually he had to seek terms. On the 29th May 1573 he surrendered unconditionally.

Both he and Maitland expected to be treated honourably, long-awaited satisfaction, as prisoners of war, but the English general washed his hands of them. With Morton had Kirkcaldy strung up from the battlements and sent Maitland in a litter to be locked up in Leith Fort to await trial and execution. Within a week Maitland was dead. One writer suggests that he look poison but it is more likely that he had a fatal stroke, for he had given up the will to live. Thwarted of the pleasure of seeing his enemy swing from a rope, Morton took his revenge by refusing to allow the body to be buried and to the frantic appeals of his widow he took not the slightest heed. It was only when Elizabeth sent him a sharp reprimand that the remains of the great statesman were interred, it is not known where. The family burying ground of the Flemings is at Biggar, but it is possible the body was secretly laid to rest, for Morton, incensed by Elizabeth's rebuke, immediately started to hound down Mary Fleming and drove her and her children out of the country to seek refuge in France.

With the fall of Edinburgh Castle and the death of

Maitland, a page of Scottish history closed. Of the participants, Knox, Moray, Norfolk, Grange and Maitland were dead. Mary was to die on the scaffold, and so was Morton. Only Elizabeth was to survive, with her haunting memories.

Time will never diminish the fact that William Maitland was a statesman without peer, the ablest man of his age. He had a tremendous influence in shaping the course of the Reformation and for this along Scotland owes him a debt of gratitude. He was an ardent patriot and upholder of the monarchy and constitutional rule. Loyalty to his Royal mistress sustained him to fight on, even when he knew in his heart the course to be lost.

The favourite weapon to discredit any politician is to attribute false motives to his actions and to Sir William Maitland's motives historians have not been kind. He lived in a violent age and tried to guide the affairs of State with the pen instead of the sword, but it was the sword in the end that broke the pen.

A controversial figure, he will ever remain one of the immortals of Scottish History.

8. THE FOUR MARIES

The old song about Mary Queen of Scots and her Four Maries, her maids of honour, is still well known. The old tune sings sadly. Should go like this:

> "Yestreen the Queen had four Maries,
> This nicht she'll hae but three:
> There was Mary Seton and Mary Beaton
> And Mary Carmichael and me."

The song ends in tragedy.

> "O often have I dressed my Queen
> And put gold on her hair;
> But now I've gotten for my reward
> The gallows to be my share."

The "me" of the song does not in fact refer to the real fourth Mary, who was Mary Fleming. It refers to a French maid at court who was publicly hanged in Edinburgh for the of her illegitimate child. During the reign of Mary, the propaganda for and against the Queen was unchecked. Not only did John Knox and the ministers thunder against the "unholy junketings in high places," but the extreme Presbyterians used any lies, any slanders, that could stir up the people. The song about the four Maries and the fate of the Mary who got into trouble is one of those bits of propaganda. As we know to-day, there was so much lying and hushing-up that it is nigh impossible to arrive at the truth about Queen Mary.

There never was a Mary Hamilton or a Mary Carmichael, who are mentioned in the song. The real facts are these. In 1547, after the disastrous defeat of the Scottish army by the English under the Duke of Somerset at Pinkie, the Scottish Lords determined to put their child Queen in a place even safer than the castle of Stirling, where she had been housed. They chose the island of Inchmahome in the lake of Menteith in Perthshire. With the utmost secrecy, she was taken to Inchmahome in September of that year. She was then nearly five years old.

Her four companions and playmates, chosen from noble Scottish families to be brought up with the Queen, went with her and later sailed with the Queen to France. They were Mary Beaton, Mary Fleming, Mary Livingstone and Mary Seton.

In his "History of Scotland", Bishop Leslie describes the matter in these words:

> "Heir all things being reddy for thair jornay, the
> Quene being as than betuix fyve and fax yearis of
> aige, wes delivered be the Quene dowarier hir moder,
> and utheris ap- pointit be the Parliament to that
> effect j Monfieur de Brezze (quha wes appointit and
> fend furth be expres commandment to have the
> conveyance of her), and wes embarqued in the

Kingis awin gallay, and with her the Lord Erlkyn and Lord Levingftoun quha had bene hir keparis, and the Lady Fleming hir fader fitter, with findre gentilwemen and nobill mennis fonnes and dochteris, almoift of hir awin aige; of the quhilkis thair wes four in fpeciall, of whome everie one of thame buir the famin name of Marie, being of four fyndre honorable houfes, to wyt, Fleming, Levingftoun, Setoun and Betoun of Creichjquho reman it all foure with the Quene in France, during her refidens thair, and returned agane in Scot- lande with her Majeftie in the yeir of our Lorde I m vc Ixi yeris; quhilk Brezze, with Vileganzeoun, ufed fie diligence in acheving thair inter- price, that finalie thay arryved with profperous wayage in the havin of Brift, quhair thay landit with that young princefle in guid faiftie, to the heich joy and gret confort of the Frenchemen. And heir is to be remembered, that the Protectur of Inglande being advertift of this jornay, caufed prepair ane gret navie of fhippes, and lend his broder than admirall thairwith, to await at the weft feyis at thaire palfage, and to haif taikin thame gif thay could ; quha did his diligence to that effect, bot yeat fo was the pleafour of God, that the ftormy wyndis blew fo gret (albeit fair frome Scotland,) that thay nevir let fayll quhill thay war cum in the faide havin of Breft jquhair thay wer reflaved verrey honorablye, and thair remanit certane fpace quhill thay wer refrefhed eftir the foir travell on the feyis."

After the Queen came back to Scotland to take the throne, three of her maids of honour were married. Mary Beaton became the bride of Alexander Ogilvy of Boyne. Lady Mary Livingstone became the wife of John Sempill, younger son of Lord Sempill. Lady Mary Fleming became the wife of Sir William Maitland, the Queen's secretary, as his second wife.

The fourth Mary, Lady Mary Seton, a daughter of the second Lord Seton and sister of Lady Martha, William Maitland's first wife, continued in attendance upon the Queen. She was so clever in dressing Queen Mary's hair and devising her wigs that the Queen praised her as "the cleverest busker I know." Towards the end of the Queen's long imprisonment in England, the faithful Mary, ill and exhausted, was compelled to leave the Queen and end her days in a French convent.

Mary Fleming came from an old Lanarkshire family. Her father was the third Lord Fleming and her mother was Janet Stewart, one of the natural daughters of King James IV. Her father was slain at the battle of Pinkie. When the Queen went to France, she was accompanied by Lady Fleming, who was an aunt of the Queen, and by Lord Fleming, Mary's brother, who died in mysterious circumstances in Paris shortly after the marriage of the Queen to the Dauphin of France. He married Lady Barbara Hamilton, eldest daughter of the Regent Hamilton, Duke of Chatelherault. Their only daughter was Jean Fleming, who married the eldest son of Sir William Maitland and Martha Seton. Thus, through two Fleming marriages, the Maitlands of Lauderdale can trace back their descent to the Stuarts.

9. LORD HIGH CHANCELLOR

"He was a man of rare parts and of a deep wit, learned, full of courage and most faithful to his King and master. No man did ever carry himself in his place more wisely, nor sustain it more courageously against his enemies."

In the rick and complex tapestry of Scotland's turbulent history there have been many famous men but rarely one who so unobtrusively left his imprint on the political and economic life of the nation as did Sir John Maitland, first Lord Maitland of Thirlestane and Lord High Chancellor.

The year of his birth is supposed to have been 1543. His parents were Sir Richard Maitland of Lethington, the blind poet, and Mary, daughter of a Border Laird, Sir Thomas Cranstoun of Corsbie. The tall, tattered fragments of Corsbie Tower will stand, perched on high ground about a mile north-east of Legerwood Kirk in the heart of Lauderdale.

It was a happy family of three sons and four daughters that grew up at Lethington. William, the eldest, who in the years ahead became Mr. Secretary Lethington, the confidential adviser to Mary, Queen of Scots; John whose fortunes brought him the Chancellorship, while Thomas taking after his father became a poet and wrote some elegant verse. The four girls married; Helen to John Cockburn of Clerkington, Isabel to James Heriot of Trabroun, Mary to Alexander Lauder of Hatton and Margaret to William Douglas of Whittinghame.

John's early education was a Lethington then in due course he went to the University of St. Andrews to graduate in Law. As was the custom of the time, he was sent to Paris to round off his studies.

At the age of twenty on his return from France, he was made joint-factor with his father of the Abbey lands of Haddington. Through the patronage of brother William he obtained the Abbacy of Kelso in commendam (tenure of benefice in absence of the regular incumbent) which in 1567 he exchanged with Francis Stewart, nephew of the Earl of Bothwell, for the Prior of Coldingham, the transaction being duly ratified by Royal Assent. He accordingly sat in Parliament as the Prior of Coldingham.

About this time also Sir Richard made disposition of the family property. Lethington was assigned to William while Thirlestane and the Barony of Blyth were gifted to John, a relatively fair division for in the Tax Roll of 1554 Thirlestane and Blyth were assessed at £5 Scots each, whereas Lethington was £10 Scots. This explains why in the lifetime of their father William was known as of Lethington and John was referred to as of Thirlestane. The income from Coldingham was divided between John and Thomas.

In April 1567 Sir Richard, now advanced in years and afflicted with blindness, resigned his office as Keeper of the Privy Seal in favour of John, who accepted it not without anxiety for the political scene was fraught with danger.

On the morning of the 19th June 1566 the Edinburgh Castle guns boomed a salute of a fair son' to Mary, Queen of Scots. In the ceaseless struggle for power the event created an unwelcome complication. For his own safety the infant Prince was lodged in Stirling Castle under the guardianship of the Earl and Countess of Mar, where he was to spend his early years, a lonely, loveless child.

January 1568 saw the marriage of William to Lady Mary Fleming, the Queen's Chief Maid of Honour. February brought the end of Darnley's short married life to the Queen, blown up in the explosion of Kirk-o-Field where he was lying ill. Whispered rumour placed the deed on the Earl of Bothwell, but no accusation could be voiced as the Earl's moss-troopers roamed the Capital. In the perplexity of the situation the Queen announced she was to marry Bothwell, newly created Duke of Orkney.

To William and John it was unbelievable that Mary could act with such incredible folly, for by this precipitate marriage it was flagrantly obvious she was either protecting, or implicating herself with, the chief suspect. Urged on by the venomous denunciations of the preachers the venal Lords hustled into action. They issued a call to arms ostensibly to rescue the Queen and bring Bothwell to justice. It was a moment for decision and both brothers felt compelled to side with the Confederate Lords. The opposing forces met at Carberry Hill near Musselburgh. To avoid bloodshed a parley was called but Mary was adamant. She would not surrender Bothwell. There was no conflict as Bothwell's loosely held followers began to desert and the Earl fled the field. The Queen was escorted back to Edinburgh where an outraged mob howled for her blood. She was lodged in the Provost's House which stood on the west side of what is now Cockburn Street at the corner of the High Street. (A plaque in the wall commemorates the site). The quarrelsome Lords revealed their treachery for they were for throwing her to the rabble. But Kirkcaldy of Grange held control with his troops while in the council chamber William strove for sanity. At length a compromise was reached. Mary was to be held in close arrest in Loch Leven Castle while an urgent message was despatched for the Earl of Moray to rerun and become Regent.

It was the best solution, for with Huntly and the Gordons in the North supporting the Queen, the Hamiltons ready to march in the West and a threat of war from Elizabeth of England if Mary was deposed, the Lords were on the horns of a dilemma. In addition the whole administration was in chaos.

Much to his relief then on the 26th August John received confirmation of his appointment as Keeper of the Privy Seal. To his legally trained mind the majesty and power of the Crown had at all costs to be re-established. This meant the suppression of violence, the administration of justice and introduction of a sound economic policy. Accordingly he pledged his support to the new Regent, trusting that Moray would seek the national good and not pursue his own personal ambition.

The Three Estates met in December and before they sat gain in August John was appointed an Ordinary Lord of Session. But the tasks of state-craft he had set himself to do were never completed. A furore of passion was unleashed by the exposure of the "Casket Letters". These were incriminating letters alleged to have been written by Mary to Bothwell the riddle of which has never been solved. They were contained in a casket decorated with twelve panels of Gothic tracery in gilded silver on silver ground (now preserved at Lennoxlove House, Haddington) and which it is said Bothwell had left in Edinburgh.

Mary's enemies made the most of them. Yielding to the mounting clamour and under duress the Queen signed an Act of Abdication in favour of her infant son, Prince James. Her reign ended on the 29th July and on the same day in the afternoon, Lady Mar carrying the child in her arms, came out of Stirling Castle and made for the Parish Kirk where the Bishop of Orkney anointed the Prince on whose head the Earl of Atholl placed the crown.

An uneasy calm followed broken by Mary's escape from Loch Leven. Once more there was turmoil. From the tangle of family alliances and feuds the Gordons, the Hamiltons and the Seatons rallied to her cause, when the tragic issue was fought out at the battle of Langside. Defeated, Mary crossed to England to throw herself on the mercy of Elizabeth who promptly imprisoned her as being too dangerous to Protestant England.

In Scotland, determined to smash every vestige of Mary's influence, Moray refused to listen to the saner councils of Lethington and his brother who argued in vain that if the succession to Elizabeth was to be achieved then Mary had at all costs to be preserved. Obsessed with hate the Regent had other ambitions and held the Maitlands to be a meddlesome pair to be exterminated. He instituted a charge of treason against the Secretary as being an accessory to the Darnley murder. When the news got abroad the Border Lairds rode in strength to the Capital and on the day of the hearing packed the court-room. To gain a verdict with such opposition Moray saw was useless so he postponed the hearing. He was immediately challenged by John supported by his cousin Robert Maitland, Dean of Aberdeen. They demanded the Secretary be discharged, for the prosecution had failed to provide witnesses or even state a case. In wild fury Moray left the Court determined to bring their downfall at a later date. Shortly after, he met his own death, shot down in the crowded High Street of Linlithgow, by a Hamilton whose estates he had impounded.

The King's grandfather, the Earl of Lennox succeeded to the Regency. He was old, ineffective, distrusted and Civil War broke out. The Catholics supported the Queen, the Protestants gave their support to the Crown, but not to Mary. Among the latter were many of the merchant class, who having a acquired wealth, desired a say in the government. Across the Border Elizabeth watched with anxious eye, for she had broken with Rome and was forceful of the united strength of Spain and France and could not afford to have a Catholic Scotland at her back. Accordingly she ordered her armies to march, to pillage, burn and ravage.

The Regent hounded the Maitlands with the old cry of treason. The Lethington property was confiscated and both brothers deprived of office. Thomas was arrested, escaped and after various adventures died in Italy. John, forewarned, sought refuge with William in Edinburgh Castle which was held for the Queen by Kirkcaldy of Grange.

So the situation remained throughout the long bitter winter. A carefully planned Marian raid on Stirling Castle in an attempt to secure the King mis-fired and in the confusion Lennox was shot.

The new Regent, the Earl of Mar did not last a year and the reins of office were grasped by the Earl of Morton, a boorish character, cruel, avaricious and revengeful, but a fit man to deal with the Lawless Scottish nobles. The tragedy of the time was that the nation had never recovered from the slaughter of Flodden, Solway Moss and Pinkie, where the cream of the nobility had fallen. Those left to inherit did so at tender age and had grown to manhood without parental curb.

Morton met the unruly situation with iron hand. He made peace with the Hamiltons then turned to quell Edinburgh Castle. He sought support from Elizabeth and with the heavy English guns battered the defences into submission. Kirkcaldy of Grange sought the honours of war but was hanged from the ramparts. William was hustled to Leith prison where he died within the week. John was incarcerated in Tantallon, a grim fortress on the sea-coast near Haddington.

Morton now continued to exert his authority. He annexed the estates of his enemies, enforced the obedience of the Kirk and laid hands on their endowments and subdued the nobles by punitive taxation. His ruthlessness brought a modicum of stability and order, but his greed bereft him of friends. Anxious to have supporters he ordered the release of John Maitland to live under house arrest with Lord Somerville at Cowthally under a surety of £10,000.

In the caller air of the Pentlands John found new strength and his health improved. There was much to learn on the political scene. He approved in principle of Morton's methods especially in bringing the Kirk to heel to acknowledge the rights of the Crown. This had been William's weakness, his failure to realise the strength underlying the Reformed Church.

But Morton had ambitious dreams. He passionately desired to get James under his power and to do this he schemed to make a 'token' resignation thus leaving a 'puppet' King, as he imagined completely helpless, who would turn to him to be manipulated as he wished. Two powerful Clan Chiefs, Argyll and Atholl however had other views. They urged the young King to accept Morton's resignation and take the government of the kingdom into his own hands and if he did they pledged him their support. James was flattered at the idea for secretly he had a high opinion of his own destiny. He also disliked the Regent. An angry Morton therefore was forced to withdraw to his country home with a mind full of crooked thoughts.

In his new-found freedom to rule in his own right James grew in stature. Atholl's influence was a steadying actor. But Morton was not to be thwarted and soon made a fresh bid for supremacy. In the violence that followed, the Earl of Mar was killed. Swiftly changing tactics Morton made a gesture of peace arranging a banquet to which Atholl was invited. A week later the Clan Chief was dead, allegedly poisoned at the feast.

Fearful of what the ex-Regent might do next the King turned for help to his father's cousin, Esme Stewart, Sieur d'Aubigny and invited him to come to Scotland. D'Aubigny was more French than Scot, soldier, courtier and a Catholic. His charm, elegance and knowledge of the world enchanted the lonely youth to whom flattery was unknown. It was not long before d'Aubigny was established as favourite, created Earl, then Duke of Lennox. But behind the blandishments lay a sinister purpose, for d'Aubigny was a pawn of the Guise Family, empowered and supplied with French gold to re-Catholicize Scotland.

Having gained his first objective, the confidence of the King with even a pretence of becoming a Protestant, he set about getting rid of Morton. To do this he sought out and be-friended the ex-Regent's known enemies. So it was that John Maitland was given his freedom and ushered into public life again. It was not long before he came into contact with the King and an association was formed which was to last for life. James quickly learned that in Maitland he had an industrious worker, whose ideas on constitutional law and order ran parallel with his own. It was pleasing to have someone who was dependable in administration, showed tact and patience and gave sound decisions. Moreover Maitland had inherited from his father the ability to write poetry, an art which James practised with a certain degree of skill. A mutual understanding and respect grew up between them. For John Maitland the moment of opportunity had arrived.

The surviving portrait of John Maitland, first Lord Maitland of Thirlestane and Lord High Chancellor of Scotland shows an expanse of face with a great nose and big upturned moustache, the eyes careful and considering. He owed much of his success to the fact that he was the first Scottish Statesman to treat King James VI., not as his contemporaries did as "a pedantic ass", but as a wise and great sovereign.

The King's adult reign began when he was a teenager desperately needing councillors on whom he could depend. He admired Maitland's swift mind and relished the cool, detached judgement. They were both lonely. From birth, the King had lived under the harsh, domineering influence of his guardian and tutors. A sickly youth, he had inherited from his mother, Mary, Queen of Scots, the distressing malady of porphyria, from which at Jedburgh in 1566, shortly after the birth of James, she had nearly died. The recognition that this agonizing disease was hereditary made him morose and melancholy. Although he over indulged he managed to preserve his health by physical exercise in his love for the hunt. His solace mostly was to be found in book learning. As he was wont to say "They gar me speik Latin 'ar I could speik Scottis". Maitland also had few intimates and from his prison life knew what it was to be cut off from the outer world. As a consequence his friendship with the King was a link of mind with mind rather than a close bond of companionship.

In September, 1579, Esme Stewart, Sieur d'Aubigny accepted the royal invitation to come to Scotland. He quickly ingratiated himself into favour for he brought with him an aura of the French Court that was fascinating to the young King. James revelled in the flattery, for he had never known affection, and rewarded d'Aubigny by creating him first Earl then Duke of Lennox.

D'Aubigny was well satisfied. The first part of an ambitious plan had been achieved. As agent of the Guise faction in France, his mission was to overthrow the Protestants and pave the way for a Catholic seizure of power. The next move was to eliminate Morton. To do this he fraternized with the ex-Regent's enemies and John Maitland was one of those singled out for favour. He was freed from house arrest and with the eventual downfall of Morton his fortunes took an upward turn. On the 26th April, 1581, he was restored to his seat on the Bench. Two years later on the 16th January he married Lady Janet, the only child of James, 4th Lord Fleming. His public image was gradually being restored but nevertheless he had to "gang warily", for in many quarters he was still regarded as "the Secretair's brother" and suspect of Marian sympathies. It took time to dispel the fears that he was a Papal agent, but conscientious work and integrity won their reward. He was made a Privy Councillor and admitted into the King's confidence. His views were pleasing to James. As a first priority he pressed for firm action to curb the arrogant nobles. Timidly James agreed to certain measures and was overjoyed when he discovered that they worked. This gave him courage to consider other reforms. At the back of his mind was the dream of the royal prerogative, the divine right of kings to rule State, Kirk and Nation. An accomplished theologian he loved to display his erudition and in Maitland at last he found a sympathetic councillor who was prepared to listen, advise and guide him. Once an agreeable compromise had been worked out, it was Maitland who drafted the necessary legislation and saw that the laws were obeyed.

Such trustworthy service did not go unheeded, for in April, 1584 Maitland became Sir John and was made Secretary of State, thus succeeding to the office so long held by his bother.

Although gratified he was nevertheless aware that he had not William's flair for foreign diplomacy. To him Elizabeth of England was an enigma. Beset by Catholic conspiracies she was devious in negotiation which made the results unpredictable. However he was able to conclude one Treaty in 1586 whereby the succession by James to the English throne was tacitly recognised.

In February, 1587 the news reached Edinburgh of the execution at Fotheringay Castle of Mary, Queen of Scots. There was a wave of revulsion for, despite her mistakes and questionable conduct, Mary still held a place in the hearts of her subjects. Repercussion was inevitable.

With the unmasking of his Catholic plotting Lennox had already fallen. The Chancellor was the Earl of Arran, bitter opponent of Maitland and envious of his growing influence with the King. The time seemed opportune to discredit him. Arran therefore accused Maitland of having complicity in obtaining Mary's execution, trusting on public support to sweep him from office. But he reckoned without James who summarily commanded him to appear at the Palace of Linlithgow to substantiate the charge. As his indictment had no foundation Arran refused and was peremptorily deprived of the Chancellorship to which the King nominated Maitland. To the higher peerage this was an affront to their prestige, for the state office was regarded as one of their perquisites. But James, who had some of his grandfather's shrewdness, made the appointment deliberately. His new Chancellor would serve more faithfully if not drawn from the clique of nobles with their vested interests. Maitland had his misgivings; he knew he would be the target of ceaseless antagonism, yet his mind was clear as to what had to be done for the good of the nation.

In making the appointment the King (James VI) directed in 1586 that, to give him assurance and security, Sir John Maitland of Thirlestane who held the Great Seal of the Realm should, as Chancellor have first place and rank in the Nation in the Order of the Precedence. The College of Justice is generally attributed to James V and the Court commenced its sittings on the 27th May 1532 and sat thereafter except from 1650 – 1661 when the powers of the Council was abrogated and its functions were handled by Commissioners for the administration of justice.

The judges consisted of the Lord High Chancellor, the Lord President, Ordinary Lords of Session and a number of supernumerary Judges, termed Extraordinary Lords.

After the Union of Scotland and England it was decided that only one seal for the United Kingdom was necessary. Nowadays, the old College of Justice, known as the Court of Session ruled over by the Lord President and a panel of

Judges, who also constitute the High Court of Judiciary, the supreme criminal court of Scotland. When presiding in the Court, the Lord President is known as the Lord Justice General, and in precedence in Scotland he ranks after Dukes' young sons & the Keeper of the Great Seal and of the Privy Seal successively if not Peers.

Patiently therefore Maitland, with this supreme authority, set to work to strengthen the power of the throne and cement the framework of central government. The more he fashioned his ideals into practical effect the more the peers showed their repugnance. The most bellicose was the Earl of Huntly and this powerful leader of the Gordons moved swiftly. With the Earls of Crawford and Bothwell he hatched a plot in which they were to gather their followers in the capital, march on the Palace of Holyrood House, seize the King and put Maitland to death. This however, and other attempts on the throne were foiled.

Unperturbed by the mischief-makers the Chancellor Maitland held to his task. Slowly the government machinery began to function and more important, was seen to fulfil its purpose. A grateful sovereign showed his appreciation for he bestowed on Maitland the ratification of the Lordship of Thirlestane the hereditary position of Baillie of Lauderdale, the barony of Stobo and the Lordship of Dunbar. As a further sign of his pleasure the King granted him the Lordship and regality of Musselburgh, with the patronage of the church and the various attached chaplainries.

Life at Court was far from smooth: James at times could be an intractable monarch. Two of the most fertile causes of friction are money and religion and on these issues James quarrelled incessantly with his Chancellor. Confronted with collision debate James would abruptly depart for his favourite pastime – hunting, leaving his Chancellor to act as he thought best, but on return the King let loose a storm of petulance and rebuke for lack of consultation.

The King also refused to come to any decision about Huntly although Maitland urged him to have done with leniency towards the troublemaker. There was an ulterior motive in James' decision. Secretly he felt that one day he might have need of him, for Huntly was a sworn enemy of the Earl of Moray of whom the King was jealous. Moray was a big, handsome, masculine man, the very antithesis of James who preferred his courtiers to be effeminate in view of his own ill health. Another cause of grievance was that Moray was a stalwart Protestant beloved by the divines with whom James was always at loggerheads. Huntly on the other hand was a Roman Catholic and this suited James for periodically he engaged in controversial attempts to reform the Kirk and many of his ideas smacked of papacy. He knew that the deep core of his subjects had a Catholic background and he believed that many were not yet convinced that the new faith was going to last. When protestations from Maitland became ominous he eluded the subject by going to the hunt.

Moreover his mind was now preoccupied over his forthcoming marriage to Princess Anne, the daughter of King Frederick II. of Denmark. Negotiations had been protracted, hindered by the interference of Elizabeth. The Princess eventually had embarked with an escort of twelve ships but when sixty miles from the Scottish coast, gales drove the convoy back to seek shelter in a Norwegian fiord. Eleven of the vessels returned to Denmark for major repairs. When James heard this he was furious and demanded that Maitland should produce a fleet for him so that he could bring his bride to Scotland. His Chancellor gave succinct reply that there were no ships available and furthermore the Exchequer was practically empty. There were also gales blowing with no sign of moderation. The atmosphere at court became electric and to soothe the King's wrath Maitland offered to provide a ship of his own, already victualed with a master willing to risk the weather. The Royal party, including Maitland much against his will, left Leith on the 22nd October and took six days to the crossing. On the 21st November James and Anne were married at Upsala, in those days an Ecclesiastical Capital and thereafter the entourage travelled to winter in Denmark. The prospect filled Maitland with gloom for he feared what might happen during the long absence, but his protestations were waved aside. During his stay he made a happy friendship with Tycho Brahe, the celebrated astronomer, to whom he penned some complimentary verse.

A return to Scotland was made in the spring and on the day after the coronation, in which Sir John Maitland carried the Queen's matrimonial crown, he was elevated to the peerage as Lord Maitland of Thirlestane.

An embarrassing situation now arose. As part of the marriage dowry James conveyed to Anne the Lordship of Dunfermline which included the Lordship of Musselburgh, but this James had already gifted to his Chancellor. The Queen claimed she had the right of dower and that Maitland should revoke it in her favour. Maitland refused contesting the legality of the demand and fought the case with tenacity and skill. Rebuffed, the Queen nursed her grievance.

About this time too, Maitland resigned the office of Secretary of State in favour of his nephew, Richard Cockburn of Clerkington, thus giving him more time for family affairs. He had arrived at a decision to remove the ancestral seat at Thirlestane Tower to Lauder Fort which he now designated as Thirlestane Castle. The site was pleasant, the foundations of the Fort being on solid rock on rising ground on the right bank of the Leader Water and close by the Royal Burgh of Lauder. Accordingly he rebuilt with extensions and made it habitable. One of the first visitors was the King in 1591 at the marriage of the Chancellor's niece to the young Laird of Lugton.

The political scene however gave no cause for satisfaction; struggle and tension continued between the aggressive nobles. The Earl of Bothwell was openly hostile while the Earl of Huntly was waiting a chance to exert his power. It was whispered the handsome Earl of Moray had taken the young Queen's fancy and the jealous James had ordered him to leave the court. He had taken up residence with Bothwell an association that gave displeasure to the King. He therefore ordered him to return to where he could keep an eye on him. But Moray, uncertain of his reception went to Donibristle in Fife, the castle belonging to his mother, the Lady Doune. The news reached James when he was hunting in the Lothians. Huntly who was in the party asked permission to execute the Royal command and fetch Moray back and rode off with a strong body of followers. The presumption is he ordered Moray to surrender then took the chance to pay off the old feud between them by besieging the castle. To hasten matters he stacked brushwood against the sanitary vents in the walls, the chutes acted like chimney flues and the flames and smoke roared up inside the castle. Trapped, the retainers created a diversion as Moray made a dash for the sea shore. He was overtaken and slain. Known as "the bonnie Earl o' Moray" a stirring ballad set to a haunting melody commemorates his tragic death.

The brutal incident created a public uproar and rumours were rife. Bothwell, quick in denouncement, accused the King and Maitland of being cognizant of Huntly's intention, even though the Chancellor was not at the hunt. Determined to do all the damage he could, Bothwell, through his coterie had pressure brought on the Queen to renew her claim to the Lordship of Musselburgh. James caught in a dilemma, pleaded innocence and moved the court quickly to Glasgow. Hoping things would simmer down he had Huntly confined in Blackness Castle but allowed him to keep his followers. To placate the Queen he asked Maitland to leave court for a while and so, exerting political sagacity and grace Maitland returned to the peace of Lethington glad to be rid of the hurly-burly of intrigue.

James soon found he could not manage without his industrious and level-headed Chancellor. His ideas of church reform alarmed the divines and when James mooted "the divine right of kings" they showed a militancy that was terrifying. Maitland was summoned to return at once. Diplomatically he eased the tension, started consultations and presented a draft Act to which he advised the King to give consent. This was passed in 1592, the Golden Act as it was named, which ratified the liberty of the Scottish Presbyterian Church. Under this the General Assembly and the subordinate courts were realised, but as a sop to James, it stipulated that His Majesty or his High Commissioner should be present at each General Assembly.

The Queen had not forgiven Maitland and again angrily put her claim for the return of the Lordship of Musselburgh. Once more the King advised his faithful Chancellor to leave court for a period but recalled him in May 1593. It was not to be for long. This time it was a domestic affair that caused the rift. James had strong views about his son and had entrusted the young Prince Henry's education to the Earl of Mar into whose care he had placed him. Anne was furious, but to her delight Maitland sided with her, insisting that the Prince should be removed from the Earl's influence. James was not to be so thwarted and roundly upbraided his Chancellor for meddling in a matter he said was not his concern. Deeply mortified, Maitland, who was feeling far from well, withdrew to Lauder. A few days later he was forced to take to his bed and lay for several weeks becoming gradually weaker. One of his last visitors was the great divine Andrew Melville. He died suddenly on the 3rd October 1595.

James was filled with remorse, consoling himself by writing an epitaph:

> "Thou passenger! That spies with gazing eyes
> This Trophy end of Death's triumphant dart,
> Consider when this outward tomb thou sees,
> How rare a man leaves here his earthly part;
> His wisdom and uprightness of heart,
> His piety, his practice of our state
> His quick engine so versed in every art
> As equally not all were in debate.
> Thus justly hath his death brought forth of late
> An heavy grief in prince and subjects all
> That virtue love, and vice do bear at hate
> Though vicious man rejoices at his fall.
> So for himself most happy doth he die,
> Though for his prince it must unhappy be".

These lines were engraved at the top of a magnificent monument situated in the aisle in the north-east side of the Church of Haddington, but later became defaced.

There is no doubt that Maitland's untimely death was a tragedy, not only to the King but to the nation, for had he lived, the breach between the King and Kirk, with all its sad and bitter repercussions would have been averted.

Maitland's great contribution was that he taught the young King James how to govern, by giving to him an administration in Scotland. For as James later boasted to the English Parliament

> "This I must say for Scotland. Here I sit and govern it with my pen. I write and it is done, and by a Clerk of the Council I govern Scotland now – which others could not do by the sword".

There could be no more fitting tribute to the painstaking work of his great Chancellor. Maitland was the creative mind which built an administration of State, which despite the confusion of the time was seen to work.

10. THE FIRST EARL OF LAUDERDALE

John Maitland, the Lord High Chancellor's eldest son, was born on August 21, 1616, at Lethington and succeeded his father in 1595.

As soon as he was old enough he joined the court of King James I at Theobalds. Not only was he the son of one of the King's most valued ministers, he was also a great-grandson of James VI, as was the King himself. A loyal man, whose youth and energy attracted King James, he received rapid advancement.

In July 1615 he became a Scottish Privy Councillor and was created Viscount Lauderdale. He became President of the Council and in June 1618 was appointed an ordinary Lord of Session. He was selected by the King as one of the Commissioners to negotiate with the Church of Scotland. The reign of James VI and I was notable for its peaceful character. The King himself had dealt ruthlessly with Border and Highland families. The court in London had drawn off from Scotland a large number of ambitious and restless young nobles. The Plantation of Ulster enticed many more to try their fortunes in a new colony and the American colonies were likewise expanding.

The King's interest in religious matters, his commissioning of the Authorised Version of the Bible, kept the Churches in England and Scotland busy in organising their affairs instead of quarrelling with the court. After all the civil warfare of his mother's reign in Scotland, the King's ability to hold the balance between rival factions followed smoothly on the reign of Queen Elizabeth. The outcome of the economic progress made was not yet seen, of course – that was to burst out in the reign of Charles I – but for the time the quiet development of society was desirable.

John Maitland had inherited the family skill for diplomacy and served the King well. In March 1624 he was created Earl of Lauderdale, Viscount Maitland, Lord Thirlestane and Boltoun. In the following year, King James died and was succeeded by King Charles, whose character seriously altered the attitude of those who were discontented with the monarchy and the court.

A curious position arose in regard to the Earl of Lauderdale as an ordinary Lord of Session. Charles I passed an Act of Parliament whereby no peer could hold the seat of an ordinary Lord of Session. Accordingly, Lauderdale was removed from the bench in February, 1626. But under the original constitution of the Court of Session, the King was permitted to appoint and removed at his pleasure. This, of course, was a device to raise money – the Stuart kings were always hard up – by selling seats on the bench, as the votes of the Extraordinary Lords could be used profitably.

The appointment of these Extraordinary Lords was eventually stopped by an Act in the reign of George I. But Lauderdale was appointed an Extraordinary Lord of Session in June 1626 until deprived of the office in November, 1628.

With the rising struggle between King Charles and the House of Commons, Lauderdale took the side of the Scottish Estates and the Presbyterians. His abilities were respected by those of moderate views and he was employed in a great variety of commissions. In 1644, he was elected President of the Estates of Parliament, an office of critical importance at that moment in the Civil War.

In June, 1610, John Maitland married Lady Isobel Seton, second daughter of Alexander Seton, Earl of Dunfermline and Lord Fyvie, who became Lord Chancellor of Scotland.

Lady Isobel's mother, Lilias Drummond, was the "Green Lady of Fyvie", whose ghost haunts Fyvie Castle.

The Earl of Lauderdale seems to have been one of the patrons of the Latin poet, Arthur Johnston of Caskieben, who dedicated his "Epigrammata" to the Earl in 1632. Johnston also wrote poems to Lady Lauderdale and one of her daughters, adding them to the wide gallery of Scottish figures whom he celebrated in Latin verse. Lady Lauderdale died in November, 1638.

Crawford describes the first Earl as "a nobleman of great honour and probity" and adds approvingly that he "managed his affairs with so much discretion that he made considerable additions to his fortunes."

Lethington was still the family home, for it was there that his eldest son was born in 1616. But his mother had purchased Brustane, near Edinburgh, in 1597. This estate was previously known as Gilberton and belonged to the Crichtons, who alienated it "to Dame Jean Flemying, Lady Thirlestane, relict of the deceased John, Lord Thirlestane, Chancellor of Scotland, for the sum of 40,000 merks."

On Lady Thirlestane taking over the old castle, the two Crichton brothers emigrated to Ulster, where they took up 2,000 acres each in the plantation of the forfeited lands of Tyrone.

When the Dowager Countess died in 1609, John Maitland succeeded to Brunstane. Some thirty years later, when his eldest son, John, married Lady Anne Home, the Earl rebuilt the old house for his son. This is evidenced by the fact that the combined arms of Maitland and Home were carved above the principal entrance to the new Brunstane House and dated, 1639.

Crawford in his Peerage tells us that at the beginning of the Civil War the charter of the Maitlands was buried for safety. When dug up again the writs had become so defaced that they were almost unintelligible. The Earl made an exact inventory of all the charters and writs and, Crawford says,

> "by reason of the character his Lordship had for integrity, the inventory was, by order of Parliament, appointed to supply the place of the ancient records of the family, the clerk register signing every page thereof."

The first Earl died in January, 1645, not long after having been chosen President of the Estates of Parliament. Both he and his Countess were buried in St Mary's, the parish church of Haddington, which was one of the largest and finest churches built in Scotland in the 15th century, the tower of which was originally capped by an open stone crown. Throughout the centuries, this beautiful church has been known as the Lamp of Lothian, although tradition claims that the title was inherited from a still more ancient church situated nearer the River Tyne, the banks of which the royal burgh of Haddington is built.

During the Reformation, the choir and transepts fell into disuse and being no longer required for public worship, they were given over to the burial of notable parishioners. Chief among these were the Maitlands, for it was here in what has become known as the Lauderdale Vault that the Earl had erected a splendid tomb in memory of his father and mother, who are to be seen in alabaster effigy, together with the epitaph which James I wrote. His own likeness and effigy of his wife have been added to the tomb.

Of a large family, only three sons and a daughter survived their parents. John was the heir. The second son, Robert, was a royalist and like his older brother was taken prisoner at the battle of Worcester in September, 1651, and held in jail. Three years later, upon payment of a fine of £1,000, Cromwell granted him a pardon and he returned to his wife, Margeret Lundin, only daughter and heiress of John Lundin of that Ilk. He is said to have died in 1658. The third son, Charles, became Lord Hatton and later succeeded his brother, John. Nothing is known of the Lady Sophia, who survived the death of her parents. Her sister, Jean, who was reputed to be a great beauty, died at the age of nineteen.

11. THE COVENANTING COMMISSIONER

John, the second Earl of Lauderdale, was born at Lethington on the 24th of May, 1616. Following the family tradition, he entered politics and this, in Scotland of the early 16th century, either meant going to court in London and seeking the favour of King James I or entering the Covenanting Kirk. Maitland became an elder of the Kirk and an active Presbyterian. Inheriting the oratorical force and diplomatic skill of his forebears, he became a leading lay figure in a Kirk which had a throng of ministers whose powers of preaching, disputation and intrigue were hard to match. At an early age, in 1643, he was one of the two lay members (the other was Sir Archibald Johnstone, who became Lord Warriston) of the eight Commissioners of the General Assembly of the church of Scotland who attended the Westminster Assembly.

Before the Commissioners could report on their endless argumentation of many months, of which the most notable outcome was the banning of the Book of Common Prayer, the Earl of Huntly had raised the King's flag in the Highlands and the Marquis of Montrose and his Highland clansman had stormed their way southwards and from Tippermuir to Kilsyth, had defeated the covenanting armies.

Meanwhile, the Earl's father had become elected President of the Scottish Estates, although he was to die in January 1645, while still in office. At this critical time in the civil war, when the menace of Montrose was more unfavourable to the Covenanters than the ease which the defeat of Prince Rupert at Marston Moor had brought was helpful to them, Maitlands occupied responsible positions on the Presbyterian side. We believe that in the counsels of their party, they stood for moderation, but this was a time of war, when the tempers of both sides were too inflamed to listen to advice about the future need of people to live together.

Montrose's great victory at Kilayth made him master of the whole of Scotland, from the military point of view, and he marched his victorious Highlanders towards the Borders to begin a Royalist invasion of England. But General David Leslie, who had brought his army from the finality of Naseby northwards to meet Montrose, surprised the Royalists at Philiphaugh, near Selkirk and not so many miles away from Lauderdale, and completely defeated Montrose, who had to cut his way through the enemy cavalry and flee up Yarrow dale.

The prisoners who had surrendered on promise of quarter would have escaped with their lives under the custom of war, but the covenanting ministers with the army insisted on their death. They were executed on the spot and their officers, after trial, were beheaded. Fear and the flush of victory were an ill mixture.

The new Earl of Lauderdale was one of the parliamentary commissioners who went to Uxbridge for further talks with Charles I. Meanwhile, the Westminster Assembly continued its meetings – it sat off and on for more than five years and held 1,163 meetings. During this time it produced the Westminster Confession of Faith and the Larger and Shorter Catechisms.

In May, 1646, Charles placed himself in the hands of the Scottish army, which was still in England, and eight months later, he was handed over to the English Parliament. While confined at Hampton Court, a commission from the Scottish Estates, headed by the Duke of Hamilton and consisting of the Earls of Lanark, Lauderdale and Loudon, arrived to enter further negotiations. The King removed himself to Carisbrooke Castle and the Scottish nobles followed him. Eventually, King Charles agreed with the Scots, to sanction in Parliament the Solemn League and Covenant. This agreement, known as the Engagement, was signed on 26th December, 1647.

The Engagement split the Covenanters. The Estates accepted it, but the militant Covenanters of the Assembly of the Church rejected it as insufficient. The King and the whole of Britain must accept the Covenant and become Presbyterian. The Assembly ordered the ministers to preach against the Engagement.

There was a rising of Covenanters in the West. Two thousand of them, under their ministers, were defeated by General Middleton at Mauchline Moor in June, 1648.

The Scottish Estates raised an army of 20,000 and marched them into England to rescue King Charles from Cromwell and the Puritans. They were defeated by Cromwell at Preston. The moderates had lost.

Perfervid Covenanters from the West now invaded Edinburgh in the "Whiggamore's Raid" and lifted the Earl of Argyll to political power. When the Estates next met, its membership was severely purged by the Act of Classes, which excluded from every kind of office all opponents unless they first did public penance to the satisfaction of the ministers.

The Earl of Lauderdale had been sent by the Committee of Estates to Holland the persuade the Prince of Wales to return. Prince Charles had played an active part in the army during the civil war and after Naseby had tried to carry on the struggle in the West of England against General Fairfax, but on the Royalists being defeated at Torrington, the Prince had fled to the Channel Islands and then to St Germain, where his mother, Queen Henrietta Maria, a sister of the French King, was in exile.

In 1648, part of the English fleet had become so discontented that it crossed over to Holland. Prince Charles eager for military action, went to Helvoetsluys, at the mouth of the river Meuse, and placed himself in command of this little navy.

He then moved to the Hague, where he was received by his brother-in-law, the Prince of Orange. It was here that the Earl of Lauderdale first met Charles Stuart. John Maitland was a man of 32, already burly of figure, with a shock of red hair and inclined to outbursts of bad temper – probably more of impatience with obdurate events and stupid humanity than of evil nature. Charles, a man of 18, already had all the good-humoured charm and intelligence that had marked his great-grandmother, Mary Queen of Scots, and his grandfather, James I, but had been so unfortunately lacking in his father. With his long Stuart nose and thick underlip, Charles was not handsome but he could win the love of women. He also could attract friends who would stay with him for a long time, in spite of the storms and treacheries, the ambitions and dismissals that surround a King. He already had in Edward Hyde, to become the Earl of Clarendon after the Restoration, a loyal adviser. Now he was to recruit to the Royalist cause a man who was capable of dealing for him with one of the thorniest problems that would beset him if he regained his crown – Scotland and the Covenanting movement.

It may never be known how the two men reacted to each other and how far Maitland at that time seceded from his Covenanting views to become a follower of Charles. But after Charles had decided to come to terms with the Covenanters and go to Scotland, the Earl of Lauderdale accompanied him.

Scotland in 1648 could be said to be without Roman Catholics. There were not ten priests in the whole country. The Highlands clans remained untouched by religious considerations: they followed their chiefs as of old. The Lowlands were divided, largely geographically – the West was for the Covenant, the East for moderation (in the event, supporters of those called the Engagers, who wanted King and Covenant or even Kind and Bishops). The Covenanters wanted government by the Kirk – in effect, they were republicans. But they wanted not only a Covenanting Scotland. They demanded the imposition of the Covenant upon the rest of Britain and Ireland. The Covenanters were led by the Earl of Argyll, who could draw upon an army from his clan as well as from the Covenanting West.

The moderate Engagers were led by the Duke of Hamilton and the Earl of Lauderdale. Argyll, head of the great family and clan of Campbell, and Hamilton, head of the Douglases, both saw themselves as the rulers of Scotland – Argyll through a Covenanting Kirk, Hamilton as the viceroy of King Charles.

There was also a Royalist party, led by the Marquess of Montrose, the Earl of Glencairn (his aunt was the Duchess of Hamilton), Lord Lorne, heir to the Duke of Argyll, and General George Middleton.

Unfortunately for Montrose, his defeat at Philiphaugh showed that an army of Cavalier horse and Highland foot was a kittle instrument for victory. Charles was willing that Montrose and the Royalists should venture their utmost in the highlands, but hoped for surer and speedier results.

The Engagers were the first of the two Scottish factions to open negotiations with the Prince. When Lauderdale arrived at Helvoetsluys, Charles was absorbed in organising his little navy for a sea victory and he would not lay aside this exciting and active project for talks round the council table. If Lauderdale wanted anything, he had to tag along. What Lauderdale and the Engagers wanted was that Charles would so far support the Covenanting position that he would be acceptable as King to the majority of Scots. He was asked to abandon such "high-flying" Royalists as Prince Rupert and Montrose, the Prayer book and episcopacy, and dismiss his chaplains.

The young Prince expressed all eagerness to go to Scotland to be received by his Scottish subjects but evaded giving Lauderdale any direct answers. He believed, from his fast growing experience of his powers, that once he was in Scotland in person, he could manage all parties by his charming ability to promise everybody what they wanted and then letting the promises take care of themselves.

Besides, Charles was in the middle of his naval invasion of England when the Duke of Hamilton and his army crossed the Border and there was no sense in agreeing with

Lauderdale if he did not represent the winning party.

All this lay behind hours and days of talks on board the "Satisfaction" on the Downs, while Charles's ships captured several London vessels and blockaded the Thames. The Parliamentary party put out their fleet under the Earl of Warwick. The seamen wanted to fight and when Lauderdale and the Earl of Culpepper, a member of Charles's court, were heard persuading the Prince to sail back to Holland, they stormed the council and swore they would throw Lauderdale and Culpepper overboard.

When Warwick's ships came in view and Prince Charles's navy pursued them, the Parliamentary fleet turned and fled, until a storm blew up and finished any prospect of battle. Upon Charles and Lauderdale returning to Helvoetsluys, they were met with the news that Hamilton and the Scots had been defeated by Cromwell at Preston. Edward Hyde, the Prince's Chancellor, was now at the Hague and the Prince met in council to receive Lauderdale. Hyde tells us in his memoirs that Lauderdale, after stating his cause and on being asked to withdraw so that the council should consider them refused to do so. There was a wordy dispute between Lauderdale and Hyde, the Earl trying to shout down the Chancellor in his loud, blustering, Scottish voice. The Prince intervened, saying it was unreasonable for Lauderdale to remain and ordering him to withdraw. Lauderdale obeyed, cursing "with much indecency", Hyde writes, and clearly without much lowering his voice.

With all the persistence of a Covenanting minister pursuing a witch, Lauderdale stuck to his task of trying to persuade Prince Charles to come to Scotland on the conditions laid down by the Engagers but after several weeks was forced to go back to Scotland empty-handed and

(Hyde sums up spitefully) "with as much rage and malice against the Council as against Cromwell himself". A middle-of-the-road position is always the most unrewarding – especially when you meet someone more in the middle of the road than you are yourself.

Then, on January 30, 1649, King Charles I was beheaded.

With the new King, the Scottish Parliament opened up new and lengthy negotiations. Charles refused to sign the Covenant. He procrastinated, hoping first that the Duke of Ormond and his papist army in Ireland would win the day and invade England for him and then, when this hope went, that Montrose, who had returned to raise the Highland clans again, would succeed this second time in defeating Oliver Cromwell and the Roundheads. Lauderdale was again one of the commissioners sent by Parliament, although Robert Baillie and the ministers were the disputants. The Duke of Hamilton had been captured after Preston and beheaded and his brother, the new Duke had openly joined King Charles's court. Lauderdale was left to speak for the Engager. His advice in private to the King was close to Charles's own view: keep the Covenant "when in Scotland".

But when Charles finally decided to go to Scotland, Lauderdale, however Royalist he might have become or however moderate, he was not in a position to help Charles very much. The Whiggamores under the Duke of Argyll were in control of Kirk and Parliament and Maitland had been an Engager. Along with others who had supported the Engagement of 1647, he was dismissed from Charles's entourage.

The execution of James Graham, the Marquis of

Montrose, a brilliant Royalist general and one of the most remarkable aristocrats of his age, has blackened the name of Charles in the histories of Scotland. He has been accused of the deliberate and cynical abandonment of his own captain-general to the vengeance of Argyle. It would seem that the sad sacrifice of Montrose was due to a breakdown in communications. We who live with a postal service every morning and hourly news bulletins on the radio have to realise that Charles had to send orders from Holland by sea to a Montrose whose camp was "somewhere in the highlands".

Montrose landed at John o' Groats on April 12, 1650. On the 27th he was defeated at Carbisdale and a week later was handed over to the Covenanters. Letters from Charles to Montrose, instructing him to lay down his arms and come to terms and promising him a post in an army to invade England, had failed to reach him. On May 1, at Breda, Charles signed an agreement meeting the terms of the covenanters. Montrose was hanged on the 21st.

This was not only an act of vengeance and fear; it was also a warning to Charles. But the Covenanters had met their match. Charles was doing something he hated. He was compromising with the Scots and with the party that had betrayed his father to an unkingly death. He did it solely for the sake of being able to march a Royalist army into England to regain his throne. He was not moved by the religious codes over which the Scots fought so bitterly. Still less did he love the overt republicanism of the Covenanters.

He was subjected to the same unceremonious indignities that had befallen his father. Intrigues round the King-to-be could have been stomached by the young Charles but plots in which he was a mere Stuart pawn, while the real cynosure of all political manoeuvre was the ferocious God of Battles of the Old Testament, this Charles could not understand.

Yet Charles, who in popular history has become known only as the Merry Monarch, showed during those months in Scotland that he could handle himself in the diplomatic sphere as well as he could in the military and naval worlds. He succeeded in uniting all factions in Scotland. But this took time.

Soon after Charles landed in Scotland, Oliver Cromwell replaced General Lord Fairfax as captain-general of the Parliamentary Army and marched into Scotland, inflicting a sever defeat on the Covenanting Army at Dunbar.

In all these events, John Maitland played a waiting part. The squint-eyed Argyll had not only purged the Estates of Engagers, but before the battle of Dunbar, the army had been screened. Excluded from active political life the Earl of Lauderdale stayed quietly at Brunstane House (Lauder) with his wife, Anne, seeing about his lands and family affairs – no doubt hoping for the sun that never came. In September, 1649, he was served heir to his father in the Lordship and regality of the burgh of Musselburgh, at the mouth of the river Esk. This was a thriving little town, with fishing, saltpans and corn mills. So that at this stage in the civil war, long before he came to stride a more prominent historical stage, the Earl began an association with the honest Toun which showed him to be a busy and comfortable landlord and superior. When, in 1670, he entered upon a contract with the provost and baillies of Musselburgh, to be confirmed later by royal charter, he was secured in his "heritable office of miller" (of the Sea Miln) and as superior of the "knaveship", as well as of an annual rent of 2,400 marks "upliftable furth of said toun ... and so furth of the said nether miln of Brunstain." We are running ahead of our narrative, but it is amusing to note that the wealthy and powerful Duke of Lauderdale, the political dictator of Scotland, held among his many offices and jurisdictions, the superiority of a "knaveship" – the time honoured payment of the miller, who received so many handfuls (neivefuls in the Scots) from every measure of corn sent to be ground.

As Cromwell followed up his victory at Dunbar by sending General Lambert to pursue the Whiggamores in the West, this had the effect of pushing all parties towards the unity Charles wished for. The Scottish Estates restored the Engagers to their political rights and Charles was crowned King at Scone, the Marquis of Argyll himself placing the crown on the Prince's head.

As soon as Charles was able to put himself at the head of an army of the united Scots, he challenged Cromwell and his New Model Army. In the manoeuvrings of war, King Charles saw his opportunity of marching into England and did so. The Duke of Hamilton and the Engagers, including the Earl of Lauderdale, went with the army. Argyll and the Covenanters refused to go and retired to sulk in their tabernacles.

But Cromwell had been prepared for such a move and four armies marched to shut up Charles in the town of Worcester, which his army had reached after a brilliantly conducted march in record time. Cromwell himself followed rapidly and took command. The Royalists were beaten. The Duke of Hamilton was killed in the battle. Among the 9,000 prisoners taken were General Leslie and the Earl of Lauderdale. King Charles himself escaped and after wandering and hiding for seven weeks, found a shipmaster at Shoreham to take him to France.

The Earl of Lauderdale, John Maitland, was sent with other Scottish nobles to the Tower of London. He was to remain in captivity for the next nine years, being later removed to Windsor and then to Portland Caste, but eventually managed to purchase his release during the time of confusion before the Restoration of Charles II.

There is a story that not only illustrates the quality of clan loyalty which pervaded Scottish society, even in the midst of civil war, but also gives a picture of John Maitland which is greatly different from that painted by the orthodox Scottish historian. The story is that of Midside Maggie and it has come down to us:

Four miles north of Lauder stands was Carfraemill Inn. Behind it runs a rough road into a wild and Longley dale, where at the summit, twelve hundred feet up, lying unsheltered on the hillside, is Tollis Hill Farm. It is a place of snell winds and harsh weather. Records show that often the harvest was not finished until the New Year and that the sheep suffered severely from the drifting snow.

Margaret Lylestone had her widowed mother had come from the south to be tenants at Westrutner, but both weather and markets were bad and misfortune after misfortune brought them to the verge of ruin. There was nothing left to sell but their only cow to pay their debts. With heavy heart, Margaret drove the beast to Kelso to be auctioned.

In the mart that day was Thomas Hardie of Tollis Hill. At the ringside he heard the gossip about the widow and her daughter and their cow. A true Border man, quiet and unassuming, nodding his head almost imperceptibly at the bidding, when the hammer fell he showed no sign of what he was thinking. But when he left the ring, he sought out Margaret and restored the cow to her. In the year 1643, they were married and to the middle farm of the three on Tollis Hill, to Midside, Thomas Hardie brought his bride. For ever after she was to known as Midside Maggie.

The pair worked hard and for a time the farm prospered. Then came a succession of bad harvest. In March, 1650, the weather "was like whereof was not usual for weets, cold frost and tempests."

As he dourly surveyed the disastrous scene, Thomas knew that he could never in a twelvemonth raise sufficient for the payment of the rent, and his landLord, the Earl of Lauderdale, was reputed to be a hard man in money matters. His heart sank as he thought of the loss of his farm and the home he had strived to build. But he had reckoned without his wife. She placed a comforting hand on his arm.

"I'll speir at him masel" she said.

Wrapping her plaid about her, she set off on the long walk to Thirlestane Castle. She was granted an interview, and pleaded her cause, modestly, earnestly and effectively. Perhaps it was her winsomeness more than her beauty that softened the Duke.

"Tis a reasonable request," he said, and then jocularly, "Since it is the snow that has brought you to my door, and the weather at Tollis Hill so bad that you cannot pay the rent, why then, if you bring me a snowball in the month of June, I will overlook the matter!"

And with a hearty laugh he dismissed her.

She toiled up the hill sides on her homeward journey, Maggie's shrewd mind was at work. The snow was lying in depth, and she paused for a moment and a grim smile came over her face.

"A snowball?" she murmured. Stooping quickly she gathered the crisp, hard snow into her hands and caked it together, kneading it into a solid lump. Hastening home, she coated it over with meal, then buried it in a deep recess on Criblaw and covered it over with sods and stones. Many must have been her anxious thoughts as the months slipped past and the spring weather turned into a gentle June. Fearfully she sought the spot on the hillside, and with trembling hands uncovered the hidey-hole. But her faith had not failed. The snowball was there intact!

Once again she took the long road to the Castle and craved an interview. To the astonished Earl she handed over her payment. A man of honour as well as a man of humour, he kept his promise and Maggie went home rejoicing with a receipt for the rent.

The years went by and the Hardies prospered. Thomas worked hard and Maggie was managing. They did not need to eat into the money that should have been paid as rent and thriftily Maggie laid the few coins by. Some day they might need them.

Meanwhile their landlord had been taken captive at Worcester and imprisoned in the Tower of London. News from the great world far from Criblaw was hard to come by but eventually word of Lauderdale's misfortunes reached the tenants at Tollis Hill. The time had come to use Maggie's little bundle of gold coins.

The arduous journey accomplished, the Hardies found a place to live near the Tower and Maggie haunted the walls and gates, disguised now as a beggar woman, seeking some means by which she could get in touch with Lauderdale. And the resourceful Maggie found a way.

One day the lonely Earl heard the faint sound of singing from the street and the Scots voice and Scottish words attracted his attention. He listened more intently. Maggie had found her way.

She sang one of the most haunting songs to come out of the Scottish Border – and the Border is famous for its songs of strife and sorrow. It had not long before been composed by Nicol Burne, or Minstrel Burne as he was known, a native of Lauderdale and one of the last of the wandering singers who roamed the countryside entertaining "Lords and Ladies gay" in their banqueting halls, singing to Lairds and famers round the ingle on a winter's even and leading a chorus in the change-houses. There is a portrait of the minstrel at Thirlestane Castle, in which he is represented as "a douce old man, leading a cow."

The tune of "Leader Haughs and Yarrow" is wistful and lingers in the memory. And when the Earl heard the verses sung in Maggie's Border voice, they brought images, sweet and poignant, of the lovely Lauder side. But more than those, that Border voice, singing so insistently, seemed to carry a hidden message from Lauderdale. To the Earl, bored to despair, Maggie's song of "Sweet Leader Haughs" transported his mind from the Tower beside the tidal Thames to his own Border torrent and filled his heart with hope.

Maggie sang:

"A house there stands on Leader side,
Surmounting my descriving,
With rooms sae rare, and windows fair,
With Daedalus' contriving;
Men passing by do often cry,
In sooth it hath no marrow:
It stands as fair on Leader side
As Newark does on Yarrow.

Park, Wanton-wa's and Wooden cleuch
The East and Wester Mainses,
The wood of Lauder's fair eneuch,
The corns are good in the Blainslies;
There sits are fine, and sald by kind,
That if he search all thorough
Mearns, Buchan, Marr, nane better are
Than Leader Haughs and Yarrow.

Sing Erslington and Cowdenknowes,
Where Humes and ance commanding;
Any Drygrange, with the milk-white yowes,
'Twixt Tweed and Leader standing,
The bird that flees through Redpath trees
And Gladswood banks ilk morrow,
May chant and sing sweet Leader Haughs
And bonnie howms of Yarrow."

When the Earl questioned the gaoler, he said, "'Tis but a silly beggar woman, my Lord."

"Bring her to me," replied the Earl. "She sings prettily. I would have her sing me some old Scottish songs."

Scottish beggars were nothing new in the London of those days and they thought no harm of letting Maggie in to please the Earl, who was generous with money when he had it.

"Leave us," said the Earl and as the door closed, Maggie dropped a curtsey and asked, "D'ye no ken me, Laird? 'Tis Maggie Hardie from Tollis Hill."

"Maggie!" cried the Earl, astounded. "What do you here, woman?"

Maggie unknotted her abundant hair and let the golden coins drop into his lap. Then she produced a Scots bannock.

"Come, pree the bannock, my Lord," she invited. And breaking open the oatmeal cake, the Earl revealed its hidden hoard of gold.

"Ye're a cleverer alchemist than Dr Dee," the Earl told her. "It was to have been a snowball."

"The bit gold will be more use to ye, Laird."

In after years, despite his brilliant attainments and tremendous power, John Maitland never forgot his humble followers, who had ventured so much for his sake. When the Restoration freed him and he was able to return to Thirlestane, one of his first acts was to give the Hardies the farm of Tollis Hill rent free for life. To his faithful Midside Maggie, as a token of his gratitude, he presented a silver girdle, which was the pride of the old woman's heart and a treasured souvenir in her family. To-day Midside Maggie's girdle, some 27 inches long and made of curiously twisted silver wire, can be seen at the National Museum of Antiquities in Queen Street, Edinburgh. It is a stored relic of the old clan feeling of humble loyalty to a Chief and of loyal gratitude of the Chief to his clansmen.

Midside Maggie was not the only woman to come to the aid of the imprisoned John Maitland. Elizabeth Murray was the elder daughter of William Murray, who had been educated with King Charles II and was created by him Earl of Dysart in 1646. In the strange ambivalence of those civil war years, like the sons of so many Scottish Covenanters who became Restoration loyalists, Lady Murray was a friend of Oliver Cromwell and as such, she was able to do something to ease the conditions of Maitland's imprisonment, sending him food and books, although it seemed she was not able to procure the release of so important a Covenanting leader.

Gilbert Burnett, Minister of Saltoun, in his "History of my own time", writes drily:

> "She had been early in a correspondence with Lord Lauderdale, that had given occasion to censure. When he was prisoner after Worcester fight, she made him believe he was in great danger of his life, and that she had saved it by her intrigues with Cromwell; which was not a little taken notice of."

The story touched upon in Burnett's book is as strange as any in John Maitland's life. Elizabeth Murray was in love with him – when his wife died she became his second wife in the 'seventies – and she was perfectly capable of carrying on the most daring of intrigues – even with the sternest roundhead of them all, Oliver Cromwell himself. Probably Burnett's description of her cannot be surpassed.

> "She was a woman of great beauty, but of far greater parts. She had a wonderful quickness of apprehension, and an amazing vivacity in conversation. She had studied not only divinity and

127

history, but mathematics and philosophy. She was violent in everything she set about, a violent friend, but a much more violent enemy. She had a restless ambition, lived at a vast expense, and was ravenously covetous; and would have stuck at nothing by which she might compass her ends."

If we add that she was married to a respectable barnet, Sir Lionel Tollemache of Helmingham, and had eleven children by him (although very large families were the custom of that time), we can realise that she was a woman of enormous lust for life.

Burnett adds:

"Cromwell was certainly fond of her, and she took care to entertain him in it; till he, finding what was said upon it, broke it off."

Was this extraordinary love affair with the Lord Protector of England more than a device for securing the release of John Maitland? Certainly it created a scandal. Elizabeth was a beautiful woman and if Cromwell genuinely fell in love with her, no shame to him. After all, he was more soldier than puritan. But a Commonwealth Caesar could not afford personal scandal – that sort of thing was for cavaliers! – and it would seem that when Cromwell broke it off, John Maitland was fated to stay in prison.

However, the Earl of Lauderdale did not fare so badly in prison. The 17th and at the date of writing, the present Earl has in his library two books which belonged to the prisoner. One is "Pia Hilaria" by Angelini Gazei, published at Cambridge in 1657, and dated by "Lauderdaill" at Windsor Castle, October 1657. The title might be translated "Pious Funny Things" or "Funny Pious Things"

– or even, "Pious Jokes" – and it suggests that in spite of the deadly seriousness of religious questions and the place that Puritanism occupied in the Civil War, there were authors who could still joke about religious matters. And there were Covenanters like Lauderdale who could enjoy them! This book must later have been in possession of the poet Robert Southey, for it has his autograph with the date, 24th November, 1797.

The other volume is "Litterae Provincials, de Morali & Politica Jesuitarum Disciplina," by L. Montaltius, published in Koln in 1658. The flyleaf of this volume is dated 4th July, 1659. As this book contains some 500 pages of correspondence about Jesuit discipline, it shows that Lauderdale was also concerned with the grave side of religion.

A third book containing the "Lauderdaill" subscription, dated Windsor Castle, 27th November 1658, was auctioned at Sotheby's in 1968, a first edition of Meric Casaubon's "A true and Faithful Relation of What Passed for Many Years between Dr Dee .. and some Spirits," a further indication of the Earl's deep studies in religious questions. Chief among the circle of alchemists and soothsayers, incidentally, was Dr Dee, Queen Elizabeth's magician.

The Earl's years in prison had not been without their useful side. In those days a nobleman who could lay his hands on a little money, smuggled into him this way or that, or simply passed to his jailers by one of his retainers outside, for no gentleman was ever completely deserted so long as feudal loyalties could find a way, was able to get books and paper. The Earl was the kind of man who would not waste time "girning" against fate. He continued his studies in Latin and Greek and Hebrew and became an accomplished scholar. But neither learned books nor poetry were to be his future. He was a man of action.

On the death of Oliver Cromwell, General George Monck, who was in command of the New Model Army in Scotland, marched on London. A new Parliament was elected. King Charles, who had been negotiating with Monck, issued the Declaration of Breda, in which he promised that the matters of dispute between Parliament and he should be decided by the new Parliament. That Parliament immediately invited him to return to England and take the crown. The Commonwealth, that sturdy attempt to establish a British Republic, was at an end.

12. THE RESTORATION DUKE

The Earl of Glencairn, hero of the 1653 campaign in the Highlands, was appointed Chancellor of Scotland; General John Middleton, created the Earl of Middleton, was appointed Lord High Commissioner to the Scots Parliament and commander-in-chief in Scotland; the Earl of Lauderdale was made Secretary of the Council. These were the men who were to carry out King Charles's policies in Scotland.

James Sharp, the minister of Crail in Fife, had worked closely with General Monck in preparing for the Restoration – he actually had met the General at Coldstream and had written his Declaration for him – and following negotiations in London, he had gone to Breda to talk with Charles. After the Restoration he brought a letter from Charles to the Scots promising that the King would preserve the government of the Church of Scotland. But already the King and Sharp were planning an Episcopalian church.

Charles's attitude towards the Kirk was best expressed in the words of Alexander Jaffray, one of the commissioners who saw Prince Charles at Breda in 1650, who wrote in his diary:

"We did sinfully entangle and engage the nation and ourselves, and that poor young prince to whom we were sent; making him sign and swear a Covenant which we knew from clear and demonstrable reasons that he hated in his heart. Yet finding that upon these terms only he could be admitted to rule over us (all other means having then failed him). He sinfully complied with what we most sinfully pressed upon him; where, I must confess, to my apprehension, our sin was more than his."

There is no doubt that Charles hated and feared the Presbyterian form of church government. It reeked of republicanism and Charles never forgot the fate of his father at the hands of Oliver Cromwell. The leader of the covenanters, the Marquis of Argyle, was sent to the Tower as soon as he went to London to see the new King and later was returned to Edinburgh, tried to treason before the Scottish Parliament and beheaded. When sentenced to death, the Marquis said, "I had the honour to set the crown upon the King's head and now he hastens me away to a better crown than his own."

The same Parliament, over which Middleton presided, passed a Rescissory Act, which repealed the legislation of the Commonwealth, so abolishing Presbytery and restoring Episcopacy. But the Committee of Estates added to this general act of restoration, an act to settle the government of the Church most suitable to monarchical government and in the meantime permitting the existing administration by sessions, presbyteries and synods. The General Assembly of the Church – that dual government of Scotland – disappeared and did not assemble for the next thirty years.

Whoever was the author of this compromise, it was fully

intended to please Lauderdale and the Engagers. Glencairn had always been a Royalist and no Covenanter and Middleton was a King's man. Between Lauderdale and Middleton there was political opposition and personal jealousy from the start. But King Charles is reputed to have told Lauderdale, that Presbyterianism was no religion for a gentleman. This was no jest, for he profoundly believed in three indispensable supports of the throne – money, armed force and bishops.

Glencairn told Lauderdale during the weeks of that fateful Scottish Parliament of 1661, "I am not for Lordly prelates, such as were in Scotland before the Reformation, but for a limited, sober and moderate episcopacy."

Lauderdale, who understood his Sharps better than the Chancellor, replied, "Since you are for bishops and must have them, bishops you shall have and that higher than ever they were in Scotland – and that you will find."

Of course, Kirk sessions in the parishes and bishops in the dioceses were an unworkable combination. Everything depended on how the compromise was observed. The ministers, especially the militant covenanters, regarded the bishops as "the limbs of anti-Christ", whose feet the King had set inside the Kirk door only to enable them to thrust their greedy, Erastian bodies into the house of God and dominate it. The bishops – a colourless lot selected to Sharp – lacked the authority of God, which the ministers fervently claimed, and had increasingly to rely on the authority of Parliament and the army. They were no more in favour of compromise that the Covenanters.

In the event, the compromise was not worth an Act of Parliament, for a soon as Sharp went to London to be consecrated as Archbishop of St Andrews, he persuaded the

King to forbid presbyteries and synods to meet, unless convoked by the bishops. At this time, Sharp had the ear of the King and he was supported in his policy by Middleton, the commander-in-chief. It was not long before Glencairn was exclaiming, "Waes me, we have advanced these men to be bishops and they will trample on us all!" His words were personally prophetic, for Sharp proceeded to wheedle out of the King a letter to the Scottish Privy Council giving the Archbishop precedence over the Chancellor Glencairn died four months later, a cynic might say.

Glencairn's heir, Alexander, had only one daughter, Margaret, who married John Maitland, the fifth Earl of Lauderdale.

While Glencairn vainly hoped for a limited and moderate episcopate, both Sharp and Middleton were high-flying episcopalians. Lauderdale held a truer policy, one far more difficult of achievement and which submitted him to all those charges of corruption and tyranny which were made against him from both sides. A loyal King's man, he supported the episcopal establishment as the best method of controlling the church by the King, although, like Glencairn, he was not in favour "Lordly prelates." At the same time, he wished the Presbyterians and their ministers to be adequately represented in the lower organs of the Church of Scotland.

When he first put forward the proposal that the question of church government should be put before a General Assembly (there had not been a General Assembly of the Church of Scotland since Cromwell's musketeers dumped the ministers on Bruntsfield Links) or before the synods, this was squashed by Middleton. At that time, according to Sir George Mackenzie (who later became Lord

Advocate), Lauderdale faced dismissal by the King. But, adds Mackenzie in his Memoirs:

> "He was undervalued by his enemies and deserted by his friends; and if prosperity ... had not betrayed Middleton and his friends to too much arbitrariness and want of circumspection, Lauderdale had fallen under the weight of his own misfortunates."

Lauderdale was able to overturn his enemy by making use of a piece of political wangling by which Middleton hoped to ruin him. In those days, decisions were come to by open voting, but James Harrington, the author of "Oceans", and Sir William Petty, the economist and mathematician, were exponents of balloting. The Chief argument for the secret ballot, of course, was that those who voted against men in power could not afterwards be persecuted and ruined, if they failed to get a majority of votes. Middleton, the soldier playing politician, seized upon this device to get rid of Lauderdale. He did not know his man. (Perhaps he was not even aware that the greatest balloteer, Harrington, was Lauderdale's cousin and Middleton put before the Estates an act for disqualifying from public office a list of men not to be trusted because of their political history. Lauderdale's name topped the list. The vote was to be taken by ballot – or billet, as it was called, from the slips on which the votes were recorded. But, alas for the secrecy of the ballot, Mackenzie recounts that the Clerk Register (Lord Carrington), "having a rooted quarrel against Southesk, did mark his billet with a nip when he received it, and thereby discovered his vote."

Lauderdale wrote a brilliant defence, all the more damaging to Middleton because one of Lauderdale's measures to ameliorate the working of the laws against the Covenanters was to defer the payment of fines by those who had refused to carry out the law, and this measure, which had received the approval of the King, was ignored by Middleton, who continued to collect the fines – in the hope that money in hand would excuse his action. King Charles, taking his usual method of dealing with difficulties, threw the billeting act into a desk and said he would do nothing about it. But Lauderdale saw to it that the Estates "raised and expunged" the act.

But Middleton was still in power and Argyle was arrested, sent to Edinburgh and sentenced to be beheaded. He was imprisoned in Edinburgh Castle, awaiting execution, while the enemies of Lauderdale were preparing their list of officers to be dismissed under the Billeting Act. For Lauderdale, this was a serious matter. If the King had been prepared to accept the action of the Estates, it could have meant not only his dismissal but thereafter, such a persecution by all his enemies – and they were all in powerful places – that he might have lost his head. Somehow, Argyle contrived to warn Lauderdale in London of the danger that was approaching from Edinburgh. The list balloted by the Estates was sealed and dispatched to the King. And Middleton had taken pains to place agents at various places on the road south to intercept messengers whom the friends of Lauderdale might send to London. Argyle got to know of this and sent a courier by side roads over the Border, who avoided Middleton's agents and arrived in time to warn Lauderdale before the Billeting Act and fatal list were handed to the King. As we know, the King flung the sealed packed into his desk unopened.

Argyle proved a good friend, as did, for example, Barbara Villiers, Countess of Castlemaine, the King's most powerful mistress. But Clarendon, the King's chief adviser, was for Middleton, as was Archbishop Sharp, who wrote to Charles and told him that the Church stood or fell with

Middleton. Lauderdale triumphed over them all in this battle because Charles always followed the same policy as Lauderdale followed himself – keep all the warring factions at loggerheads. It was true that Charles was bitter against the Covenanters and could not forgive the first Marquess of Argyle for the humiliations of the fifties, but he had no wish to see Sharp and Middleton in complete control. There was always the possibility of a new rebellion across the Border!

Lauderdale's brand of politics suited him far better, especially as he had more faith in Lauderdale's loyalty. If the bishops and ministers could be kept quarrelling and their pretensions separated from Parliament, that would prevent the covenanting menace. If Argyle were restored to his Earldom, he would remain a Royalist and push the squint-eyed bogey from Inverary into the past. Lauderdale could be trusted, insofar as the King trusted anybody, to keep the Scottish Estates in line.

Middleton was replaced by the Earl of Rothes, a follower of Lauderdale and son of that Rothes who has been called Father of the Covenant. His first act was to sign the warrant releasing Argyle from Edinburgh Castle and a few months later, Argyle was restored to his title of Earl and part of his estates.

On the day after the passing of the act of expungement, Lauderdale wrote to the King:

> "loth of September, being the day after St Billeting's Day, begins in some remarks spun round the text of that which I am ravished with, that you govern this poor kingdom yourself."

Clearly, Lauderdale delighted in "breaking jests" in his political career and it is just as plain that King Charles enjoyed them. He enjoyed Lauderdale just as he enjoyed Buckingham, his boyhood friend and contemporary, who was also a prodigious breaker of jests. Lauderdale continued:

> "By yesterday's Act you will see that billeting is dead, buried, and descended; ... We durst not move what was so positively illegal without a clear order. But if it be your will, you shall see we know no law but obedience."

Middleton was replaced as Lord Commissioner and it was the Earl of Rothes who opened the next Parliament in 1663.

While this Parliamentary struggle was going on, Lauderdale was being attacked in another sphere. The new Earl of Argyle was related by marriage to Lauderdale. His wife was Lady Mary Stewart, daughter of the Earl of Moray, who had married a sister of Lauderdale's wife, Lady Ann Home. Their marriage had taken place in 1650, when Argyle was Lord Lorne, heir to the Covenanting Marquess of Argyle. Lorne strangely enough, had been a good Royalist from his youth and had been an officer under Glencairn and Middleton in their Highland campaign, but because of his father's record, he was not trusted by Chancellor Clarendon and his men in Scotland, Glencairn and Middleton. They were naturally eager to destroy the power of the house of Argyll, which in Campbell country was almost an independent state, and after the execution of Lorne's father, there was the possibility of forfeiture and rich grants to the King's favourites.

Lauderdale as naturally aided with Lorne. During his imprisonment, Lorne had kept in touch with him, in spite of Lorne's own difficult and dispersed existence during the

Commonwealth. As soon as Lauderdale was released from Windsor Castle, in March, 1660, Lorne had written to him, asking Lauderdale's advice and reminding him that he had "good eyes" and that he could be written to through "Johne Michell, stable in the Cowgate of Edinburgh." There is no doubt about the friendship and trust between the two men – in spite of the trickery of the first Marquess of Argyll – for as we know, Lorne's good eyes were used later to save Lauderdale from his enemies.

In the struggle to obtain his father's forfeited estates, Lorne, now second Marquess of Argyll was accused by Middleton's Parliament of "lease-making" – that is, causing discord between the King and his subjects – and when the matter was considered by King Charles in Council, while the Middleton faction demanded Argyll's arrest, Lauderdale argued that Argyll's promise to appear before Parliament would suffice and he would stand cautioner.

In the 1663 Parliament, Lauderdale felt free to make a speech outlining his policy on church government, in which he declared the unlawful nature of the covenanting oath and pointed out that this oath carried no obligation to change the settled form of government. As this Parliament passed an Act ordering everybody to attend their parish churches or pay heavy fines – a quarter of a Laird's rental, a quarter of a tenant's goods – Lauderdale made clear that he was not going soft towards the Whiggarmores of the West. They promptly nicknamed the Act, the Bishops' Dragnet, and did their best to evade the paying of fines.

Lauderdale, in private memoranda for the King, declared his policy of short parliaments so that the country could return "to the good old form of government by His Majesty's Privy Council". Long Parliaments only served to create division by carrying on private interests. Lauderdale looked forward to the next Parliament as one in which the Estates would be completely loyal to King Charles. The bishops and temporal Lords were now in agreement. The power which the officers of state and nobleman had on the election of the representatives from shires and burghs would obtain a royal majority. This secured the negative vote. Then, the Lords of the Articles (or Committee of the Estates) who prepared the legislation for the Estates, was entirely Royalist, so securing the affirmative vote. In short, both Government and opposition, executive and legislation, were controlled by Lauderdale.

John Maitland had demonstrated his political genius by bringing about in practice and by writing down in theory the solution to the combination of monarchy and Parliament, which for three centuries has existed in varying degree in Great Britain and which hundreds of statesmen, writers and crators have described as the great achievement of the British parliamentary system.

As soon as the Commonwealth had gone, the question of the absolute rule of Parliament, or republicanism, had gone with it. The problem was how to enable King and Parliament to exist together. King Charles I had faced that same problem by inflexibly clinging to his royal power – and had lost his head. His son had no intention of doing so or of becoming an undignified exile touting the courts of Europe, as he had done, or of again going to war. King Charles managed it, in his own insinuating way. There is no space to go into his methods and contrivances. Nor into the similar policies of Lauderdale in Scotland. It is enough to say that the whole political question behind the Civil War was not simply King or Parliament – although, of course, for the extremists on both sides, it was so – but: how could King and Parliament exist together? That was a debate which consumed not only the 17th century but the 18th century as well, right up until the watershed of the 1832 Reform Act.

Lauderdale, with his church government separated from the civil Parliament, with a government and cabinet system in the Committee of Estates and the Privy Council, had achieved a workable system, the skeleton of the British constitution as it remains to-day in our own time. All the political struggles from his day have been struggles of factions, great leaders and social classes to obtain power over this structure and modify it, extend this or contract that, to suit their own ideas and aims.

How much of this was Lauderdale's own and how much was due to King Charles, who was a King of acute intelligence, it is difficult to know. How much of it was simply Lauderdale following the general trend of politics, balancing the obvious – King and Parliament – and doing it, during his period of power in Scotland, better than others, it is difficult to assess. But we have quoted enough of what he clearly wrote down to show that he was doing more than intriguing from day to day to keep himself in the seat of office, that he was following a well thought out policy.

His frequent assertions that the King's will was everything to him, the whole of his policy, was that a gross flattery to obtain his own way with Charles and to confound his enemies with royal approval? Or was it a genuine acknowledgement of the extent of Charles's part in this formation of policy? Was it a genuine joint policy? Or was it more the King's than Lauderdale's?

In a short biography, it is impossible to follow these fascinating questions, but we raise them to show that the Duke of Lauderdale was far from being the blundering buffoon and brutal despot which is the picture of him we have inherited.

The suppression of conventicles and the forcing of the people into the parish churches did not go well. The peasantry, burghers and Lairds of the West County were able to carry on a resistance movement which varied from boycott to taking to the hills. Lauderdale found that the measures designed to force the episcopal clergy, the landowners and Lairds to carry out the laws would not work where the whole people was against them. Too often the men supposed to enforce the laws were in sympathy with the people.

Lauderdale used military force. Much has been said about the covenanters and their sufferings during the occupation of the West by troops under Sir James Turner and Col. Thomas Dalziel. The Covenanters fought back. Civil war is a terrible thing, when brutalities are committed by both sides. But when the defeat of the Covenanters at the Pentland Hills was followed not only by hangings but also by the torture of prisoners by the boot and thumbkin, this was something for which Lauderdale can be justly attacked, though we do not know how far his personal, immediate responsibility went. At that time Rothes was not only Commissioner, but also Treasurer, Commander-in-Chief and Privy Seal.

In any case, the torturing arose from fear, that basest of all political motives, because the Covenanters at the Pentland Hills were within a few miles of the Canongate of Edinburgh.

Rullion Green was followed by the dismissal of Rothes and the appointment of John Hay, Marquess of Tweeddale, as commissioner, who was no friend to Lauderdale. The King now issued an Indulgence, counter-signed by

Lauderdale, which allowed the outed ministers (who promoted the prescribed conventicles) to return to their manses and glebes, with an annual sum allowed to them by the government out of the stipend fund they collected.

In 1669, Lauderdale was made High Commissioner to Parliament for that year. His administration in Scotland continued the policy of suppressive legislation against the open-air preachings and outed ministers, alternating with indulgences designed to seduce the ministers into the episcopal church and back to their parishes. Acts against "intercommuning" with rebel covenanters, designed to starve them out of the hills, and for the bonding of property holders to guarantee their families and dependents were tried. All three measures failed to pacify the West and bring the people back the to the parish churches.

Lauderdale was now approaching the height of his career and powers. In 1670, he had signed for Charles the secret treaty of Dover, by which Charles received a subsidy from the French King, Louis XIV, on agreement to keep the peace and Charles's promise, which he never kept or meant to keep, that he would declare himself publicly to be a Catholic. With the dismissal of old Clarendon, the Lord Chancellor, and Lauderdale's own high standing in London, his power in Scotland became nigh absolute.

He began the work of enlarging Thirlestane Castle. This was done in as magnificent a style as the times allowed. And by then Lauderdale was very rich, for the perquisites of high office were great. Besides the office of secretary of state and Lord high commissioner to the Estates, he was an Extraordinary Lord of session and governor of Edinburgh Castle, first commissioner of the treasury and president of the council, as well as being one of the Lords of the King's bedchamber. All were lucrative offices.

Sixteenth century Thirlestane was placed in the hands of Sir William Bruce of Kinross, who was soon to be commissioned by King Charles to rebuild the parts of the palace of Holyroodhouse which had been damaged by fire by Cromwell's troops. Bruce was to become a kinsman of the Earl of Lauderdale during the years in which he and his masons renovated Thirlestane, for he was a cousin of the Countess of Dysart, who became Lauderdale's second wife.

Bruce was an ardent royalist and had worked for the restoration of Prince Charles, his activities taking him frequently to the Continent to contact the exiled royal family. During these visits he had ample opportunity to indulge in his bent for architecture and gave close study to the design and layout of famous buildings, storing away ideas which he some day hoped to use. At Thirlestane, he used the technique which he had so successfully achieved at his old home, the house of Balcaskie, before he acquired Kinross. This was the creation of a dignified approach and entrance with side extensions which turned the old unwieldy fortalice into a stately residence – a Thirlestane which was to become the home of a Duke before Bruce's plans were completed. The existing towers and turrets, which still do so much to keep the medieval look of Thirlestane, he matched up in his additions to obtain symmetry. And for the interior he designed some remarkable plasterwork ceilings.

Historians have the curious habit of regarding Scotland as a barren, savage, poverty-stricken country in almost every age. It is amusing to listen to the view of Hester W. Chapman, whose "Tragedy of Charles II" was published in 1964.

"That kingdom ... was then a wilderness partially inhabited by illiterate savages, whose loyalty to their chiefs was so exploited as to keep them in perpetual warfare: living like beasts and fighting like demons, superstitious, tormented and hideously cruel, the clans had long submitted in atavistic terror to the voice of the Kirk, who ministers, after a century of frenzied effort, had achieved power over nobles, Parliament and the Stuart dynasty."

She goes on to describe the ministers as "malicious witch-doctors –

"… these imitation Old Testament prophets had brought conceit, hypocrisy and tyranny to a fine art; their vanity was boundless, their ranting eloquence as tedious as it was repetitive, their horror of natural instincts and healthy enjoyment ludicrous and disgusting."

Then, at the bottom of the same page, page 161, she writes:

"Campbells, Grahames, (unkindest cut of all!) Maitlands and many more – all were in the grasp of Kirk; and so their leaders, many of them highly educated, widely travelled, sophisticated and intellectual persons, whose surroundings and manner of life reflected European culture and cosmopolitan taste, persuaded themselves, or decided to pretend, that their God was that of the Covenanters; like the priests of Baal, they too were prepared to howl and weep and cut themselves with knives in degraded ecstasies of self-abasement before their awestruck followers, whose subjugation was thereby complete."

We are compelled by all this nonsense to try to follow the example of that Maitland priest of Baal who was prepared to howl and weep and cut Miss Chapman's literary ecstasies with the knife of common-sense. Scotland never was a wilderness of savages living like beasts and fighting like demons.

True, the Covenanting ministers tried to dominate the Scottish people; their pretensions of infallibility were as all embracing as the Pope's; their sermons were interminable. Their chief defect was their lack of humour – a fatal defect in Scotland. And all their attempts at totalitarianism failed.

Lauderdale was not the only one to fall asleep during the sermons, but on one occasion when in attendance on Charles II at divine worship he had to be peremptorily roused from slumber because his loud snores were reverberating through the church. The incident is recorded for us in the epigram by Richard Graves in "A Court Audience," which appeared in "The Festoon, a Collection of Epigrams, Ancient and Modern," published in 1767. The preacher was the well-known Dr Robert South, who was in high favour with the restored royalists. He held strongly to the belief of the divine right of kings and preached with vigour, often seasoned with sarcasm. Grave's epigram, therefore, was one to please King, Duke and Bishop.

> "Old South, a witty churchman reckon'd
> Was preaching once to Charles the Second,
> But much too serious for a Court,
> Who at all preaching made a sport:
> He soon perceive'd his audience nod,
> Deaf to the zealous man of God.
> The doctor stop'd; began to call,
> 'Pray wake the Earl of Lauderdale:
> My Lord! Why, 'tis a monstrous thing!
> You snore so loud – you'll wake the King!'"

Far from being a savage land, Scotland was a cultivated and prosperous country. Upon the Restoration, the Estates agreed to pay the Royal treasury £40,000 a year in customs and excise duties. During the secretaryship of the maligned Maitland, the prosperity of Scotland was growing and the genius of all classes was burgeoning to such an extent that they gave birth in the following century to the first wave of Scottish cultural achievement. Sir William Bruce was the forerunner of William Adam, father of the Adam Brothers, and of James Gibbs. Michael Wright shared with Lely and Kneller the honours of being court painter during the reign of Charles II. The collection of poetry which Sir Richard Maitland made in the previous century was surpassed by and his own poetry was a prelude to that of William Drummond of Hawthorden and Robert Sempill of Beltrees, who Habbie Simson inaugurated the great era of Scottish poetry. The volume of sermons, polemics and histories published was so enormous that it would have filled a Kirk.

In medicine there were Dr Archibald Pitcairne and Sir Robert Sibbald, founder of the Royal College of Physicians in Edinburgh. In law, there was the work of Sir George Mackenzie of Rosehaugh and of James Dalrymple, who became Viscount Stair.

The wealth which came to men like Lauderdale was amassed from the industry of an intelligent tenantry and class of sailors, for modern industrial production was not yet in sight. The huge quantity of surplus wealth flowing into the towns began the growth of cities like Edinburgh, Glasgow, Aberdeen and Dundee. It was every man's ambition to become the Laird of an estate of his own and to build one of the new mansion houses in the middle of a park. The existence of a large class of penniless beggars, pointed to by Andrew Fletcher of Saltoun, the utopian writer, and, we should add, two generations of civil war

147

during the 17th century, do not contradict the increase in agricultural production and the increase of surplus wealth.

For historian to write of Scotland as Miss Chapman does is absurd and gives the world a totally wrong idea of our history. As the new walls of Thirlestane were going up, Lauderdale and his family could take pride in the Scotland that was being formed during the two decades after the Restoration. In spite of the difficulties, mistakes and crimes that occurred, as occur they must in all periods of social change, the people of Scotland were about to stride into a period of achievement which placed them, in the front rank of history. And a Maitland was there – John Maitland, soon to be Duke Lauderdale – as there was to be a future Maitland – James Maitland, eighth Earl of Lauderdale.

What was this John Maitland like, who played such a dynamic part in Restoration history? He was certainly no handsome and romantic hero. Like the lugubriously visage King, he was an ugly man. But the faces of both men belied their intelligence and contradicted their wit and humour.

Lauderdale was described by Lord Fountainhall as "the learnedest and most powerful minister of state in his age." He did not look the part, though his actions proved his power and his reports and letters to King Charles showed his learning.

Gilbert Burnett, Minister of Saltoun, in his "History of my own time", described Lauderdale as:

> "the Earl of Lauderdale was believed [to be] the chief adviser. So he became very popular in Scotland."

In modern times, Gordon Daviot, in his "Claverhouse"

published in 1937, has this to say:

> ".. Scotland .. was ruled nominally by Charles the Second, but in fact by that magnificent scallywag, John Maitland, Duke of Lauderdale, King's Commissioner. Nothing happened in Scotland that those small pale eyes buried in the bloated face did not see; inside that clumsy red head were all the secrets of two kingdoms and all the guile of a continent; and to that fat palm stuck ten per cent. Of every saleable commodity from Berwick to Thurso. ... For nearly twenty years this grand-nephew of Mary's Lethington had kept himself in office with all the Maitland dexterity, if less than the Maitland grace.'

It is difficult to know if this is an attack upon Maitland or the rease of an admiring fellow Scot. But it is the fact that historian after historian condemns and blames Lauderdale for all the crimes committed in Scotland after the Restoration and for all the sorrows of the land.

It is necessary to stop for a moment and consider the Duke's evil character. There is hardly one writer who has any good to say of him. Naturally, we want to defend the good name of the Duke but it is no part of our purpose to whitewash him because he was a Maitland. There is no need for us to do so, for in historical fact the Duke of Lauderdale was not the devil whom the Covenanters railed against.

When Henry Hallam in his ponderous "Constitutional History of England, says that "the period .. of what is usually denominated the Cabal administration .. is justly reckoned one of the most disgraceful in the annals of our monarchy," this pontification is sheer nonsense. In the first place, the powers and cohesion and endurance of the so-Called Cabal has been stretch by historians beyond reality. The coalition Lord Clifford, treasurer; the Earl of Arlington secretary of state; the Duke of Buckingham; Lord Ashley, Chancellor of the Exchequer, and the Duke of Lauderdale, whose initials made the mystic Cabal (we who are more than accustomed to initial and portmanteau words have no idea of the fascination of that word "cabal" for historians and writers of schoolbooks), this coalition existed only from the fall of Clarendon in 1667 until 1673 at the longest and at no time were the five men completely in agreement. They were a cabal of individual schemers who soon became enemies. In short, the Cabal is a historical fiction. Secondly, we can point to a score of other political combinations just as devious, sinister, self-seeking and unscrupulous as the Cabal.

And when Hallam, inveighing in lofty terms against the profligacy of the court of Charles II, speaks of "the great ultimate security of English freedom, the expulsion of the house of Stuart," again he misses the mark. If Charles had many mistresses, when he fell out of love with them, he did not send them to the Tower or hack off their heads; he gave them titles and settled estates on their bastards. In modern, if not in Victorian eyes, he was an amiable sinner compared with a sadistic monster like Henry VIII, whom it is now the fashion on television to picture as "Bluff King Hal", rollicking through high politics and acting God – or at least, the Divine Arbiter of England – while everybody conspires to forget that he tortured or murdered six wives. As for "freedom", Hallam forgets the dictatorship of the Tudors and the period of first three Georges, the Hanoverians, in his eagerness to blacken the Stuarts.

The Duke of Lauderdale was a devoted supporter of the Stuarts, as his forebears had been. All the odium thrown upon Charles II was likewise cast upon Lauderdale. There is no need to defend his moral character. He was no worse than a thousand others of his day and, as his friendship for Argyll shows, better than many. He has been described as "coarse" and there is no doubt that he was a rough-tongued quick-tempered, high-handed autocrat. Again, there have been thousands like him.

He was not a Scotsman for nothing. He knew how to be caustic and crude, he enjoyed a drink, he proposed to make his way in the world.

The age of the Restoration was not the only historical era during which it was every man for himself and the devil take the hindmost. If Lauderdale was more subtle and more far-seeing, more able to stay the course and see other intriguers who opposed him fall into disfavour; if he was able far longer than most to retain the support of Charles II, this was achieved not out of pure chicanery, but rather out of ability in alliance with a strange loyalty to Charles Stuart – a loyalty which I think started their first acquaintance in the boisterous adventure of Prince Charles's navy putting out of Helvoetsluys to conquer his kingdom and ending in chaotic disaster.

When Lauderdale, supposedly the staid Covenanting commissioner, stepped aboard Prince Charles's flagship, it was the first crack in his covenant. To go through that naval exploit with Charles, face death by drowning and defeat by mismanagement, could not but draw the two together, like sharing a mistress. Besides, it must have captivated Lauderdale's bold, intriguing spirit to watch the 18-year-old Prince make those fledgling moves in the game of diplomacy which sent Lauderdale back to Scotland checkmated.

But in his loyalty to Charles II, Lauderdale did not forget other things. He made himself wealthy by the perquisites of his office, as did the rest. He maintained the loyalty of Scotland to the monarchy – the historians would have it, the subservience of Scotland. He was for moderation in religion, the great battlecry of the period. And if he pleased no one in Scotland because he strove to balance the bishops and the moderate Presbyterians and the whiggamore covenanters against each other, with himself, acting on behalf of the King, at the top of the pyramid, all he did was to carry out of the tactics of divide and rule which could be learned from the pages of the Old Testament and have always been a prime strategy of the world's rulers.

He is held up as the arch-persecutor of the Covenanters, so many writers following the ridiculous exaggerations of Hallam, who seems never to have heard of Ireland or 1743, though even Hallam says, "the tyranny of Lauderdale far exceeding that of Middleton, as his own fell short of the Duke of York's." In fact, if such things can truly be compared, a comparison of the fate of the extreme wing of the Covenanters under Cromwell, Glencairn, Middleton, Monmouth, and York, with their treatment by Lauderdale shows that Lauderdale has suffered severely in the hands of historians.

The probable reason for this was the total irreverence of Lauderdale. C.P. Hill, in his "Who's Who in History," declares that King Charles "found him an amusing oddity and something of a butt in council." In other words, Lauderdale was a sort of Scots comedian at the court of King Charles. The Earl of Clarendon, in his memoirs, says that Lauderdale "called himself and his nation a thousand traitors, and Rebells," and also that he "scornfully spoke of the Covenant, upon which he brake a hundred jests." The dichotomy between the unscrupulous persecutor and the oddity of a hundred jests; between the bloody tyrant and the King's boon companion, is something the historians do not seek to explain. Unless they wish to imply that Lauderdale was a man who could sign a death warrant with a jest. The truth is that they have no understanding of the Scottish sense of humour.

What is more striking than Lauderdale's loyalty to Charles Stewart, is the loyalty given to him by Archibald Campbell, Earl of Argyll, a loyalty which Lauderdale fully returned until the day of his death; the loyalty of an open and courageous minister like Gilbert Burnett, who moved away from Lauderdale only when he went on to the road of becoming Bishop of Salisbury, and the loyalty of a man like Robert Murray, his Deputy Secretary and first President of the Royal Society, whom John Aubrey wrote of as "the only man that would do a *kindnesse gratis* upon an account of Friendship," and who only left Lauderdale's circle over the scheme for uniting the two countries, which proved then abortive.

Perhaps a cynic would say that Lauderdale was the best of a bad lot. It would be interesting to know what Lauderdale himself would say, if he were able to look upon his history and "brake a jest", no doubt a hundred jests, upon it.

Whatever the verdict, we believe that the Maitlands have no cause to be ashamed of their great Duke.

That is not to say that everything Lauderdale did is to be admired. It was his aim, as the King's Commissioner in Scotland, to place the resources of Scotland at the disposal of Charles II and to so play off all oppositions against each other that they would not be able to interfere with this policy.

The Act of Indulgence of 1669 was resented by the Scottish Bishops and Archbishop Sharp dared to criticise it at the Parliament of that year. Lauderdale replied by proposing and having passed an Act of Supremacy, which placed the final voice on church affairs with the King.

Charles, continuously involved with his struggle with the English Parliament – the main bone of contention always being the granting of funds to meet the royal extravagances – now wished for a union of Parliaments, with the intention of having a controlled Royalist faction from Scotland to vote against the English members. But such a union would have done away with the King's Commissioner in Scotland and Lauderdale deftly passed through the Scottish Parliament a Militia Act, which provided the King with 20,000 men "who would march when and where he might be pleased to command." This was much more to the purpose and King Charles dropped the union idea.

But the storms of intrigue never ceased to agitate round the Commissioner's chair of state. If old friends, like Elizabeth Murray, who had prevailed upon King Charles upon the death of her father to create her the Countess of Dysart in her own right, had become friendly with Lauderdale again – her husband had died and her resentment of Lauderdale's ungratefulness for what she had tried to wheedle out of Cromwell was forgotten with Lauderdale's power and wealth – then old enemies, like Tweeddale, and new enemies, like the new Duke of Hamilton, were also active. But so long as he had the favour of the King, friends could expect preferments and enemies could rage regardless.

Sir Lionel Tollemache, husband of Elizabeth Murray,

died in 1668 at Helmingham, and a year later her father, the Earl of Dysart, died, leaving her Ham House, near Richmond. Elizabeth's marriage to Sir Lionel had not come up to her expectations, for he preferred the life of a country squire to that of a court intriguer. He lacked the drive and zest to better himself and lacked the ambitions of power and splendour which she herself possessed.

But now, a widow possessed of a splendid mansion like Ham, still with enough beauty and more than enough vivacity and wit to make her way in King Charles II's court, the Countess cast her eye about for someone who could help her to fulfil her ambition. Her glance fell on her old friend, John Maitland. An invitation to Ham House was quickly followed by more and presently the Earl was so much under her influence and so great was the scandal of their liaison that his wife, Anne, left him to go and live in Paris.

At the end of 1671, Lady Lauderdale died, and within six weeks, on February 17th, 1672, Lauderdale and the Countess of Dysart were married. On the 2nd of May, Lauderdale was created Duke and Marquess of March. He chose his secondary title to do honour to the family of Dunbar, Earls of March, from whom he was descended. On the 2nd of June, at Windsor, he was installed a Knight of the Garter.

But in the following year, with the Second Dutch War going badly and King Charles's stock running low as against Parliament, Lauderdale's rivals began to organise opposition to him, in England under the leadership of Clifford, the Earl of Shaftesbury (the "C" of the so-called Cabal) and in Scotland by the Duke of Hamilton. Lauderdale replied to his Scottish enemies by a fresh Act of indulgence to deal with Kirk affairs and the adjournment of the 1673 Parliament. The Scottish Parliament was not to meet again until 1681, when politics had drastically changed.

In 1674, the English Parliament passed an address asking the King to dismiss Lauderdale but Charles replied to this by creating Lauderdale the Earl of Guildford and Baron Petersham and making him a member of the English Privy Council.

At the height of these manoeuvres against Lauderdale, King Charles wrote him,

> "I could not let this expresse go to you without a line under my owne hand to assure you of the continuance of my kindness to you which nothing shall alter."

But circumstances were to alter kindness. The troubles in Scotland, particularly in the South West, continued in spite of Lauderdale's "stop-go" policies. The measures against "intercommuning" were followed by the appointment as Lord Advocate of Sir George Mackenzie, whose zeal against the conventicle holders earned him the nickname of Bloody Mackenzie. As the conventicles were regarded by the government as "nurseries of rebellion", there was no intention of letting up on the measures taken against them. Burnett records that Lauderdale once, in a fit of exasperation, exclaimed, "Would to God they would rebel, so I might bring over an army of Irish papists to cut all their throats."

This cry of any angry man had no response in action, but Lauderdale set about a scheme for an army of occupation. He got the Marquess of Atholl to raise an army of 6,000 Highlanders, who, along with force of militia, were quartered upon the South Western countries for some five weeks. This was the "Highland Host" whom the anti-

Lauderdale writers accuse of the most frightful crimes, but who seem to have done little more than eat their hosts out of house and home and when they left, take with them everything they could life and carry!

The Popish Plot in 1678 was ably used by the party of Whigs to attack Lauderdale and in Scotland helped to foment the rebellion in which a troop of dragoons were defeated at Lesmahagow. This was followed by the killing of Archbishop Sharp at Magus Moor and a Covenanting victory over Graham of Claverhouse at Drumclog. The Earl of Linlithgow, commander-in-chief in Scotland under Lauderdale, was replaced by the Duke of Monmouth, who defeated the Covenanters at Bothwell Brig, June 1679.

The Whigs, who supported Monmouth, were ambitious for power at court, but the Duke of York was recalled from Brussels and sent to Scotland, on the advice of Lauderdale himself, who supported York in spite of James's hatred and unthankfulness.

But the illnesses of old age were creeping upon Lauderdale and in October, 1680, he resigned his office as Secretary for Scotland, being succeeded by Alexander Stuart, the Earl of Moray, who was his nephew, the Earl's mother being Margaret Home, co-herress with Anne Home, Lauderdale's wife, of the Earl of Home. Lauderdale was soon deprived of all his other posts. This was to be expected by a political figure when he had become too old for service, but when, in 1682, the pensions granted to him and his Duchess were taken away, that was wicked ingratitude, if it were knowingly agreed by King Charles and not a dirty trick of Lauderdale's enemies. Perhaps it was due to the behaviour of his second wife, Elizabeth Murray, who made his fall from power more bitter and more tragic than it need have been.

Burnett says of her:

> "The Lady Dysart came to have so much power over the Lord Lauderdale that it lessened him much in the esteem of all the world; for he delivered himself up to all her humours and passions. ... As the conceit took her, she made him fall out with all his friends, one after another. From that time to the end of his days he became quite another sort of man than he had been in all the former parts of his life."

Fountainhall says brutally in his memoirs:

> "... discontent and age (corpulency also, it is said) were the chief ingredients of his death, if his duchess and physicians were free of it; for she abused him most grossly, and had gotten all from him she could expect, and was glad to be quit of him."

It is to be wondered if Charles II was also glad to be quit of the old warhorse who had stuck to him since the days on the Downs when he had snuffed the war trumpets.

Lauderdale had no son and when he died at Tunbridge Wells on 24th August, 1682, his Dukedom and marquisate of March and the English honours of Guildford and Petersham became extinct.

13. THE THIRD AND FOURTH EARLS

Charles Maitland, Lord Hatton, succeeded his older brother at the age of 62. Charles and his son, Richard, had both shared in the success of the Duke of Lauderdale but they had also contributed a great deal to the aggrandisement of the head of their house. While the Duke was at court in Whitehall, close to the King, Charles kept a watchful eye and stern hand on events in Scotland. His loyal support was of the greatest advantage to his brother. But when he himself succeeded, all the work he had done was of little advantage to him.

Charles succeeded only to the Scottish titles, as third Earl of Lauderdale, Viscount Lauderdale and Viscount Maitland, and Lord of Thistlestane and Boltoun.

As soon as he succeeded his brother, he had to face the demands of his brother's second wife, the former Countess of Dysart. Shortly before the death of the Duke she had induced him to obtain a charter under the Great Seal under which she became Duchess of Lauderdale and Baroness Brunstane for life. She wasted no time in claiming the baronies of Brunstane and Duddington to the exclusion of the rights of the new Earl. He was immediately pursued by the Duchess of Lauderdale, who laid claim to certain of the family estates. And the enemies of the Duke now rounded upon the brother who had supported him.

Born in 1620, Charles married on 18th November, 1652, Elizabeth Lauder, the only daughter and heiress of Richard Lauder of Halton (or Hatton) in Midlothian. On the death of Lauder, Charles Maitland came into the considerable property of Hatton and Platts. With the Restoration, he was given the post of Master General of the Mint in Scotland and became a member of the Scottish Privy Council in June, 1661. Eight years later, when he was admitted an Ordinary Lord of Session, he took the legal title of Lord Hatton.

The increase in his fortune enabled him to begin the task of reconstructing and extending the old house of Hatton. This seems to have been completed in the year after his death, for on the keystone of the gateway leading to the house there is the date, 1692.

During his brother's absences from Scotland, Lord Hatton presided over the Privy Council. He was a close and loyal supporter of the Lauderdale policies and incurred all the odium of his brother's enemies. In May, 1672, he was created a baronet. Fountainhall, in his "Historical Notices", says of the Duke:

> "All persones cryes shame upon him for ruining the memory and standing of his family by giving away Dudston, etc., in property to his Duchess, and Leidington to her son Huntingtour."

Charles Maitland, the heir, took the matter to court but the Duchess, an expert in litigation and the use of influence, gained the day. He had to pay debts on the property at Brunstane and Duddington, a decision which induced Sir George Mackenzie, the Lord Advocate, to say,

> "to make the Earl ratify, and likewise pay the English debts, was to make his ratification the winding-sheet of the Earldom."

The Duchess's greed was not to be the winding sheet of the Earldom but it cost the Earl a great deal. The Dysart family remained in possession of the House of Brunstane and the lands of Duddingston for the next forty years.

The Duchess's daughter, Elizabeth Tollemache, married Archibald Campbell, heir to the Marquess of Argyle, in 1679, and she went to live in Brunstane. Argyle was in exile but owing to the influence of the Duke of Lauderdale, the son was able to stay on a Brunstane. However, after his father's arrest and execution in 1685, he thought it safer to move to Holland, where he remained until he was able to return with William of Orange in 1688.

During these years, the Duchess, widow of the Duke of Lauderdale, lived at Brunstane and it could have been her influence, as well as the traits which her daughter inherited from her, which led to the quarrels between her daughter and her husband, for ultimately they separated from each other.

The Duchess quarrelled with one of her neighbours, Sir James Dick of Prestonfield, about the swans of Duddingston Loch and again took the dispute to the Court of Session. She took out of the Loch five swans and used the skins of two of them as a gift to General Drummond in his sickness, to keep his breast warm. The swans or their parents has been put in the loch by the Duke. Sir James Dick broke into her yard and took the remaining three swans back.

In court he claimed that though the first swans has

been put in the loch by the Duke of Lauderdale, their progeny belonged to him as the owner of the loch. Fountainhall notices the decision.

> "The Lords of Council fund if they had come of their own accord and bigget there, then they were Sir James's, but since the owner who put them in was known, they fund they belonged to the Duchess."

Sir James's hatred of the "Dutchess" was plain for Fountainhall adds that he turned all the rest out of his loch.

But then the Duke of Hamilton, as hereditary keeper of the King's Park, decided to step in. Declaring that the loch of Duddingston was within his jurisdiction, he took possession of the loch in the King's name and put the swans back in again.

The Duchess died in June, 1696, and was succeeded in her estates by her son, Lyonell, the second Earl of Dysart, who during his mother's lifetime had held the title of Lord Huntingtower.

In the years the Duke's death, although he had fallen into disgrace at court, the Maitlands of Hatton continued to flourish. Richard the eldest son of Lord Hatton, was made Lord Justice General in 1681 and his brother, John, who also had entered the legal profession, was admitted to the Faculty of Advocates in 1580. The Earl built a town house in the Canongate of Edinburgh, which in those days was the fashionable residential quarter for the nobility. It still stands, modernised, under the name of Queensberry House.

In July, 1861, the faction of the Duke of Hamilton attacked Lord Hatton. He became the central figure of a tangle of intrigue and litigation, typical of the period, when every man was for himself in the tussle for favours and stopped at nothing to gain power. One of the charges brought against him was that when in 1678. Mitchell was tried for firing a pistol at Archbishop Sharp, both Hatton and his brother, in examining Mitchell in council, promised him his life if he confessed the crime and when Mitchell came before the court, they denied making any such promise, with the result that Mitchell was hanged, on the insistence of the Archbishop.

Whatever the truth in the allegation, Alexander Bruce, Earl of Kincardine, pursued the matter with malice. In his account of his own times, Burnett stated that Lord Kincardine had in his possession from the Duke and the Duke's brother which requested him to ask the King to make good the promise. Anderson, in "The Scottish Nation" adds that James Boswell, Lord Auchinleck, a grandson of Lady Kincardine, observed that she gave a copy of the letters to the Duke of York who showed them to King Charles, "who was stunned at the villainy, and ashamed he had employed such a minister, and immediately ordered all his posts and preferments to be taken from him." This sounds a strange story and strangely points to what we would now call a frame-up. If the Lauderdale letter asked Kincardine to get the King to make good the promise of pardon for Mitchell, why did not Kincardine do so, instead of saving up the letters to use against Hatton? And to say that King Charles was "stunned" and "ashamed" at one broken promise to a criminal, when his own career was littered with broken promises of greater and graver importance, is little more than nonsense.

Nevertheless, Hatton's political enemies triumphed. His prosecution before Parliament was stopped with the adjournment of that body and the case went directly to the

King. Hatton was deprived of the presidency of the Privy Council and an investigation of the Treasury accounts was ordered. Upon the report of the commission, the Lord Advocate was ordered to proceed against him for misappropriation and he was found liable in £20,000. He was deprived of all his offices. During this time, the Duke of Lauderdale was in disgrace and ill and was unable to do anything to help his brother.

The disgrace of the Duke of Lauderdale did nothing to alter the persecution of the Covenanters. On the contrary, Lauderdale's enemies, now in the seats of power, were responsible for such an increased terrorisation by a military force under Graham of Claverhouse that the ten years or so following the Duke's death became known in Scottish history as the Killing Time. The men then responsible were the new favourites of King Charles and then of his brother, King James VII – William Douglas, third Earl of Queensberry, who became a Duke in 1684; George Gordon, created Earl of Aberdeen in 1682, and James Drummond, the Earl of Perth. Yet Lauderdale and Claverhouse has been picked out by historians as the men chiefly responsible for the whole period of persecution. The great difference between Lauderdale and the enemies who took his place was that he had a genuine policy, to which he adhered for twenty years, while they were men of the moment, willing to grab at honours as the price of their policy of greater persecution.

Two years before the revolution of 1688, the third Earl had so far restored himself in favour that he was readmitted a Privy Councillor.

Charles II died in 1685 and his brother James, who succeeded him, was openly a Catholic. He reigned for only three years, all the factions opposing Catholicism uniting to support the landing of William, Prince of Orange, and his wife Mary, who were Protestants, William being a nephew and Mary the daughter of James II.

The *coup d'etat* of 1688 has been nicknamed the Glorious Revolution by liberal historians but in fact it solved very little. The division of loyalties only became more complicated. The Maitland family was split in two by the usurpation of William and Mary. Richard, the eldest son, who became fourth Earl on the death of his father in June, 1681 was a royalist and together with his brother Alexander, another Jacobite, died in exile. John, the second son, was a supporter of the 1688 Revolution and stayed at home, to become in turn the fifth Earl of Lauderdale.

Nothing is known of the early education of Richard Maitland, but it is likely that he had a classical education at St Andrews University, like his forebears. He was an adept scholar and in later life became a man of learning and culture, his leisure being devoted to a translation into English poetry of the poems of Virgil. This was printed after his death. John Dryden, who saw the original manuscript, was so impressed by its quality that he adopted many of the lines in his own translation in compliment to Lauderdale.

Richard was sworn a privy councillor in October, 1678, and was appointed general of the mint jointly with his father. He married Lady Anne Campbell, second daughter of the 9th Earl of Argyll, the Covenanting leader who was executed in 1661. By one of those curious quirks, which serve to confuse readers and at the same time add spice to history, Lady Anne's brother, the tenth Earl, married Elizabeth Tollemache, a daughter of the Duchess of Lauderdale by her first husband, Sir Lionel Tollemache. As we know, the Duke of Lauderdale was a friend of the tenth

Earl, who in his youth was an active royalist as against his covenanting father.

Not only did Lauderdale and Argyll help each other in politics, but they were personal friends. We find Argyll sending down to London for Lauderdale and the King salt herrings and whisky from Inveraray. "On one occasion," writes Henry Willcock, in his life of the 9th Earl of Argyll, "Argyll sent honey from his own bee-hives along with the spirits in order that Lauderdale might enjoy the compound now known as 'Athol Brose'." Lauderdale was godfather to one of Argyll's sons, called John in Lauderdale's honour, a John who later was father to another John, the fourth Duke of Argyll.

Upon the fall of the Duke of Lauderdale, the Earl of Argyll found himself attacked. John Hay, Earl of Errol, who married a daughter of the Earl of Perth, laid a false claim upon the Argyll estates for a debt of Argyll's father for which Errol had been cautioner. The Committee of the Articles tried to get Parliamentary control over the Argyll estates on the ground that on his father's forfeiture they had become Crown Property. These attempts failed.

But when, in 1681, Argyll himself opposed the Test Act, his enemies, including the Duke of York, then in Scotland, and King Charles himself, united to destroy him. He was arrested and confined in Edinburgh Castle. Tried and found guilty of treason, Argyll contrived to escape while the court (under Lauderdale's enemy, the Justice General, Queensberry) waited to hear from King Charles in Whitehall what the sentence would be.

Argyll had married, as his second wife, the widow of Alexander Lindsay, Earl of Balcarres, who had been made the hereditary governor of Edinburgh Castle. Argyll's step-daughter, Lady Sophia Lindsay, went to visit him in his cell, accompanied by a young man as page and a servant carrying a lantern. Argyll and the page changed clothes and the Earl walked out of Edinburgh Castle with his step-daughter, to reach a horse and ride for the Border.

Whether Lord Richard Maitland (as he then was) had a hand in Argyll's escape, is not clear but it is certain that afterwards he followed Argyll's career closely and in spite of their political opposition to each other – Richard remaining a royalist while Archibald Campbell becoming increasingly the champion of the Covenant, as was his father – Richard aided Argyll when political dangers menaced family safety.

In exile in Holland, Argyll became involved in plots against the King. In June 1863 a plot to murder the King and the Duke of York at Rye House on their way back from the races at Newmarket was disclosed to the King. Argyll was suspected of being concerned with this and letters of his in cypher, which had been intercepted by government agents, were sent to the Scottish Privy Council in order that the Countess of Argyll could be questioned for the purpose of discovering the key to the cypher. She was forced to admit that one of the cypher letters referred to Lord Maitland, her son-in-law. Maitland's papers were then seized and examined but as nothing could be found which incriminated him, he was left unmolested.

In 1685, with the rebellion of the Duke of Monmouth against his uncle, James II, the Earl of Argyll landed in Scotland with his son, John, and a small army, raised a force of Highlanders from his own country and entered upon a disastrous campaign which ended in his capture, trial and execution. Like his father, he died for the Covenanting faith – and also, be it said, for the right of Argyll and other great chieftains to rule as kings in their own territories.

During the years in which he managed Scotland, the Duke of Lauderdale had kept Argyll friendly while diplomatically excluding him from office, but when the Duke of York came to Scotland, the Duke saw at once that Argyll, as a Covenanting leader, and with a Campbell army at call, was a real danger.

His friends in the Scottish Parliament had tried to remove Argyll's heritable jurisdictions but they had failed. Their success would have undermined the power of all the Highland chiefs. Scotland was to endure another sixty years of struggle before the legal power of pit and gallows was taken from the chiefs.

Richard, Lord Maitland, was present at the execution of Argyll. After the Earl has been condemned, he was taken to Edinburgh Town House, where eight of his friends were allowed to meet him and go with him to the scaffold. Maitland was one of them. At the place of execution, Argyll gave some souvenirs to Maitland for his wife and children and then knelt down before the guillotine, which was nicknamed the Maiden, remarking as he did so that it was the sweetest maiden that ever he kissed.

When Dutch William came to England, the Scots waited to see what he would do, for it was generally known that he distrusted the Scots and was plainly afraid of the "Highland menace." Though they accepted him as King, his disruption splintered Scotland. Among these who held that the Stuarts in the main line of hereditary were the rightful monarchs was Richard Maitland. Upon the invasion of William of Orange, James II had fled to France, where Louis XIV gave him a pension and allowed him to establish a court at St Germains. Maitland followed the King to his court in exile. He was there when he succeeded his father in the title.

But even at St Germains, he remained a Maitland. He still believed in the old policy, so steadily followed by his uncle, the Duke, that government in Britain could only continue by compromise, by holding to a middle course, by them down when they could not be balanced. Maitland was not particularly welcome at court, for James as Duke of York had been one of the Duke of Lauderdale's enemies, but he did not hesitate to give the exiled King the best advice he had to give. He had not approved of the extreme measures of James while he was on the throne and now he advised the King to come to an agreement with the Protestants at home. This was not to the liking of James fanatical spirit. From his knowledge of the Scottish nobility and their political sincerity, Maitland even went so far as to nominate three peers as men who would genuinely work for the King's return. They were Charles Home, Earl of Home; Henry Sinclair, Lord Sinclair, and Charles Carnegie, Earl of Southesk. All were opponents of the revolutionary settlement and remained so faithfully.

King James ordered Lady Lauderdale, whose connection with Argyll he hated, to leave Paris and return to England and Lauderdale was forbidden the court. The Earl retired to Paris, where he sought to alleviate his disappointment and the boredom of exile by continuing his literary studies. He died in Paris in 1695.

Nothing is known about three others sons of third Earl. William Maitland married, as his first wife, Lady Christian Makgill, eldest daughter of the second Viscount Oxford. The first Viscount was a companion of Charles II in exile and was created a viscount in 1651 for his services during those years. The second Viscount married Lady Henriet Livingstone, daughter of the Earl of Linlithgow, and had one son, who died without issue, and three daughters.

On the death of the second Viscount in 1706, the title became extinct. But this marriage of William Maitland and Christian Makgill began that connection with the Makgills which in succeeding generations brought about an immense ramification of relationships.

The two daughters of the third Earl of Lauderdale married Scottish peers. Isobel married in 1670, John, Lord Elphinstone, and Mary married Charles Carnegie, who became the fourth Earl of Southesk. This marriage brought with it interesting historical connections with the Grahams as well as with the Carnegies.

It was through Mary Maitland's marriage to the Earl of Southesk that the Maitland safe connected with the Murrays of Scone. Southesk's aunt, Jean Carnegie, married first James Murray, Earl of Annandale, who became third Viscount Stormont, and then upon his death, secondly, David Murray, Lord Salvaird, who inherited and became fourth Viscount Stormont. William Murray, third son of the fifth Viscount, who was born at Scone in 1705, entered the English Bar and attained with unprecedented rapidity the highest reputation in his profession. He became Lord Chief Justice of England and was created Earl of Mansfield. It was he who changed the nickname of "the muckle mou'd Murrays" to that of "the silver tongued Murray" by the eloquence and persuasion of his pleading.

14. THE FIFTH EARL

John Maitland, second son of Lord Hatton, succeeded his brother as fifth Earl of Lauderdale. A lawyer, he had shared in the family good fortune under Charles II, being admitted to the Faculty of Advocates in July, 1680, and in the same year buying the estate of Ravelrig, just outside Currie, Midlothian. Unlike his brother, he supported the revolutionary settlement and King William III. When he was appointed a Lord of Session in October, 1689, he assumed the judicial title of Lord Ravelrig.

He also became a baronet of Nova Scotia and a member of the Scottish Privy Council. And, to show that he had not abandoned the camp for the court of session and Parliament hall, he became Colonel of the Edinburgh Militia. This was one of the key military posts in Scotland, like the governorships of Edinburgh Castle, Dumbarton Castle and the Bass Rock.

The fifth Earl married Lady Margeret Cunningham, only daughter of the Earl of Glencairn, the third son of heir of the Glencairn who was Lord Chancellor after the Restoration. Her uncle, John Cunningham, who was then Earl of Glencairn, had supported the Revolution so fervently that he had raised a regiment of 600 men for the service of the government and received a commission as Colonel of the regiment. He was made governor of Dumbarton Castle.

When he took his seat in the Scottish Parliament in September, 1696, Lauderdale found that the Duke of Queensberry and Sir John Dalrymple of Stair were in command of the government in Scotland. The defeat of the Jacobite army at Dunkeld, following the death of Graham of Claverhouse at Killiecrankie, and the victory of William III over James II at the Battle of the Boyne in Ireland had damped down the Royalist movement and the so-called massacre of Glencoe had cowed the clans for a generation. The Covenanting turmoil in the South West had been neatly diverted by the creation of a regiment of Cameronians. As for the religious question in general, the Church in Scotland was fully occupied in disputes between the Presbyterian and Episcopal ministers over their livings after the formal abolition of episcopacy. So that the way was left open for political and parliamentary questions.

Under Queen Anne, the English Government wanted the ending of a separate Parliament in Scotland, with separate officers of the crown. Queensberry and Dalrymple were strongly in favour of the union. In this, he followed a long established political tradition of his family. It was Sir Richard Maitland of Letherington, secretary to Mary Queen of Scots, who negotiated so doggedly with Queen Elizabeth's secretary, Cecil, for agreement between Scotland and England – an agreement which even then could have gone beyond a mere dynastic accommodation over the succession to a closer union of the two countries. And if the Duke of Lauderdale had thrown cold water of proposals for unity, it was to protect his immediate interests: although he may have been realist enough to recognise that King Charles's notion of having a phalanx of Scottish votes at his command at Westminster would serve Scotland far less than the worst of Parliaments in Edinburgh. However that may be, the John Maitland of 1707 was no fire-eater.

Described by a contemporary as "a well bred man, handsome in his person, fair complexioned, a gentleman that means well to his country," he would have stated his views for union with clarity and common sense, without seeking to create enemies.

His eldest son, James, married Lady Jean Sutherland, a daughter of the Earl of Sutherland, and there was one child of the marriage, a daughter, Jean, who was only six years of age when her father died in 1709, leaving his brother, Charles, heir to the Earldom. The third brother John, a Colonel in the Guards, died in 1756 without issue. The only sister, Elizabeth, married James Carmichael, Earl of Hyndford, who following a military career.

15. THE SIXTH EARL

Due to the death of his elder brother, Charles Maitland, the second son, who was born in 1688, succeeded his father as sixth Earl. He was then 22 years of age and he was still a young man when the Jacobites raised the standard of rebellion against the new Hanoverian King, George I.

Scotland had not swallowed its discontent over the union of the two Parliaments in 1707, which had centred authority in London, when the death of Queen Anne in 1714 made George, Elector of Hanover, the next Protestant heir to the throne of Great Britain. The exiled James II had died in 1701 and the Jacobites had in James III, the Old Pretender, one of the finest of the Stuarts, a balanced and tolerant thinker and writer; who may not have been a military genius but who certainly would have made a King of an entirely different kind from the sadistic idiot from Hanover.

When the Earl of Mar, dismissed from his office as Secretary of State by George I, raised the standard of King James VIII of Scotland, the Maitland family again found itself divided. Lady Mary Maitland, the Dowager Countess of Southesk, was an active Jacobite and, as we have said, her son was a regimental commander in the army which Mar raised, mostly of Highlanders and men from the North East of Scotland. The Earl of Lauderdale was an officer in the Hanoverian army, which was under the command of the

Duke of Argyll, a military tactician of some ability. Through a snowbound November, the Duke advanced his troops slowly and eventually brought the Royalists to battle at Sheriffmuir, about four kilometres east of Dunblane amid the Ochil Hills of Perthshire. The contest was indecisive, both sides claiming victory, for the casualties were so heavy in the two armies that it was impossible to say who had won. At Sheriffmuir the Earl of Lauderdale fought as a volunteer and it is on record that "he behaved himself with great gallantry."

He had already shown his interest in military affairs by becoming a member of the Royal Company of Archers, a quasi-military elite. There is a difference of opinion about the date of origin of this body, some holding to the tradition that it was a bodyguard formed by James I, while others maintain that it was recruited from the Scottish Guard of archers who attended upon the French King, the famous Garde Ecossaise. It was known as the Royal Company of Archers before 1676 and in 1822 George IV, as part of his royal descent upon Edinburgh, made the company into the King's Bodyguard for Scotland: in 1830 they were placed on the same footing in military precedence as the Household Brigade.

Following the family tradition, the sixth Earl was appointed General of the Mint and Lord Lieutenant of Edinburgh. The first appointment was a sinecure which had become practically hereditary in the Maitlands. The second shows the persistent connection of the Maitlands. The second shows the persistent connection of the Maitlands with the capital city. It would be true to say that for a long period, through their stay at Letherington and Hatton and membership of the Scottish legal trade and Parliament, they were more a Lothian family than a Border one. But following the Union of Parliaments and 1715, they came a great change in the role which Scotland played in history. During the 18th century, Britain was engaged in constant wars against France and Spain, which included wars all over the world for the annexation of colonies. Large armies were required and it became government policy to recruit Scottish Highlanders as the finest fighting men they could find.

Scottish regiments, officered by the sons of Scottish chiefs and nobles, were the principal force for the foundation of the British Empire. And for the next century and more the name of Maitland is constantly to the fore in the lists of officers and heroes who won the colonies. This tradition started with the family of the sixth Earl.

He himself was elected one of the sixteen representative peers for Scotland in 1741 but had only a short carder in the House of Lords, as he died in July, 1744.

Exactly 34 years before to the day, he had married Lady Elizabeth Ogilvy, daughter of James Ogilvy, Earl of Findlater and Seafield. Lady Maitland survived her husband by 34 years, continuing to look after a large family of active and brilliant sons and daughters, whose careers would fill volumes of history and whose family notation fills three pages of Burke's Peerage.

As the 18th century could well be described as the Golden Age of the Maitlands, it is extremely interesting to follow the lives of some of them. Leaving the career of the eldest son, James, who became seventh Earl, to a further chapter, we may begin within the second son, Charles.

Charles married Isobel Barclay, the heiress of Sir Alexander Barclay of Towie, Aberdeenshire. According to the custom where large estates were involved, he adopted

the surname and arms of Barclay, becoming Charles
Barclay-Maitland. His son, an officer in the Dragoon
Guards, was known as Charles Maitland of Tillicoultry. His
son Charles, born in September 1810, became rector of
Little Longford, Wiltshire. He died in 1844 and the
inscription of his tombstone in Hanging Longford
Churchyard, in the Wylye Valley, reads as follows:

> "To the Memory of Rev. Charles Maitland, late
> Rector of this Parish, who died December 16th,
> 1844, aged 88. On the north side of this grave rests
> the remains of Harriet, who died April 12th 1839,
> aged 19, and of Elizabeth Mary who died July 18th
> 1841, daughters of the above Rev. C. Maitland and
> Anne his wife."

Anne, his wife, who died in September, 1857, is buried
beside him. Their son, Charles, succeeded to the Earldom
as the twelfth Earl of Lauderdale, in 1878.

Charles Maitland, the progenitor of this Barclay line,
was married three times. In 1765, about four years after the
death of his first wife, he married a daughter of Patrick
Haldane of Gleneagles, and thirdly he married Janet
Moncrieffe, a daughter of Sir Thomas Moncrieffe of that
ilk, but there was no issue from these marriages. He died in
November, 1795.

The third son of the sixth Earl was George Maitland,
who entered the Church and became Archdeacon of Larne.
"A dignified clergyman in Ireland" – so runs his epitaph.
He died unmarried in 1764.

The next son, Richard, born in 1724 was a colourful
figure. He chose a military career and played an important
part in the foundation of British Canada. As a captain he

served under General Wolfe at the taking of Quebec in September, 1759. The French had settled Canada and when the British invaded the country in 1758, they first captured Louisburg and then sailed down the St Lawrence river to attack the town of Quebec, where the Marquis de Montcalm had gathered an army of French Canadians and Indians. The town itself, built in cliffs above the river, was well fortified and considered impregnable. Wolfe's strategy was to strike the enemy at the very point considered to be safe. During the night, the Fraser Highlanders and a regiment of light infantry climbed the cliffs, the heights of Abraham, and formed into line of battle in challenge of the French. In the ensuing battle, the French were defeated and General Montcalm killed but unfortunately Wolfe was also killed.

Upon the consequences of Canada in the following year, Captain Maitland was appointed deputy adjutant general of the Army in Quebec and four years later became adjutant general for all the troops in North America. He was promoted Colonel in 1772.

By Mary McAdam, his wife, Richard Maitland had a numerous and interesting family, most of whom went into the Army. Captain Richard Maitland, of the Durham Fencibles, died without issue in 1802. Fencibles were troops raised for home defence only during the 18th century and particularly during the Napoleonic Wars, and disbanded when the need for service was over.

Patrick Maitland became a partner in the firm of John Palmer and Company, bankers, Calcutta, and afterwards retired to live at Kilmaron Castle, Fife. His son, Major-General Frederick Colthurst Maitland, of the Indian Army, married Anne Deering Williams and by her had a son, Frederick Henry Maitland, born in December, 1840, who succeeded his cousin as the thirteenth Earl of Lauderdale in 1884.

The two youngest sons of Col. Richard Maitland – John and James – distinguished themselves in the Navy and in the Army.

John first saw action in the Royal Navy as a midshipman on board the "Boyne", of 98 guns, the flagship of Sir John Jervis, during an expedition against the French West Indies. He was quickly promoted Lieutenant and transferred to the frigate "Winchelsea" and then to the "Lively." He was serving on board that ship in 1795 when, after a hard-fought action of three hours, the French man-of-war "La Tourterelle" was captured.

Two years later he was promoted captain of the "Kingfisher". At that time, Napoleon was preparing his expedition against Egypt, which he carried out under the guise of a proposed invasion of England. The British Army and Navy were mustered. Infected by the revolutionary ideas from France and more directly by the terrible conditions on board ships of war, which are now well known to readers of historical novels, British seamen were in mutinous mood. The whole navy was roused by the prolonged hardships endured since the beginning of the war. There were mutinies in the fleet at Spithead and at the Nore in the summer of that year. On the first of July, mutiny flared up on the "Kingfisher." The men would not listen to reason and in the dangerous clash of wills, Captain Maitland realised that he was faced with the loss of his ship if he did not act incisively. Drawing his sword and calling on his officers to follow, he attacked the mutineers, killing and wounding several of them. In a few minutes of bloody fighting, he became the master of his ship again. This spirited conduct won for him the approbation of his old commander, Jervis – now Admiral Earl St Vincent – who in a special order recommended to the Fleet "Dr Maitland's recipe" for administration in similar circumstances. It is pleasing to add that in the years that followed, other recipes were used to improve conditions in the lower deck.

Captain Maitland was stationed in the Channel and then on the "Barfleur" in the Mediterranean until the end of the Napoleonic Wars in 1815. He was later promoted Read-Admiral. He was twice married, his first wife being his cousin, Elizabeth Ogilvy, of Inchmartine, a grand-daughter of the sixth Earl of Lauderdale.

His brother, James, receives in Burke's Peerage the brief sentence:

"James, Lieut-Col. 75th Regiment, Born 1772, killed at the siege of Bhurtpore. Died unmarried."

But behind these curt words is hidden much that was valiant.

Nothing is known of James's early life except that he joined the Army. In February 1804, at the age of thirty-two, he was in India, where he commanded the 75th Regiment, of Foot the forerunner to the 1st Battalion of the Gordon Highlanders. Shortly after, the regiment embarked at Surat bound for Calcutta, whence they proceeded by boat up the Ganges River on the long journey to Cawnpore.

From there they linked up with Lord Lake's Army which was lying between Deig and Bhurtpore, facing the threat of an attack by Rao Holkar and his warlike Mahrattas.

Having secured his reinforcements, Lord Lake took the initiative by launching as assault on Deig, strongly held by the enemy. The fighting was bitter and lasted two days, the town and fort eventually being carried. The next objective was Bhurtpore, about 35 miles west of Agra, a formidable obstacle, for surrounding the city was a deep ditch surmounted by a massive mud wall which was practically shot-proof.

Attempts were made to batter a breach, so that a storming party could go in, but these proved abortive, for any damage done was quickly repaired during the night by the defenders. Lord Lake then determined to make an all-out attack. A fresh bombardment began on the morning of the 9th January 1805, and on its cessation storming parties raced forward, led by Colonel Maitland and his Gordon Highlanders. Nothing could be finer than the vehement courage of this assault. It is best told in Lord Lake's despatch to the Marquis Wellesley, the Commander-in-Chief:

> "I determined on the storming of the place yesterday evening. I chose this time, in order to prevent the enemy from blockading the breach during the night, which had hitherto been the case. I am sorry to add, that obstacles of an insurmountable nature were opposed to the storming party on their arrival at the breach; the water in the ditch was exceedingly deep, this difficulty was speedily surmounted, and the party gained the foot of the breach, but though every exertion was made by both Officers and Men, the breach was so imperfect, that every effort to gain the top proved fruitless, and the column, after making several attempts with heavy loss, was obliged to retire, which they did in excellent order.
>
> Among the many brave men who have fallen on this occasion, it is with sincere grief I report the

death of Lieut-Colonel Maitland of the 75th Regiment, who commanded the storming party; his exertions are described by all to have been of a nature the most heroic, and his example animated the men to persevere in their attempts, which nothing but difficulties of a nature the most unexpected could have rendered unsuccessful.

The gallant Officer, though he had received several severe wounds, continued to exert himself until he received a shot in the head, which proved instantaneously mortal. Although we unfortunately failed in gaining possession of the place, we were not wholly unsuccessful, a flanking column on the right gained possession of the enemy's battery, and succeeded in spiking their guns and in destroying the greatest part of the enemy who were opposed to them. I beg to assure your Lordship, that the conduct of our Officers and men employed last night, has been as exemplary as on every former occasion, but circumstances of an unexpected and unfortunate nature occurred, which their utmost efforts could not surmount, but I hope in a few days their excellent conduct will be rewarded by the possession of the place."

His expectations were realised, for Bhurtpore fell shortly afterwards and peace was concluded in April.

16. THE GIBSONS AND RAMSAYS

The fifth son of Charles Maitland, the sixth Earl, Alexander was born in 1728 and died in 1820. Throughout his life he rose through the ranks of the British Army achieving the rank of General in 1793. The first of the Maitland Baronets of Clifton was created for him, General the Hon. Alexander Maitland, in the County of Midlothian, in the Baronetage of the United Kingdom, on 30 November 1818.

Sir Alexander's youngest son, Frederick, followed his father into the Army and there is no doubt that his Maitland character found good play. After seeing active service as a Lieutenant of solders acting as marines during the three-year siege of Gibraltar by the Spaniards, which was brought to an end in February, 1783, he thereafter saw much service in Jamaica and the West Indies, acting as military secretary to General Sir Ralph Abercromby in his West India campaign.

In 1805, the year of Trafalgar, he was returned to the West Indies as Governor of the island of Grenada and promoted to Major-General. In 1809 he was once again on active service, commanding the brigade at the capture of Martinique and in the operations at Les Saintes, for which he was voted the thanks of the House of Common for his gallant conduct. In the highly responsible post of Governor of a new colony, Maitland quickly gained the reputation of being an upright and painstaking administrator. Although his legal knowledge was self-acquired, it is to his credit that his decisions were never questioned or reversed save in one case, on a high technical point of law.

In 1811, he was moved up in rank to Lieutenant-General and in the following year he was brought back to the Mediterranean theatre of war as second-in-command to Lord William Bentinck. Unfortunately his health broke down and he was sent home on sick leave. But his abilities and experience of administration in the West Indies were not to go unrecognised, for he became Governor of Dominica in 1813 and advanced to full General in 1825.

On his retirement he went to live at Hartfield, Sussex. He died at Tunbridge in January, 1848, at the age of 84, and was buried in the parish church at Hartfield.

General Sir Alexander Maitland was succeeded in 1820 by his eldest son, Alexander Charles, who married in April, 1786, Helen, the heiress of Alexander Gibson Wright of Clifton Hall, West Lothian. Their eldest son, Alexander Gibson Maitland, advocate, died at the age of 41 in 1828 and two years later, his wife, Susan, the eldest daughter of George Ramsay of Barnton, Edinburgh, also died. Their son, Alexander Charles Gibson Maitland, succeeded his grandfather in 1848 as third baronet.

His brother, George Ramsay Gibson Maitland, was a Writer to the Signet, whose eldest son, John Nisbet, succeeded as fifth baronet. His brother, George Keith Ramsay Maitland, an architect and tea planter in Ceylon, married in 1877 Christina Mary McDonell, daughter of Angus McDonell of Keppoch, Chief of one of the oldest and most famous clans in Scotland. Of their family, the second son, Captain Keith Andrew Ramsay Maitland, was killed in 1917.

Angus Charles Majoribanks Maitland, his brother, was a pioneer of motor cycling. We are happy to say that, at the date of writing, he is still with us.

Before dealing with the third Baronet, we must deal with the younger sons of the second baronet, Sir Alexander Charles Maitland. Keith Ramsay Gibson Maitland entered the Army and ended his career as Colonel of the 79th Regiment, which became the 1st Battalion Cameron Highlanders. He won the Crimea Medal with three clasps and the India Medal with clasps.

The Sixth son, who called himself John Maitland, was a pioneer in accountancy. In Scotland the first accountant to set up professionally was George Watson of Edinburgh towards the end of the 17th century who later founded George Watson's College for Boys. During the 18th century the practice of accountancy, as distinct from book-keeping was mainly in the hands of a few family concerns.

It was here John mastered his initial training and after some experience decided in 1834 to launch out on his own.

About this time public interest was being focussed on the National Security Savings Bank movement. Attracted by the scheme John devoted much time and thought to it, for he saw that if the Savings Banks were to succeed then they must be run on a system that was reliable and trustworthy, otherwise the confidence of the public would never be gained. Accordingly he drew up a carefully compiled method of accounting suitable to the needs of Savings Banks immediately adopted by the Edinburgh Savings Bank, becoming in time a model procedure for other like institutions. The Edinburgh Savings Bank owes its success to John Maitland's business-like and as near as possible fraud-proof system of book-keeping. In recognition of his service, he was appointed actuary of the Bank in 1839, a position he held for ten years.

Observing that the savings movement was gaining momentum throughout the country, he circulated in 1841 a memorandum to all the newly formed Savings Banks setting out suggestions for accountancy procedure and conduct. The memorandum was received with enthusiasm and his proposals adopted by many, including the Glasgow and the Manchester Savings Banks, two of the largest operating at the time. As honorary treasurer of the Edinburgh Savings Bank, in 1858, he gave evidence before the Select Committee on Savings Banks.

He was now firmly established as an authority, so it was natural that when in 1850 the public office of Accountant to the Court of Session was created, the Crown nominated him to fill the post. This position he held until his death fifteen years later. His ability was further recognised when he was asked to join the Boards of Directors of the Commercial Bank of Scotland and of the North British Insurance Company.

Accordingly in 1854 the first professional accountancy body of modern times was established, the society of accountants, Edinburgh, of which John Maitland was a founder member. The Institute of Accountants and Actuaries in Glasgow came the next year, followed by the Society of Accountants in Aberdeen in 1867. In 1951 there was an amalgamation of the three bodies and the name altered to the Institute of Chartered Accountants of Scotland.

Like his relative, David Makgill Maitland Crichton of Rankeillour, John Maitland played an active part in the

Disruption of 1843. The crisis in the Church of Scotland was the burning topic of the day and when the Free Church was formed, he gave all his energies towards building the new church. In this he joined James Maitland Hog of Newliston, who had married his sister, Helen, in 1827. His services were eagerly sought, not only because of his business acumen but also for his capacity for calm thinking and planning. He was appointed a deacon in the new Free St George's Church, Edinburgh, and in 1846 was elected Ruling Elder.

The major problem facing the new Church was how it was to be financed and maintained, for there were no churches and no manses for the ministers who had left their established Kirk and there was no money. To all this Maitland directed his every effort.

Several pamphlets came swiftly from his pen, remarkable for clearness, terseness and pith setting out the necessity for creating a sustentation fund for the clergy and outlining the method of contribution and operation. His proposals were unanimously approved and his sustentation fund became a model.

He was a great believer n systematic giving and practised what he preached by following the scriptural dogma of donating a set portion of his yearly income towards philanthrophie and church objects. A few years before his death he made a special benefaction by building, at his own expense on a site which he had secured in close proximity to the New College, commodious and handsome premises for the various offices of the Church, including a spacious hall. Part of the arrangement was that the former and less suitable offices in Frederick Street were handed over in part exchange. Nevertheless, Maitland contributed from his own means some five to six thousand pounds towards the final cost.

A contemporary writing states: "The whole Church was thus placed under great obligation to him for this munificent gift, and will always associate his memory with that substantial and noble structure. An excellent portrait of the donor, by Mr. Norman Macbeth, graces the Presbytery Hall, and another portrait, in full length by Sir John Watson Gordon, has been placed in the principal room of the adjoin National Security Savings Bank, as an expression of the value attached to his long services there by the directors of that institution".

Generally Maitland enjoyed fairly good health, but on Tuesday 29th August 1865, having carried out his official duties, he returned in the afternoon to his summer residence at Swinton Bank near Peebles complaining of what appeared to be an influenza cold. By the week-end he was seriously ill. He died suddenly on the 6th September. He is buried in the Grange Cemetery, Edinburgh, by the north wall where near-by Dr. Chalmers and other true and good men of the Disruption lie at rest.

The third baronet, Alexander Charles Gibson Maitland added "Ramsay" to his name on inheriting the estates of his grandfather, George Ramsay of Barnton and Sauchie. On his son dying without a male heir, the baronetage passed to his cousin in 1897, Sir John Nisbet Maitland. His daughter, Claire, married Field Marshall Lord Milne, an Aberdeenshire man who became famous as commander of the British forces at Salonika in 1916, when the Bulgarian Army was defeated.

The only daughter of the fourth baronet, Mary, married in 1901, Sir Arthur Herbert Drummond Steel, who added Maitland to his name and who, as Arthur Steel Maitland, had a distinguished political career before his death in 1935. After holding various cabinet posts, he was Minister of Labour during the General Strike of 1926, when he played a leading role in that industrial drama.

The widow of the second Baronet, Lady Matilda Ramsay Steel Maitland, lives at Gogar House, near Edinburgh. Her surviving second son, Sir Keith, the third baronet, of Sauchieburn, Stirling, died unmarried in April, 1965, when the baronetcy became extinct.

Sir John Nisbet Maitland was succeed by his elder son, John, who after serving in the First World War, was a housemaster at Alleyn's School, Dulwich, and when he died without an heir, his brother, George Ramsay Maitland, became seventh baronet. He had a distinguished military career, becoming Lieutenant-Colonel of the 14th Jat Lancers. For the South African War he held the Queen's Medal with five clasps and in the First world War, he won the D.S.O. and the Belgian Croix de Guerre. He retired to Burnside, Forfar, and did in 1960.

He was succeed by Major Sir Alexander Keith Maitland, who served with the Queen's Own Cameron Highlanders from 1940 to 1950.

Posted to the 1st Battalion, he sailed to India early in 1942. After a period with 'Special Forces' he rejoined his regiment at Kohima, and took command of A 'Grenadiers' Company during the Irrawaddy crossing, and led them to the capture of Ava Ford at Mandalay. Later he took part in the occupation of Japan, and held staff appointments in Singapore and Hong-Kong. Returning home in 1950, he married Miss Lavender Mary Jex, the youngest daughter of Francis Jex Jackson of Kirkbuddo, Forfar, in 1951. Resigning his commission, he took a year at the Royal

Agricultural College, Cirencester, before taking up residence at Burnside, where he became one of the most progressive landowners in the North-East. He was a pioneer of the Scottish Broiler industry.

The present baronet, the ninth, is Sir Richard John Maitland, born 1952.

17. GENERAL FREDERICK LEWIS MAITLAND

The sixth son of the sixth Earl was Frederick Lewis Maitland. He was born on the 19th of June, 1730, and immediately became a son of fortune, for his godfather was the Prince of Wales, after whom he was named Frederick Lewis, Christian names which were to be repeated many times in future generations in honour of the Prince, who unfortunately died before he could succeed his father, George II, on the throne. Frederick Lewis Maitland entered the Royal Navy as a youngster and soon showed his mettle, being promoted Lieutenant at the age of nineteen and captain ten years later.

Between 1763 and 1775, he was in command of King George III's royal yacht. In 1767, he married Miss Margeret Dick, the only daughter of James Dick of Colluthie, Monzie, Fife. It is here where the fun really begins, to put it light-heartedly, for the earnest student of the Maitland family tree. The gallant sailor little realised the tremendous "genealogical furore" he was to create by his marriage, for in time the families of Maitland, Makgill, Crichton and Heriot were to be united un ramifications of relationships that to an outsider represent complete bamboozlement. It is only possible without becoming wearisome to sketch these relationships and pick out a few outstanding figures, which is a pity, for each family separately and conjointly has produced men and women whose life stories would make fascinating and compulsive study.

Service in the Royal Navy has always included in it the celebrated "beer and skittles" and if rum and water became the Navy drink through generations of service in the West Indies, native tipples in other parts of the world were not neglected. The introduction of port into Britain and its popularisation as a fine drink owe a great deal to Captain Frederick Lewis Maitland.

It was the English merchants in Oporto, Portugal, who developed the vineyards of the Douro in order to create a wine suitable to the English palate and climate. The first outlet they had for their wines was in supplying the English fleet, which made Oporto a regular port of call.

On the 27th December 1703, the Methuen Treaty was signed, whereby a preferential rate of duty was levied on all port shipped to England, compensated by the importation to Portugal of the previously prohibited English woollens. The result was an immediate boom in trade between the two countries. In Oporto, as in most places where Englishmen were engaged in commerce, the merchants formed a Factory, a kind of Chamber of Commerce and exclusive club rolled into one.

In 1761 the "Third Family Compact" was signed, aligning France and Spain together with Naples and Parma in a defensive alliance, which at once brought Spain into conflict with England. The first victim was neighbouring Portugal, who had refused to join the pact on account of the lucrative Methuen Trade Treaty with England. French and Spanish troops crossed the border, and the French fleet moved in to blockade and take Oporto. The English reaction was swift and the Navy, ever ready, brought instant succour to the threatened port, while at the same time covered the landing of an expeditionary force. The enemy was routed at the battle of Valencia, and the survivors harried out of Portugal. Peace was sought, and a Treaty signed on 10th February 1763.

Colonel H.D.M. Crichton-Maitland, of Ightham, Sevenoaks, Kent, possesses a momento of these events in the Oporto Cup, a splendid presentation vessel made of Scottish silver weighing seven pounds and seventeen inches high. The whole cup is heavily embossed and the Maitland crest in engraved below the following inscription:

> "Presented by the British Factory of Oporto to the Hon. Frederick Maitland, Commander of His Majesties Ship 'Renown', as a small acknowledgement of his great services to the Trade on the coast of Portugal in the year 1762."

It is to be hoped that the gallant Captain was, never after, in lack of his glass of port.

Another of Frederick Lewis Maitland's exploits, of which he was very proud, occurred one morning when he was sitting down to breakfast in his cabin aboard the "Elizabeth", of 74 guns. There came a hail from the lookout that a hostile French ship was in sight. Captain Maitland, although suffering at the time from a severe disability of his legs which crippled him, immediately gave orders that he should be hoisted up to the poop and propped in a chair, from which he bellowed his command though a speaking trumpet to raise aloft every stitch of canvas. The "Elizabeth" bore down on the enemy and after a brisk exchange of shots, in which the enemy vessel was outmanoeuvred, the British seamen boarded her and forced her surrender. Then, having received the French captain's sword, Captain Maitland allowed himself to be lowered below to finish his interrupted breakfast.

The capture turned out to be the treasure ship of the French fleet.

The captain's share of the prize money came to some £4,000 and with this he built the house of Nether Rankeillour, Fife. In showing friends and guests over the house, he would take delight in relating that he had gained the money for it one morning before breakfast. It is sad to think that he died on 16th December, 1786, unaware that the brevet of his promotion to Rear-Admiral was only awaiting his Sovereign's signature.

His wife's father, James Dick of Colluthie, was the son of the Rev. William Dick, minister of Cupar Fife, and of Isabel Makgill, of Rankeilour. In the course of time, Margaret Maitland became heiress to the ancient family of Makgill which, like the Maitlands, had a long record of service to the Crown.

Her eldest son, Colonel Charles Maitland, served in the West Indian campaign of 1794 as aide-de-camp to his cousin, Major-General Thomas Dundas. His son, David Maitland Makgill, heir to the family of Makgill, was also served heir to the Crichtons of Frendraught and added Crichton to his name. Their son, David Maitland Makgill Crichton, was a champion of the Disruption, when 420 ministers of the Church of Scotland, because they refused to acknowledge the right of patronage and desired that church members should freely choose their ministers. It is interesting to know that one of the ancestors of his Makgill great-grandmother was Alexander Leslie, the Covenanting general who led the Scots army in the Civil War and is regarded as the victor at Marston Moor.

David was the fifth child to be born in a family of fifteen but in those days of high infant mortality he became the eldest before he was grown up. He was educated at St Andrews Grammar School and finished his law studies at Edinburgh University, becoming a member of the Faculty of Advocates in 1822. His father's death and that of his elder brother, Frederick, a midshipman in the Royal Navy, at the age of 22, left him heir to Rankeillor and the death of his grandmother, Margeret Maitland-Makgill, in 1825 brought a further change of circumstances, as under the settlement he had to assume the name of Makgill and so became David Maitland-Makgill of Rankeillor.

In 1827 he gave up his legal practice and in the same year married Eleanor Julian Hog, daughter of Thomas Hog of Newliston. The happiness of his married life was saddened by the illness of his wife and in September, 1832, he let Rankeillor and went to Madeira but in January of the following year his wife died of consumption and was buried in Madeira. He remarried in December, 1834, Esther Coventry, daughter of Dr Coventury, professor of agriculture at Edinburgh.

In 1837 he successfully claimed to be served heir in line to James Crichton, Lord Frendraught, and added Crichton to his name. He was elder of the Church and not only organised a daily ration of soup to the needy, but also established Sunday schools and day schools. He converted a large area of moorland into arable and let it to the villagers at a small rent. He also introduced reforms into the management of local road trusts that secured improved roads at a greatly reduced cost. But his major interest was in the controversy over the Non-Intrusion Act, which tore Scotland in two. The peak of action was the Disruption and in this David Maitland-Makgill Crichton played his part. He contributed generously to the erection of the Free Church, manse and school at Collessie.

In 1844, his health broke down. The people he had helped in their struggle for a free church rallied to pay their respects to him. A testimonial, for which the subscriptions were limited to one shilling, took the form of a silver candelabra with statues six inches high of Knox, Luther and Calvin, inscribed: "To David Maitland-Makgill-Crichton of Rankeillor, from ten thousand members of the Free Church of Scotland, 1845", a full-size portrait in oils and a large volume containing the autographs and names of the subscribers. Not to be outdone, the farmers of Fife presented him with a dinner service in gratitude for his work in saving them high road taxes.

He died in July, 1851, and was buried in the family grave at Monimail. His memorial stone bears the phrase:

"The Poor Man's Friend."

18. THE HERIOTS

Margaret Dick, the wife of Captain Frederick Lewis Maitland, was not only heir to the Makgills of Rankeillour but also heir in line to the Heriots of Ramornie, Ladybank, Fife. Her grandson, David, succeeded to Rankeillour and his brother, James, while still a minor, was served heir to Ramornie. Under the entail, he was obliged to assume the name and arms of Heriot, thus becoming James Maitland-Heriot of Ramornie, though he preferred to be known simply as James Heriot.

And so, to the confusion of Makgill Maitland Crichton and Makgill Crichton Maitland, the additional surname of Heriot gave increase. The Heriots of Trabroun, in Lauder, were a family as old and as distinguished as the Maitlands. They had held Trabroun for a century and a half before James Heriot granted a discharge, dated 8th March, 1560, to Sir Richard Maitland of Letherington for the receipt of money due to him according to the contract of marriage between Isobel Maitland, his daughter, and James Heriot younger of Trabroun. The receipt was witnessed by Patrick Cockburn of Clerkington, John Maitland and others. The actual marriage took place in October of that year.

In 1611, James Heriot, with the consent of his wife, sold the lands of Trabroun to John Hamilton, his grand-nephew, a son of the first Earl of Haddington. The balance of the purchase money was paid in 1623 to the two surviving daughters and the property passed entirely from the family. This branch of the Heriots now appears to be extinct.

Heriot's will, written in his own hand, left estate consisting chiefly of farming stock to a sum of £4,932. Stating that he was "of a great age," he left his soul Eternal to God and his body "to be honourably buried in the burial place of my father at Haddington Kirk at the south-east side thereof." He nominated Isobel Maitland, his well beloved spouse, to be his "only executrix and universal intromitter" and recommending her "to the protection and maintenance of the Great God Almighty and to the protection of the Hon. Lord John Maitland of Thirlestane and Sir Thomas Hamilton of Byres, Secretary to our Sovereign Lord, earnestly requesting them for God's cause and kindred and for the love and goodwill he bears them that they would fortify, maintain and assist her in the using of the said office of executrix that she sustain no wrong in the ministration thereof, for she has been an honest, virtuous, godly, good wife and helper and brought up her three daughters in virtue and knowledge of God's Word."

But the Heriots of Ramornie, whose founder was Walter Heriot, burgess of Cupar Fife, who obtained a charter for his estate round about 1501 to 1512, eventually merged with the Makgill Maitland line by the marriage of Janet Craig, heiress to Ramornie, with Sir David Makgill of Rankeillour, the third baronet. Both the Makgill Crichton and Makgill Heriot branches of the family produced generation after generation of distinguished officers in the Navy and Army and the military traditions continues to this day.

James Heriot married in 1813, Margaret Dalgleish, of Scotscraig, Fife. Two of their sons, both of whom preferred to call themselves Heriot-Maitland, distinguished themselves in the second Chinese War, which ended in the capture of Peking in 1860. Major-General Sir James Makgill Heriot-Maitland, K.C.B., served not only in China, but in Canada and then in the Egyptian campaigns. He was several times mentioned in despatches, once for "extreme gallantry."

His brother, Admiral William Heriot-Maitland, married Elizabeth, eldest daughter and heiress, of William Stark Dougall, of Scotscraig, and he added the further name of Dougall to Maitland, thus beginning a new line of Maitland-Dougalls.

No fewer than six Maitlands served in the South African War.

19. A MAITLAND AT WATERLOO

Before continuing our story of the Lauderdale Maitlands, we must bring in General Sir Peregrine Maitland, held to be of the Pittrichie branch, who commanded the Guards at the Battle of Waterloo. He completes the trio of Maitlands who figured so brilliantly in that period of history – James, the eighth Earl, Napoleon's "bon garcon", the diplomat; Captain Frederick Lewis, of the "Bellerophon", who received Napoleon's surrender after Waterloo; and General Peregrine, of "Up, Guards, and at 'em!" fame, of whom we shall, in the following chapters, discover more of.

Writing in the Clan Maitland News Letter of October, 1963, Mrs W.P. Maitland Russell, of Edinburgh, said:

> "The ancestry of Sir Peregrine Maitland is still uncertain. There seems to be evidence that he derived from the Pittrichie Branch of the   First Cadetship. The College of Arms indicates that a Grant of   Arms was made on the 20th January 1818 to Sir Peregrine, and   reports that according to constant tradition his family was   descended from the ancient family of the same name seated at   Pittrichie in Aberdeenshire, a branch of the Noble House of   Lauderdale."

Mrs Russell is a widow of Captain Wilmot Peregrine

Maitland Russell, M.C., M.A. (Oxon.), who was an officer in the Gordon Highlanders during the First World War and then was in the diplomatic service in Finland. His father Captain T.S. Russell, Chief Constable of the West Riding of Yorkshire, and his mother's mother, Georgine Louisa Maitland, was a daughter of Sir Peregrine.

It is known that Peregrine's grandfather, Richard Maitland, a London merchant, was educated at Marischal College, Aberdeen, from 1725 to 1729, when he graduated Master of Arts. Peregrine's father, Thomas Maitland, married Jane Matthew, of Felix Hall, Essex, who mother was Lady Jane Bertie, a daughter of Peregrine Bertie, second Duke of Ancaster and Kesteven. Lady Jane's twin sister, it is interesting to record, married Rev. James Austen, brother of the famous novelist, Jane Austen.

The family name of Peregrine thus had its origin in the Bertie family and goes back to Tudor times. Catherine, Baroness Willoughby de Eresby married in 1535 Charles Brandon, Duke of Suffolk, brother-in-law to King Henry VIII. After the death of her husband, she married Richard Bertie, a descendant of whom was created Duke of Ancaster in 1715.

Mrs Maitland Russell relates that Bertie and the Duchess had to flee from England in the reign of Queen Mary to escape persecution, as they were staunch Protestants. In Wesel in 1554, their first son was born and "rather whimsically, they named their first-born, Peregrine, on account of their wanderings."

This Peregrine Bertie grew up to be the 11th Lord Willoughby de Eresby and towards the end of Queens Elizabeth's reign, Warden of the English East March on the Borders and Governor of Berwick, in which office he died.

Peregrine Maitland was born in July 1777 at Longparish House, Hampshire, and at the age of 15 became an ensign in the 1st Foot Guards, the Grenadiers. He served with the regiment in Flanders and in Spain, when the Grenadier Guards took part in the retreat to Corunna in 1809. By 1812, he was a brevet-Colonel and again in Spain.

At the British Army's passage of the Bidassoa in October, 1813, he commanded the First Brigade of Guards and was in command at the following battles on the Nivelle and the Nive. In 1814, he was promoted major-general and in the following year was created a Companion of the Bath.

The life of a fighting soldier during the Napoleonic Wars was not easy, for there was little leave and the periods of peace were not extensive. However, in June, 1803, during an interval in war but while Napoleon was collecting the Grande Armee around Boulogne for the threatened invasion of England, Maitland found time to get married at St George's, Hanover Square, London, to Louisa Croften, daughter of Sir Edward Crofton, Bt., M.P. for County Roscommon. The marriage was soon to end in tragedy, for Louisa died in November, 1805, and her infant son, born on the first day of May, 1804 died soon after her.

In the spring of 1814, Wellington and his Army from Spain occupied Bordeaux and the Germans under Schwarzenberg took Paris. Napoleon abdicated and was retired to the island of Elba. And Europe had a breathing space from war. But the restless little Corsican was not content to remain Emperor of Elba. On March 1, 1815, came the news that Bonaparte had landed in France and that the magic of "L'Empereur" was drawing his old soldiers in their thousands back to the eagles, ready to die for France *an la gloire*.

The British Army was mustered in Belgium under Wellington. The final issue was to be fought out round the small village of Waterloo. The battle began on June 16 at Quatre Bras, where a mixed force of British, Belgians and Dutch held off the French, and at Ligny, where the Prussians were forced to retreat, thus widening the gap between the allied armies. The engagement reached its climax on the 18th at Waterloo, where Wellington's infantry held desperately to the Chateau of Hougoumont in spite of furious attempts by the French to dislodge them, while the main body of British infantry, formed in squares, held off repeated attacks by the French cavalry.

General Peregrine Maitland was in command of the First Brigade of Guards. Towards the end of that nerve-grinding day of noise and carnage, with victory a matter of holding on and summoning the last reserve of strength, Wellington gave his old comrade in arms and the Guards the order that was to turn the tide of battle.

On the other side, Napoleon and Marshall Ney had expended their artillery and cavalry. The British squares, although decimated, stood firm and would not be broken. Like Wellington, Napoleon called upon the last and finest troops. He flung into the field the battalions of his Imperial Guard. If any force could give him victory, it was the flower of the Army. They advanced, an awe-inspiring sight, over the ridge wreathed with smoke, ready to give the British the coup de grace. From their ranks came the cry of *"Vive l'Empereur!"*

A grim faced Wellington cantered over to where General Maitland's guardsmen were crouching and nodded their commander. "Now, Maitland, now's your time," he said.

Maitland gave the order. But if the order was yelled in parade ground style, the language was Wellington's own. "Up Guards, and at 'em!"

The long red line of the Foot Guards rose as one man as if they had sprung from the ground. There was a crush of fire that cut a swathe in the formidable ranks that were almost upon them. The British bayonets fell to the level and before the onward rush of steel, the French guardsman wavered, then broke and ran. They carried with them the defeat of their Emperor.

There has always been controversy over that command: "Up, Guards, and at 'em".

Dr Fitchett, in his book on the Battle of Waterloo, denies that the Duke of Wellington used the phrase, although it has been attributed to him by many others. But it seems unlikely that Wellington having given the order, "Now, Maitland, now's your time," about which most writers agree, would have issued a second order over the head of one of his most trusted commanders, a seasoned campaigner of the Peninsular Wars, whose duty it was to lead the Guards into attack.

Captain Leonard Garbett, CBE, RN (ret), a descendant of General Maitland, has this to say about the famous order.

"I expect I am the only great-grandson living who knew the sons and daughters of Sir Peregrine and Lady Sarah. As children we were   given to understand that our great-grandfather, Sir Peregrine, gave   the order, "Up, Guards, and at 'em," probably after Wellington had said, "Now, Maitland, now's your time', but I have   no documentary evidence of this. Maybe we heard it from Sir Peregrine's son, Horatio, who became an Admiral and who lived close to us."

This appears to be as authentic as anything.

It was completely in line with Maitland's fighting spirit to give such a command to his men and this is borne out by what Colonel J.A. Stanhope says in his letter to the Duke of York.

> "Were it possible for me to add anything to the reputation of Maitland by stating the gallantry he has shown in cheering on his men with his hat off … I could not dwell long on the subject."

Until it can be proved otherwise, we shall give General Peregrine Maitland the credit. Besides, whatever the words of command might have been, it is certain that he led the Guards in the final assault upon their French counterparts and that their victory won the battle of Waterloo. And ended Napoleon's attempt to regain the imperial throne. Nearly a month later, he surrendered his sword to Captain Frederick Lewis Maitland of the Royal Navy on board H.M.S Bellerophon.

Meantime, General Maitland was in Paris, helping his commander-in-chief to organise the occupation of the city and to negotiate with the Bourbonists.

For these services he was awarded the Waterloo Cross and the KCB.

There was no doubting Peregrine Maitland's courage and resource as a soldier but it might have been that the added dash of that "Up, Guards, and at 'em!" was due to his being in love. Tradition says that he met and fell in love with Lady Sarah Lennox at the famous eve of Waterloo Ball given in Brussels by Lady Sarah's parents, the Duke and Duchess of Richmond. Tradition also says that in his bravery he proposed to Lady Sarah at the Ball – and was accepted.

Both knew of the dangers that were ahead for the General on the field of battle but the menace of those shakoed imperial guardsmen they could face. What was more difficult for them was the hostility of the Duke and Duchess. The proposed marriage of their daughter to an Army General with only his service pay – and a widower at that – was not at all pleasing to them. The proposal was rejected. But there was never a Maitland yet who didn't get his own way.

Lady Sarah was now in Paris and General Maitland and she resolved to get married in spite of her parents' disapproval. Maitland took her to his friend Paymaster of the Guards in Paris, whose wife and daughter looked after Lady Sarah and became delighted and eager conspirators for bringing about so romantic a match.

Maitland went to seek the support of the Duke of Wellington, who was surely a match for the aristocratic Richmond. The Duke was intrigued by the romance and annoyed that Richmond should not be prepared to accept one of his best and most trusted Generals. As virtual ruler of France, he saw no difficulty in arranging the desired marriage.

So, on the ninth of October, 1815, Peregrine Maitland and Sarah Lennox were married at the British Embassy in Paris. The Duke of Wellington saw to it that the Ambassador signed as a witness, to make sure!

Later, when they saw the happiness of their daughter, her parents forgave what they considered to be a misalliance and gave Lady Sarah and her husband and their growing family the warmth of their affection. Wellington, too continued a good friend of the Maitlands and they and their family were frequent guests at his house.

After the official ending of the war, Maitland had a period at home before being appointed Lieutenant-Governor of Upper Canada in June, 1818. The war between the United States and the British in Canada had ended in 1814 but the ambitions of both governments had not been met. The Earl of Selkirk's Red River scheme was stretching Canada into the middle of the continent and the rivalry between the two great fur trading companies which emerged as the United Hudson Bay Company was tearing the young colony apart. It was no easy task for General Maitland, in his own province of Upper Canada, to keep the balance.

That he was considered a complete failure is the strange conclusion outlined in the Oxford Comparison to Canadian History and Literature, where Norah Story accuses Maitland of a series of "high-handed acts" from the very time he arrived in Canada until the day, ten years later, when "these incidents ... led to his recall." As they read like a catalogue of crimes committed round the parish pump, including "the stopping of halfpay to Major John Matthews who had called for the singing of 'Yankee Doodle' during a convivial benefit for a touring company of American actors who were stranded at York (Toronto)", it seems unlikely, however much a military disciplinarian Maitland was and however parochial was Canadian politics, that this was the reason why General Maitland finished his term as Governor of Upper Canada, he was appointed Lieutenant-Governor of Nova Scotia until retired in 1834, "after being absent on leave since 1832" – this is a parting kick from the Oxford Companion.

In any case, General Maitland's memory has been honoured by both provinces. In Upper Canada, on the St Lawrence River a community in Greenville County, Ontario, has been named after him and Menesatung River, one of the most important waterways flowing into the Lake Huron was renamed Maitland River. In Nova Scotia, the once thriving shipbuilding community in Hants County near the mouth of the Shubenacadie River was called Maitland.

General Maitland was now able to have a well-deserved rest at home but years of idleness did not suit him and when he was offered the first-class post of Commander-in-Chief of the Madras Army, he was happy to accept. But his appointment ended abruptly in December, 1838, after he had held it for only two years. He felt it obligatory upon him to resign over a serious difference of opinion with the East India Company, which was still largely the ruling power of India. The Company ruled British India from 1600 until 1784, when its powers were shared with the Crown. This made life very difficult for the Army.

The company had made an order exempting Christian natives from compulsory attendance at native religious festivals and Maitland took strong exception to its failure to enforce its order. The issue roused public feeling at home, the newspapers ran a campaign and the matter was raised in Parliament. There the Government came down strongly on Maitland's side, approving the stand he had made against the Company. Incidentally, the East India Company's rule was abolished altogether in 1858 and Queen Victoria became Empress of India.

In March, 1844, Maitland was sent to South Africa, this time as both Governor and Commander-in-Chief of the Cape Colony. His first task was to deal with the warlike Kaffirs in the Eastern Province and he devised a treaty to ensure peace and amity between the administration and the tribes.

20. GENERAL SIR PEREGRINE MAITLAND'S FAMILY

Charles Lennox Brownlow Maitland, the eldest son of Sir Peregrine Maitland and Lady Sarah Lennox, was born in 1823. At the age of 18 he became an ensign in the Grenadier Guards and rose to be their Lieutenant-Colonel in 1863. From 1844-7 he was military secretary to the Commander-in-Chief and Governor of Cape Colony and was D.A.A.G. in Crimea, 1854-55. He was Lieutenant-Governor of Chelsea Royal Hospital from 1868 to 1871 and Lieutenant-Governor of the Tower of London from 1876 to 1884. He died in January, 1891, and was buried at Tongham, Surrey.

His Brother, Horatio Arthur Lawrence Lennox Maitland, born in March, 1834, became an Admiral in the Royal Navy. He was severely wounded at the siege of the naval fortress of Sevastopol during the Crimean War and later served in China waters. He died in March, 1904, and was buried at Tongham.

Sarah, the eldest daughter, born in October, 1816, married Colonel T. Bowes Forster, who was ADC to her father when he was Commander-in-Chief of the Madras Army. She died in April, 1900, and was buried in Tongham. Of their family, the eldest son, Bowes Lennox

Forster (1837-1919) became a Lieutenant-general. The eldest daughter, Susan, married the Rev. Charles Garbett, who was a chaplain with the East India Company for 25 years and in 1869 became the first Vicar of Tongham. Their eldest son, Cyril Forster Garbett (1875-1955) was Bishop of Southwark and then of Winchester before becoming the Archbishop of York.

Sarah Forster married Edward Haworth Greenly of Titley Court, Titley, Herefordshire. One son, Walter Howorth Greenly (1875-1955), entered the Army and rose to the rank of major-general. Another, John Henry Maitland Greenly (1885-1950), was a civil engineer, became Lieutenant-Colonel during the First World War and later was chairman of Babcock and Wilcox Ltd. He became a K.C.M.G. in 1941.

Jane Bertie Maitland, the next daughter of Sir Peregrine and Lady Sarah, born in 1825, died unmarried at Tongham and 1885 and was buried there.

Caroline Charlotte Maitland (1817-1897) married John George Turnbull (1790-18772) of the Indian Civil Service. This was another romance which started in Madras, for the young Turnbull was Accountant-General there during Sir Peregrine's term as Commander-in-Chief. The Turnbulls retired from India to live in Tongham. There they retained some of the splendour of colonial life, for Caroline kept a carriage and pair with groom in yellow livery sitting beside the coachman and two Pomeranians running in front. They are buried at Tongham. Their sons carried on the military tradition, as did several of their grandsons, and a number of them are also buried at Tongham.

Emily Sophia Maitland (1827-1891) married Admiral Lord Frederic Herbert Kerr, a son of the sixth Marquess of

Lothian. Their third son, Frederic Walter Kerr, became Colonel of the Gordon Highlanders and their eldest daughter, Emily Georgina, married Francis Edmund Cecil Byng, who became 5th Earl of Stratford.

Eliza Mary Maitland married Major-General John Desborough and their family, too carried on the military tradition by sons and grandsons serving in the Army and daughters marrying officers in the Services.

The youngest daughter of Sir Peregrine and Lady Sarah, Georgine Louisa, married the Rev. Sir Thomas Eardley Wilmot Blomefield. Their eldest son, Thomas Wilmot Peregrine Blomefield (1848-1928), a civil servant, married Lilias, grand-daughter of the 7th Lord Napier. The Napiers, descendants of Sir John Napier of Merchiston, the famous inventor of logarithms, were already allied to the Maitlands, Colonel Charles Maitland of Craigieburn having married Isabella Scott Napier in 1797. Their grandson, Thomas Edward Peregrine Blomefield, became fifth baronet on the death of his grandfather in 1928.

Louisa Charlotte Emily Blomefield married Captain Theodosius Stuart Russell, D.L., Chief Constable of the West Riding of Yorkshire.

Their second son, Charles Lennox Somerville Russell (1872-1960), after a distinguished career in the India Civil Service, was Knighted. Captain Wilmot Peregrine Maitland Russell, M.C., M.A. (Oxon.), was serving in the British Legation in Peking during the siege in 1900 and served with the Gordon Highlanders during the first World War, winning the Military Cross. After the war he went to Helsinki as First Secretary to the Embassy and then as acting Charge-d'Affaires. He wrote many articles on military and foreign affairs. In 1932, he married Miss Amy

Moncrieff Penney, daughter of Scott Moncrieff Penney, Sheriff-Substitute of Argyllshire. Another son, Archibald George Blomefield Russell (1879-1955), entered the Dimplomatic Service and became Lancaster Herald at the College of Arms. He was an authority on William Blake, the poet and engraver, and wrote several books.

During June, 1965, the 150th Anniversary of the Battle of Waterloo was marked by military ceremonies at Brussels, Antwerp and the battlefield. Sir Roderick Barclay, the British Ambassador to Belgium, and Lady Barclay held a ball at the Embassy in Brussels on 15th June, to commemorate the famous Duchess of Richmond's ball on the eve of the battle. Among those present were Lieutenant-Commander David McWilliam, of the Royal Navy, and Mrs Veronica McWilliam, and Mr David S. Milligan, representing the family of Sir Peregrine Maitland.

Lt-Commander McWilliam's great-great-grandmother was the Eliza Mary Maitland who married Major-General John Desborough in 1857. Mr Milligan's great-grandmother was Caroline Charlotte Maitland, who married John George Turnbull. Their grand-daughter, Sylvia Nora Evelyn Turnbull, married Lt-Col Stanley Lyndall Milligan, son of Robert Angus Milligan, a solicitor of Aberdeen.

21. CAPTAIN MAITLAND AND NAPOLEON

Rear-Admiral Sir Fredrick Lewis Maitland K.C.B. was one of those Naval Officers destined by fate to shape the course of history.

He was born at Rankeillour, Fife, on the 7th September 1777 the third son of Captain the Honourable Frederick Lewis Maitland R. N., sixth son of the 6th Earl of Lauderdale and whose Godfather was H.R.H. Frederick Lewis, Prince of Wales.

Raised in the Naval tradition of his father, the bot had no ambition but to go to sea. Accordingly and as soon as he was old enough, arrangements were made for him to join the Royal Navy. It was not long before he made his mark. As midshipman he served on the "Southampton" and took part in the decisive action off Ushant on the Glorious 1st of June 1794, when Lord Howe broke the strength of France's Channel Fleet. On the 3rd April following he was promoted to Lieutenant of the "Andromeda", then transferred to the "Venerable". Flagship of Admiral Lord Duncan, and two years later posted to the Mediterranean under Lord St. Vincent.

But it was in 1801, covering the landing of Sir Ralph Abercrombie's forces in Egypt, under the most hazardous conditions, that he displayed such cool daring and courage that won for him special praise and opened the way to post rank.

In August the same year, he took the "Carrere" a recent prize, to England and was then given the "Loire", a 46-gun frigate with instructions to capture or destroy the privateers and coastal batteries on the west coast of France and Spain. At the beginning of the summer of 1805 he was on a northward course off Muros when news reached him that there was a French privateer of 26-guns in the Bay and making ready for sea. The information excited him for once before he had actually been into Muros and know the harbour. The plan formulated in his mind that this might be a chance to give his crew a stimulating cutting out expedition to relieve the monotony of being the eternal watch-dog. Accordingly he gave orders to make anchor, sent for his officers and got out his charts, giving them detailed and precise orders.

At nine o'clock the next morning having briefed his crew, he stood into Muros, but immediately came under fire from the guns of a small fort at the Point. Three boats were ordered away, manned with as many sailors as could be spared together with a detachment of the Royal Marines, with instructions to land and spike the guns. As they pulled away, Maitland reminded them that the day was the 4th of June the birthday of H.M. King George III, and for his sake, as well as their own, they should make it a memorable day.

As 'La Loire' continued to draw in, Maitland observed a corvette and a large brig, but concluded, as they appeared to be in the process of fitting out, that their guns were not ready for action. A second fort at this moment opened up with an accurate fire. Manoeuvring for an advantageous position Maitland gave the order to engage the enemy.

Meantime the cutting out crews had landed. The sailors and marines tumbled out, scrambled up the slope and fell upon the astonished Spanish gunners. The battery was carried and swiftly silenced. Lieutenant James Yeo in command of the raiding party observed the heavy fire of the second fort and decided something must be done about it. Calling to his men he raced across the intervening ground, reached the outer gate of the fort and stormed into the defences. The fighting was sharp and severe, and the Spaniards finding the pace too hot, broke and surrendered. The British colours were run up to hearty cheers.

Maitland came in closer and sent off boarding parties. The brig was found not to be sea-ready, so he ordered her destruction. The privateer, 'La Confiance' was taken to sea.

'La Loire' had every reason to be satisfied with the day's work. The Spanish fort of twelve, 18-pounders had been put out of action, the smaller fort at the Point destroyed, 'La Confiance' a fast ship of 26-guns taken as prize and 'Le Belier' of 26-guns burnt. In addition 40 barrels of powder, 2 small brass cannon and 50 stand of arms captured. Casualties were slight, two seamen seriously wounded and thirteen others with minor wounds. The enemy suffered twelve killed and thirty wounded.

The following years showed a continuous pattern of naval success, and in 1814 he commanded the "Goliath" on the Halifax and West Indies stations. In the beginning of 1815 he was back in Cork, assembling a fleet of transports and merchant ships, but bad weather prevented sailing.

In the interlude came the dramatic news that Napoleon had escaped from Elba Bay, and had landed in France.

Maitland immediately posted to "Bellerophon" a 74-gun ship with a fighting record and sailed from Cawsand Bay under orders of Rear-Admiral Sir Henry Hotham. He received instructions to station off Rochefort.

On the 28th June he learned of Napoleon's defeat at Waterloo, and that the Emperor might attempt flight to America. His attention was directed to Bordeaux as the likely port of embarkation, but it was Captain Maitland attempted, it would be made from Rochefort. He therefore sent the "Myrmidon" to watch Bordeaux, the "Cephalus" to cruise off Arcasson, while he himself in the "Bellerophon" stood off Rochefort. He therefore sent the "Myrmidon" to watch Bordeaux, the "Cephalus" to cruise off Arcasson, while he himself in the "Bellerophon" stood off Rochefort.

His intuition proved correct. At daylight on the 10th July the Officer of the Watch informed Captain Maitland that a small schooner was standing out from the French squadron towards the "Bellerophon". A flag of truce was observed. By 7a.m. General Savary Dub de Rovigo and Count Las Cases, Chamberlain to the Emperor, were aboard to present a letter to the Admiral commanding the cruisers off Rochefort. The missive stated that the Emperor Napoleon had abdicated, had chosen the United States of America as a retreat, was embarked on board a frigate, and expected a passport from British Government, and whether the Admiral had knowledge of such passport.

Captain Maitland replied that he had no knowledge of his Government's intentions, but as the two countries were in a state of war, it was impossible for him to permit any ship to put to sea from Rochefort. Meantime, all he could do was to forward the dispatch to his Admiral, who was at

Quiberon Bay.

The days went past with tense vigilance. There were further negotiations, the French trying to inveigle him into a compromise, but they met their match in the resolute Captain of the "Bellerophon". He would promise nothing without authority. The port was under blockade and if the Emperor was determined to sail, he would have to fight his way out.

On the 14th July the following letter was received under a flag of truce:

> "Count Las Cases has reported to the Emperor the conversation which he had with you this morning. His Majesty will proceed on board your ship with the ebb-tide to-morrow morning, between four and five o'clock.
>
> If the Admiral, in consequence of the despatch you forwarded to him, should send the passport for the United States therein demanded, His Majesty will be happy to repair to America; but should the passport be withheld, he will willingly proceed to England, there to enjoy the protection of the laws of your country."

But Captain Maitland was not to be caught. "You will recollect," he said briskly to the envoy, "that I am not authorized to stipulate as to the reception of Buonaparte in England, but that he must consider himself entirely at the disposal of His Royal Highness The Prince Regent"

"I am perfectly aware of that," was the reply, "and have already acquainted the Emperor with what you have said on the subject."

Satisfied that the position was clear, Captain Maitland went to his cabin and wrote a despatch to the Admiralty.

The despatch was as follows;

> H.M.S. 'Bellerophon'
> Basque Roads,
> July 14th 1815.

Sir,

For the information of my Lords Commissioners of the Admiralty I have to acquaint you that the Count Las Cases and General Lallemand this day came on board H.M. ship under my command with a proposal from the Count Bertrand for me to receive on board Napoleon Bonaparte, for the purpose of throwing himself on the generosity of H.R.H. the Prince Regent. Conceiving myself authorised by their Lordships' secret order, I have acceded to the proposal and he is to embark on board this ship to-morrow morning. That no misunderstanding might arise I have explicitly and clearly explained to the Count Las Cases that I have no authority whatever for granting terms of any sort, but that all I can do is to convey him and his suite to England to be received in such manner as H.R.H. may deem expedient. At the request of Napoleon Bonaparte, and that their Lordships may be in possession of the transaction at as evenly a period as possible, I despatch the Slaney, with General Gougaud his aide-de-camp, directing her to put into the nearest port and forward this despatch by his First Lieutenant, and shall in compliance with their Lordships' orders proceed to First Lieutenant, and shall in compliance with their Lordships' orders proceed to Torbay, there to await such directions as the Admiralty may think proper to give me.

Enclosed I transmit a copy of the letter with which General Gougaud is charged from Napoleon Bonaparte to H.R.H. the Prince Regent, and request you will acquaint their Lordships that the General informs me he is entrusted with further particulars which he is anxious to communicate to H.R.H. I, am etc.,

F.L. Maitland

The next morning, the 15th July 1815, soon after 6 o'clock, the barge, in charge of the First Lieutenant, returned from the shore bringing Napoleon with him. As the colours had not been hoisted, there was no ceremony. The scene is described in Captain Maitland's Narrative:

"General Bertrand came first up the ship's side, and said to me, 'The Emperor is in the boat'. He then ascended, and, when he came on the quarter-deck pulled on his hat, and addressing me in a firm tone of voice, said 'I am come to throw myself on the protection of your Prince and laws'. When I showed him into the cabin, he looked round and said, 'This is a hand-some cabin.' I answered, 'Such as it is, Sir, it is at your service while you remain on board the ship I command.' He then looked at a portrait that was hanging up, and said, 'Who is that young lady?' 'My wife,' I replied. 'Ah! She is both young and pretty.' He then asked what countrywoman she was, begged to know if I had any children, and put a number of questions respecting my country, and the service I had seen. He next requested I would send for the officers, and introduce them; which was done according to their rank."

Breakfast was served at nine, but it was observed that the Emperor ate little, and on enquiry it was found that it was his custom to have a hot meal. Orders were immediately given to allow his *Maître d'hôtel* to give directions to prepare the dishes which the Emperor was accustomed to have an which would be most agreeable to him. On that day, as usual, the Captain sat at the head of the table, but the following day and thereafter, at his request, he sat at the Emperor's right hand.

> "He conversed a great deal.... Among other things, he asked me where I was born. I told him in Scotland. 'Have you any property there?' he said. 'No, I am a younger brother and they do not bestow much on people of that description in Scotland.' 'Is your elder brother a Lord?' 'No, Lord Lauderdale is the head of our Family.' 'Ah! You are a relation of Lord Lauderdale's. He is an acquaintance of mine, he was sent Ambassador from your King to me, when Mr. Fox was Prime Minister. Had Mr. Fox lived, it never would have come to this, but his death put an end to all hopes of peace. Milford Lauderdale *est un bon garçon.*" Adding, 'I think you resemble him a little, though he is dark and you are fair.'"

On the 16th July orders were received to sail to Torbay and await instructions.

> "During the time we were heaving up the anchor, and setting the sails, Buonaparte remained on the break of the poop; and was very inquisitive about what was going on. He observed, 'Your method of performing this manoeuvre is quite different from

221

the 'French,' and added, 'What I admire most in your ship is the extreme silence and orderly conduct of your men; on board a French ship, everyone calls and gives orders, and they gabble like so many geese.'"

The weather was favourable. The Maitland Narrative continues:

> "Buonaparte amused himself by playing *vingt-un* after breakfast, and he proposed I should play with him and his party. But I told him I had no money, making it a rule to leave it all with my wife before I went to sea; on which he laughed, and good-humouredly offered to lend me some, and trust me until we arrived in England. I, however, declined his offer, having the numerous duties of the ship to attend to."

On July 18, Capt Maitland wrote to Lord Keith:

> M.S.S. Bellerophon, At sea,
> July 18, 1815

My Lord,

Having received directions from Sir Henry Hotham to forward the companying despatch to your Lordship by an officer, I avail myself of the opportunity to explain the circumstances under which I was placed when induced to receive Napoleon Buonaparte into the ship I command.

After the first communication was made to me by Count Bertrand that Buonaparte was at the Isle d'Aix and actually embarked on board the frigates for the purpose of proceeding to the U.S.A., my duty became peculiarly harassing and anxious from the numerous reports that were daily brought from all quarters of his intention to escape on vessels of various descriptions and from different situations on the coast, which the limited means I possessed, together with the length of time requisite to communicate with Sir H. Hotham in Quiberon Bay, rendered the success of at least possible and even probable.

Thus situated, the enemy having two frigates and a brig, while the force under my command consisted of the Bellerophon and Slaney (having detached the Myrmidon to reinforce the Daphne off the Maumusson Passage, where the force was considerably superior to her and whence one of the reports stated Bonaparte meant to sail) another flag of truce was sent out for the ostensible reason of enquiring whether I had an answer to the former, but I soon ascertained the real one to be a proposal from Bonaparte to embark for England in this ship.

Taking into consideration all the circumstances of the probability of the escape being effected if the trial was made either in the frigates of clandestinely in a small vessel, as had this ship been disabled in action there was no other with me that could produce any effect on a frigate, and from the experience I have had in blockading the ports of the bay, knowing the impossibility of preventing small vessels from putting to sea, and looking at it as of the greatest importance to get possession of the person of Bonaparte, I was induced without hesitation to accede to the proposal as far as taking him on board and proceeding with him to England, but at the same time stating in the most clear and positive terms that I had not authority to make any sort of stipulation as to the reception he would meet with. Under all the circumstances I am happy to say the measures I have adopted have met with the approbation of Sir Henry Hotham, and will I trust and hope meet with that of your Lordship, as well as of H.M. Government. I have etc.,

F. L. Maitland.

On the 20th the "Bellerophon" met and spoke to the "Swiftsure" on her way to reinforce the "Bellerophon" in the blockade at Rochefort. Her Commander, Captain Webley, was rowed across.

"Well, I've got him," was Captain Maitland's greeting.

"Got him? Got Whom?"

"Why, Bonaparte; the man that has been keeping all Europe in a ferment these last twenty years!"

"Is it possible?" said the startled Webley. "Well, you are a lucky fellow!"

Lieutenant John Bowerbank of the "Bellerophon", in his "Extracts from a Journal", gives some interesting sidelights on Napoleon aboard his ship.

On Sunday the 23rd July the 'Bellerophon' passed Ushant and on Monday the 24th was close into land.

"Buonaparte appeared delighted with the prospect, and his approach to England. Looking through his glass, he frequently exclaimed in French 'What a

> beautiful country'.... At 8a.m. we anchored and were immediately surrounded with boats. He seemed struck with the beauty of the women, repeatedly crying out 'What charming girls! What beautiful women!' and bowing to them."

> Tuesday the 25th "How very curious these English are."

At daybreak on the 24th July, the Bellerophon dropped anchor in Torbay, where she lay under a tight security ring, until the 26th, when she proceeded to Plymouth Sound.
During this period the Government were deliberating what action to take. Their decision eventually was that Napoleon should be transferred at sea to the "Northumberland" and should be taken to and held prisoner on the island of St Helena. On receiving this news, the Emperor was furiously angry. He protested that he had been tricked.

Lieutenant John Bowerbank diary reveals his response:

> Friday 28th July, About eleven a.m. Lord Keith came on board. He was introduced to Napoleon. Buonaparte was, I understand, very pressing in his enquiries relative to his own probable fate, and avowed his determination of never being conveyed to St Helena."

> Sunday 30th July. It had been said that he read English with ease, though he could not speak it. I suspect, however, that his knowledge of it is very imperfect, because pointing to some of the most common words in the newspapers, he frequently inquired of Captain Maitland their meaning.... For the first time since he has been on board he was not shaved. This surprised us, as we had been

accustomed to remark his great and peculiar personal neatness. During the night he sent out to request that no noise might be made over his head. We were told he had taken ill.

Monday 31st July. He looked extremely ill and dejected. I should scarcely have imagined that so great a change could have taken place in so short a period. He was still unshaven, and his countenance naturally sallow, had now assumed a death-like paleness.

Wednesday 2nd August. We were all now in full expectation of some tragical event. The general conjecture was that he would end himself, by poison. It was believed that he had his possession a large quantity of laudanum. Madame Bertrand hinted that ere morning we should find him a corpse. Whilst at supper Bertrand waited on Captain Maitland with a request of Buonaparte that the sentinels should be forgiven to call out every half hour, as it prevented his rest.

Thursday 3rd August. As we are now in hourly expectation of the arrival of the 'Northumberland' he had, I understand, been frequently requested to name those officers of his suite whom he might wish to accompany him. He obstinately refused to do so, protesting his determination never to quit this ship."

Saturday 5th August. "Napoleon still remained shut up within his cabin. Madame Bertrand said to me 'I promise you, you will never get the Emperor to St. Helena; he is a man, and what he says he will perform.'

Sunday 6th August. At breakfast the information was communicated viz that he had at length consented to name his companions, and intended quietly to leave the ship. This indeed is not the finale we expected. For although I am not prepared to say that he ever personally declared his intention of destroying himself, yet it had been an intention which his adherents have taken such pains to insinuate, that the persuasion of his doing so, in preference to be forced from the "Bellerophon", had taken full possession of our imaginations.

In a later interview with Lord Keith, Napoleon and Las Cases protested that they were not prisoners but merely passengers on the "Bellerophon" and that Captain Maitland had tricked them. But this argument fell on stony ground for Lord Keith told them that "nothing like a promise was made by Maitland on his part, but on the contrary a simple offer of good treatment and being carried to England."

Napoleon had the grace to say to Captain Maitland, before leaving the "Bellerophon":

> "Certainly I made no conditions; how could an individual enter into terms with a nation? As for you, Captaine, I have no cause for complaint; your conduct towards me has never been that of a man of honour."

The "Bellerophon" set sail for the rendezvous with the "Northumberland" off Berryhead and soon after breakfast the Emperor sent for Captain Maitland.

> "I have requested to see you, Captaine," he said, "to return you my thanks for your kindness and attention while I have been on board the 'Bellerophon', and

likewise to beg you will convey them to the officers and ship's company you command."

About noon, arrangements having been made, Napoleon walked out of the cabin with a steady, firm step, again thanked Captain Maitland for his conduct towards him, and went forward to the gangway. Here he turned and bowed to the ship's company before going down to the waiting barge. When the boat pulled clear, he stood up, pulled off his hat and once again bowed, to the Captain and Officers, and then towards the men. A few minutes later he was aboard the "Northumberland".

So ended the surrender of Napoleon to the Britain. To clear up the many misunderstandings which arose, most of them circulated by the jaundice of jealously, Captain Maitland published in 1826, "A Narrative of the Surrender of Buonaparte, with a detail of the Principal Events between 4th May and the 8th August, 1815." Sit Walter Scot's called this book "as fine, manly and explicit account as ever was given of so interesting a transaction."

The next few years saw Captain Maitland in South American waters. Then he was called back to the Mediterranean with orders to sail to Naples and embark the King of the Two Sicilies and take him to Leghorn. It was a rough passage of seven days but so pleased was the King that before going ashore he invested Captain Maitland with the insignia of a Knight Commander of St Ferdinand and presented him with his portrait set in diamonds in a gold box. Continuous service eventually brought Maitland his Rear-Admiral's flag in 1830.

He then became Admiral Superintendent of the Dockyard at Portsmouth, before going into retirement.

Meantime, the "Bellerophon" had reached an unhappy end. Five weeks after she parted company with the "Northumberland" off Berryhead, her serving life came to an end. Captain Maitland wrote the last words in his ship's log on the 13th September, 1815:

> "At 11 came on board the Pay Captain and Clerk and paid the Ship's Company. Sunset – hauled down the Pendant."

Soon afterwards the gallant old "Bellerophon" was handed over by the Admiralty to the Transport Board for use as a convict hulk. Under the name of "Captivity" she served this dismal use until 1836, when she was sold for £4,030 to be broken up.

It was fortunate that her Old Captain, now Sir Frederick Maitland, was superintendent of the Portsmouth Dockyard at that time and he was able to save one or two relics of the old "Bellerophon." The figurehead and stern ornaments are now to be seen in the Victory Museum at Portsmouth.

In July 1837, Sir Frederick was recalled from retirement and appointed Commander-in-Chief, East Indies and China, and hoisted his flag on the "Wellesley."

During the First Afghan War, early in 1839, he covered the landing of troops and in assisting the Army's advance from Bombay into Afghanistan, he reduced the town of Kurrachee by naval action.

But his long and devoted service to his country came to end during this campaign. He died on board the "Wellesley" and was buried in St Thomas's Cathedral, Bombay. A monument to his memory is inscribed.

"This monument is erected by the Officers of the Indian Navy as a token of their respect and esteem for the memory of this distinguished Officer and particularly to mark their sense of the kind and considerate conduct uniformly shown to their corps during his command and service with them 1839-39."

Captain Maitland of the "Bellerophon" showed, by his respect for his officers and men as well as for Kings and Emperors, that he belonged to the type of men who are the strength and pride of Scotland. The secret of his life was the simplicity and sincerity of his character, his calm indifference to either gain or fame and his self-forgetting patriotism.

22. THE SEVENTH EARL

James, the seventh Earl of Lauderdale, succeeded his father in 1744. Born in 1718, he joined the Army and served for 25 years, eventually being appointed Lieutenant-Colonel of the 16th Foot (Bedfordshire) Regiment, but he abruptly ended his military career by resigning his commission when a junior officer was promoted over him. In those days a successful military career depended not so much on ability as on knowing the right people at Court, whose influence was the deciding factor in the advancement of officers to the higher commands. James Maitland had either plenty of the old Maitland forthrightness and made enemies or his marriage to the daughter of a wealthy London citizen was displeasing – whatever the reason, his military career was not a successful one, unlike those of other members of the family.

Probably the Earl was more interested in commercial affairs, to which he had been introduced by his father-in-law, Sir Thomas Lombe, an alderman of the City of London, whose only daughter, Mary, inherited his substantial fortune. He was one of the founders of the British Linen Bank, which is now merged with the Bank of Scotland. The preliminary organisation for the company was carried out during the 1745 Rebellion, under a Government plan to develop Scottish industries, and was designed to encourage the growth of flax and handle the sale of linen.

A charter was obtained by the Duke of Argyll and Andrew Fletcher of Milton, dated 5th July 1746:

> "whereby James, Earl of Lauderdale, William, Earl of Panmure, and others were constituted a Body Politic and Corporal by Name, Style and Title of The British Linen Company."

The authorised capital of the company was £100,000, but only half of this was offered for subscription by the Court of Directors, who were also authorised to borrow money on bills and bonds. The company's first warehouse was in Halkerston's Wynd, in the High Street of Edinburgh, but it was cleared away in 1898 upon the construction of the North Bridge.

In the warehouse there were to be "a book-keeper and an accountant, two staplers to give out the yarn and a porter." But the linen business was swiftly overshadowed by the banking side. In 1750, the company began to issue its own bank notes and by 1763 and mercantile operations were brought to a close.

It would seem that Lady Mary Maitland was addicted to the fashionable novels of the day, for her first son was named Valdare Charles Lauder Maitland. Unfortunately, he died when two years of age. The next son, James, succeeded. Then there was Thomas, who won renown in the public service overseas and whose life is described in another chapter. And William Mordaunt, who became an enthusiastic soldier. He started his career as a cornet in the 10th Dragoons. During the war of 1781-92 against Tippoo Sahib, the Sultan of Mysore, he transferred to the Seaforth Highlanders, in which his brother, Thomas, was a captain. He also commanded a company and at the assault of

Seringapatam, Tippoo's capital, Captain Maitland was wounded in the arm. While Thomas left the Army, Mordaunt continued in the service and died in 1841 a Lieutenant-Colonel. By his first wife, Mary Orpen, daughter of the Rev. Richard Orpen, Killowen, and widow of John Travers, Fir Grove, County Cork, he had one son, Thomas, who in 1863 succeeded to the Earldom.

23. "CITIZEN" MAITLAND

James, the eighth Earl of Lauderdale, is described somewhat drily in William Anderson's "The Scottish Nation," as "a distinguished public character." He was a good deal more than that. He was one of the founding fathers of English Liberalism and one of the earliest writers on economics when that field was dominated by Adam Smith.

Born at Hatton House on 26th January, 1759, he studied at both Edinburgh and Glasgow Universities. He was a student at a wonderful time. The Scottish Universities were then at their most formative and most earnest work and, helped by the rivalry between the colleges of Edinburgh and Glasgow, they produced a generation of brilliant professors in every field.

Adam Smith, who had been Professor of Moral Philosophy (an old Presbyterian title which to-day would be Professor of Social Science), published his "Wealth of Nations" in 1776. At Edinburgh, Dr William Robertson, the historian; Dr Thomas Reid, the philosopher of common-sense; Dr Matthew Stewart, the mathematician, and his all-round son, Dugald Stewart, headed a cohort of the talents. James Maitland attended the lectures of Dugald Stewart, who remained his friend. Stewart was one of those who accompanied the young Viscount on his grand tour.

At Glasgow University, Maitland listened to John Millar, whose "History of English Government" and Origin of the Distinction of Ranks" were in those days as important in the field of politics as Adam Smith's book on economics. As with Dugald Stewart, Maitland remained a life-long friend of John Millar. Perhaps it was to Millar, with his Scottish shrewdness and candour, that Maitland looked for that intellectual sustenance and refreshment which men of talent require, for when in Scotland, Maitland went often to visit his old professor. Then there must have been a sharpening of acute minds!

Another teacher had a strong influence on Maitland. When he went to Paris, he was accompanied by Andrew Dalzel as tutor. Dalzel the son of a Kirkliston Wright, who became Professor of Greek at Edinburgh University, university librarian and the first layman to be Principal Clerk to the General Assembly of the Church of Scotland, was a brilliant example of the Scottish "lad o' pairts" who made his way in the world by his native abilities. In his youth Glasgow University was pre-eminent for its Greek: he made Edinburgh even more famous as a centre of Greek Studies.

In those days, all gentleman spoke French as a matter of course and all students learned the language with their Latin and Greek, for France was the land of Voltaire, Rousseau, the Encyclopedists, and all up-to-date and advanced thinkers looked to France.

No wonder the young Viscount Maitland became an ardent Whig in his teens. All the more so because the world in which he was voracious and intelligent pupil was one of intense change. Britain, France and Spain were struggling to seize colonies from each other and to occupy new colonies and their struggles were taking their armies and navies and settlers to the far corners of the world. The settled colonies in North America were at war with the British Government, demanding their independence, which they had declared to the world in revolutionary terms in the famous Declaration of Independence, of July 4, 1776.

While other men in his family were serving in the Army and Navy, James must have felt it right that he, as head of the family, should be struggling to gain an understanding of the central power which dominated and controlled all those military efforts, now taking place on a scale and to an extent never known in history. It was the most natural thing for him to become a man of politics.

At the age of 21 he entered Parliament as member Newport, Cornwall, a seat in the patronage of the Duke of Northumberland. It is to be remembered that 1780 was before the days of universal franchise or of any franchise worth speaking about it all. Seats were sold and bought and votes were sold and bought as a matter of course. This was not so terrible as it sounds to our democratic ears, for the only people who could possibly be represented in Parliament were the wealthy and if the elections were expensive, rowdy, violent and bitterly contested, all this went on at the expense of members of the aristocracy battling for their personal ambitions.

So there was nothing untoward in the Earl of Lauderdale buying his son a seat nor anything strange in Maitland becoming Member of Parliament at the ripe old age of 21.

Pitt became a member of the House of Commons at the same age and Charles James Fox, reckoned to be the founder of British Liberalism, entered the House at the age of 19. Of course it was in many ways the age for aristocratic youth, for a man could become a Captain in the army or navy before his majority.

In the Commons, Maitland became a staunch supporter of Fox and helped in the political aims of the Whigs – peace with the Americans and the French and more power to Parliament. He supported Fox's India Bill, designed to replace the rapacious rule of the East India Company with a commission appointed by Parliament and then the Crown, but this Bill was thrown out by the Lords and led to the defeat of the coalition Government in which Fox was Foreign Secretary. William Pitt then became Prime Minister.

Maitland was to be a thorn in Pitt's flash during the whole of his career, especially over the questions of financing the wars against Napoleon Bonaparte.

In 1790, the seventh Earl of Lauderdale died and James succeeded to the Earldom. In the same year he was elected a representative peer for Scotland and went from the Commons into the House of Lords, where for the next six years he was one of the Whig peers.

Meantime, the political storm in France was slowly brewing. Lauderdale went to Paris in August, 1792, in expectation of action by the political clubs and he was not disappointed. Three days after his arrival in the French capital, the Parisian mob invaded the Tuilleries and the revolutionary government imprisoned Louis XVI and his family. Throughout the rest of August, Lauderdale remained to witness events, to absorb the revolutionary drama, to keep in some contact with his friends and to help where he could. For the aristocrats were now fleeing for safety and those who remained had to face the possibility of death. It was not long in coming. After the September 2 massacre, Lauderdale left Paris, but he only went so far as Calais, where he stayed for several weeks. There is no doubt that he acted the Pimpernel for his friends and when the uproar in Paris seemed to have subsided, following General Dumouriez' success at Valmy over the Austrians and Prussians and the establishment of the Republic and of the National Convention, he returned to Paris. He was there when the Convention offered their assistance to all peoples who wished to overthrow their monarchist governments. On December 5, he left Paris for London. Louis XVI was now under trial for his life by the Girondists, the moderate revolutionaries, the Whigs of France, if you like.

Lauderdale came back from revolutionary Paris a more ardent Whig than ever and a friend of the Convention government.

To understand the general position of Lauderdale and the Whigs, we have to appreciate the historical background to events. As we have already seen, from the time of Secretary Maitland of Letherington onwards, the struggle between King and Kirk, between King and commons, between bishops and ministers between nobles and commoners, St Stephen's and the City, had continued. The republic of the Commonwealth in Britain in the middle of the 17th century had failed to establish a permanent bourgeois republic. It was too early, for the British merchant and yeoman classes were not sufficiently powerful and distinct from the landowners. The Commonwealth, it could be said was a bourgeois republic without a bourgeoisie. The Restoration was followed by the Glorious Revolution (so-called) of 1688, a compromise which enabled the aristocracy of wealth to mingle with the aristocracy of birth.

The true development of Britain in the 18th century was

the spread of its empire, principally in India, which was a storehouse of wealth to be raided, and in America, which was the natural market for British trade. But while the triumphs of Clive and Hastings produced only a colonial India, George Washington and Benjamin Franklin were the representatives of a true republic – the United States of America.

The peace between Britain and the United States was signed in Paris in 1783. Six years later, the Constituent Assembly in Paris debated the preliminaries to the French Revolution. Although Baroness Orczy, Hollywood and Elstree have always presented the French Revolution to us as merely an uprising of a hungry mob, intent only on plunder and murder, the French Revolution was essentially concerned with destroying the power of a complete monarchy and its aristocratic shell and replacing them with a republic – a commonwealth, a nation – in which the wealth gained by commercial and industrial enterprise would have full play. It was 1560 in Scotland and 1640 in England writ large in French.

In this political sense. The French revolution had its counterpart in Britain, where the Whigs represented the republican and moneyed forces, while the Tories represented the monarchy and aristocracy. The fact that the Whigs were themselves mostly aristocrats reproduced the extent to which money had bought its way into the aristocratic developing the British aristocracy on the continent, a class gradually enriching and renewing itself by marrying commercial wealth and by ability recruited by royal patronage.

The reflection of the French Revolution in Britain, therefore, was a mild one. It was openly expressed by the organising of a club, called the Friends of the People, by the

Earl of Lauderdale, his brother Thomas, Charles Grey, Samuel Whitbread, Richard Brinsley Sheridan, Lord Kinnaird and Lord Buchan. The subscription was a guinea and a half and their principal aim was a reformed House of Commons.

In the political maelstrom of that day, when every kind of gossip, accusation and slander was permissible, when insults in the clubs and duels in the parks ere frequent, no one played politics in a low ley. The Friends of the People were roundly attacked. Fox, the great individualist and verbose opportunist, did not join, of course. It was left to Whitbread to do donkey work in the Commons, while Lauderdale managed the Lords.

Lauderdale's speeches in the Lords on the war with France, his talks in the clubs, his Whig friends in the City, brought him notoriety. And when he appeared in the House in the plain dress of a citizen, he was swiftly nicknamed "Citizen Maitland" – a nickname he enjoyed. The newspapers, as outspoken as a Wilkes and a Fox, accused him of investing his fortune in French assignats! It was even gossiped around St James's that he intended to renounce his title.

But for Lauderdale, being a Whig was not a political adventure. In August, 1782, he had married Eleanor Todd, only daughter and heiress of Anthony Todd, secretary to the General Post Office.

But in revolutionary times, events happen swiftly and changes which lagged for a century take place in a month. In France, a new constitution and its new Directory called in the "little Corsican" to defend it from the Paris mob and the first snots of the Napoleonic era were fired. On both sides of the Channel, the war was settling into a more serious struggle. In the General Election of 1796, the Tories, as the war party, won an immense victory over the peace with France Whigs. Lauderdale lost his seat in the House of Lords.

He then became pamphleteer for the Whigs on financial questions and produced a series of sharp criticism of Pitts financial Acts. To further understand the economic essays of Lauderdale, we must appreciate that they were as much political as economic. They were essays to argue the case of the moment and not attempts to set out general laws of the behaviour of money, commodities, interest and credit. They emphasised one argument at the expense of the others. Hence those inconsistencies which economic students if to-day may discover.

The reason for those inconsistencies is not any inconsistency in the character of Lauderdale but the natural changes brought about by his personal reaction to changing historical conditions. While a Price, a Millar, an Adam Smith, in their academic solitude, could write economics in general terms, as more or less objective observers, Lauderdale was hardly in a position to do so. Not only was he a landholder and stockbroker, he was also a party leader, an important member of the ruling class. While Adam Smith could look upon the public wealth and private riches as things outside his study to be didacted upon, Lauderdale was arguing about his own riches, his own position in society and the effect of public events – war, taxation, mercantile policy, the rate of interest, the public debt – upon his own fortunes and those of others, like himself and Lord Kinnaird, who were peers and landowners and also closely connected with the City of London.

In 1796, there was no state machinery in Britain, no Civil Service, as we know it to-day. Government proceeds in the modern world by means of official surveys, expert inquiries and parliamentary commissions. In 1796, there were the pamphlets of a Wilkes, a Burke, a Lauderdale. It was perfectly natural that Lauderdale, a Whig leader, and a rival and enemy of Pitt, the wartime Prime Minister, and of Dundas, his Home Secretary, who had the task of suppressing the excesses of Whiggism and Jacobinism, should tackle economics from the standpoint of his own position rather than from the basis of the laws of economics.

After all, when Pitt imposed an income tax or a forced loan, it was not the mass of people who was paying: those moneys came directly from the coffers of Lauderdale and his fellow politicians of immense wealth, like the Dukes of Bedford, Devonshire and Portland. In Lauderdale's day there were no huge joint stock companies, insurance companies, great banks, no universal taxation system and civil service (except for excise officers, who formed a large body for that time of some 12,000). We who are accustomed to budgets of thousands of millions of pounds and huge investments in industrial developments, must think back to the time when all industrial enterprise was the work of individuals and of small groups of individuals risking their own private capitals. Social thought had already grasped the power of capital amassed by the individual landowner, merchant, banker and millowner. But only a Hume and a Lauderdale were alive to the enormous power of social capital, which is a commonplace of to-day.

The essence of Lauderdale as an economic writer can be summed up in his own words:

> "... if to him (David Hume) the power enjoyed by a man of one hundred thousand a year, seemed to exceed so wonderfully the proportion of power

enjoyed by a hundred men of one thousand a year ...
Can any man believe that he would have differed
from me in pronouncing, that it must be attended
with despotic authority? ... Those who conduct the
Government are at present in possession of more
power than would attend a property of Twenty-five
millions a year."

For Lauderdale, to tax the landowners, merchants and
bankers in order to place the enormous power of the State
revenue into the hands of his political rivals was something
to be attacked. For him, that was a tyrannical power. He
well knew the power of wealth. His family fortune and that
of his wife meant power. He had for friends some of the
richest men in England, like Francis Russell, the Duke of
Bedford, and Thomas Coke, Earl of Leicester. But even
they could not lay their hands on more than some £75,000
in cash in a year, whatever their credit. Pitt was going to
have £25 millions! If a couple of thousand pounds could
buy a seat in the House of Commons, a commission in the
Army or Navy, the City of London – everything would be
at his beck and call. This was no financial theory. This was
real. And Lauderdale saw it clearly.

By reacting against this kind of governmental power,
Lauderdale was true to his Whig principles. Gradually he
reacted, too, to the growth of Bonapartism in France,
leaving his political Jacobinism to concentrate on the
economic education of the Whigs. A great difficulty was the
fact that Fox, the flamboyant, under-rated Lauderdale, while
making use of his talents as an organiser and economist. On
one occasion, a contemporary relates, when Lauderdale
proposed to draft a document, Fox wrote to Lord Holland,
his nephew: "If he does it, it should be done in time for you
or somebody else to put it into English." This was the pot
calling the kettle black with a vengeance, for Fox's famous

speeches were unprintable without being rewritten.

Napoleon's defeat of the combined Austrian and Russian armies at Austerlitz was followed by the death of William Pitt on January 23rd. Lord Grenville formed his coalition Government for All the Talents, which included leading Whigs – Fox, Gray, Erskine, with the Earl of Lauderdale as Secretary for Scotland. Napoleon's successes in Austria had been accompanied by the defeat of his sea power at Trafalgar. There was now stalemate. Napoleon was confirmed to Europe: the rest of the world belonged to Britain. The Grenville Government opened negotiations for peace.

Was it again a slighting of Lauderdale that made Fox, the Foreign Secretary, choose Lord Yarmouth to undertake the negotiations with the French? In any case, Yarmouth proved to be unequal to the task and Lauderdale was sent to Paris in August 1806, with full powers to conclude a peace. But peace was far from Napoleon's plans. He was still striding the path of the conquest of Europe and the peace negotiations were only further diplomatic manoeuvres between campaigns. The negotiations were still continuing with Talleyrand when Prussia declared war again upon France. Napoleon at once departed for the front. Lauderdale left Paris on October 9. On the 14th, Napoleon completely routed the Germans at the twin battles of Jena and Auerstadt. From Berlin in November, he proclaimed the blockade of Great Britain and the ban of British imports in Europe. Britain's retaliatory measures were instrumental in bringing the United States into a new war against the British, which was motivated also by the Yankee hope of capturing Canada.

While Fox wished to replace Lauderdale in the Paris negotiations with his nephew, Lord Holland, it seems that

Napoleon thought more highly of Lauderdale. It could be, of course, that Napoleon's good opinion was not brought about by Lauderdale's high quality as a negotiator; on the contrary, like all dictators, Napoleon was inclined to like those whom he could either bully or outwit. Perhaps Fox distrusted those economic theories? To reach a true appreciation of those negotiations would require such a knowledge of the characters and motivations of those concerned, over and above the actual events and their results, that it is doubtful if it ever could be attained at this time of day.

But it seems certain that the Whigs were correct in believing that that was the most favourable time for a general peace. In continuing the war, Napoleon was compelled to over-reach himself. Yet, as we have said, Napoleon was then imbued with his imperial destiny and peace was not possible.

In September, 1806, Fox died and in the following March the Ministry of All the Talents resigned on the question of Catholic rights. By this time, the imperial struggle between the English and French was more than plain and the old Jacobin ideas had been lost sight of in the growing industrialisation of Britain.

It has been often said that Lauderdale went from the Left of Whigs to end up as a Tory. This is not really true. In the Government of All the Talents, he remained a Whig.

Afterwards, he was never again in office. Not only had the character of the war changed, but the Whigs had supported the Prince of Wales against George III and when the King became insane and the Prince was appointed Regent and later, when he became George IV, Lauderdale continued to support him. But Lauderdale gradually began to retire from active work in the House of Lords. In 1814, he published a pamphlet on the corn laws and again in 1829, he published "Three Letters to the Duke of Wellington" on government income and expenditure.

Lauderdale lived to see the passing of the first Reform Act of 1832, when his former colleague on the Government of all the Talents, Charles Grey, the Earl of Howick, was Prime Minister. But Lauderdale played no part in the political campaign which preceded it. He had retired to Thirlestane Castle, where he died on 13th September, 1839, at the age of eighty, having lived to see the beginning of the reign of Queen Victoria.

24. "KING TOM"

We have just mentioned that the younger brother of the eighth Earl was Thomas Maitland. Thomas was one of those who formed with him the Society of the Friends of the People. Born at Hatton House barely a year after his brother, James, the two boys were brought up together and were close to each other. It was natural that when Thomas sought a Parliamentary career, he should join with his brother in the Whig Party.

The two Maitlands made a brilliant and vociferous left wing in the House of Commons all by themselves! Yet the young fire-eater was to become Lieutenant-General Sir Thomas Maitland, G.C.B., G.C.M.G., G.C.H., P.C., one of the greatest of colonial administrators in the early days of the British Empire. His life proved to be even more spectacular than that of his brother.

Tom Maitland was in every way a "character". His nickname throughout his career in the colonial service was "King Tom", "a title which he earned by his arbitrary decisions, especially on the interpretation of orders, about which he was a law unto himself. On the other hand, he was known to his staff and colleagues as "Honest Tom", another nickname which he deservedly earned as a colonial governor who proved himself to be a man of vision and a nation-builder in the truest sense.

At first Thomas Maitland wished to follow in the footsteps of many of his forebears and adopt the law as his profession.

In 1774, he entered Lincoln's Inn but the atmosphere of the Law Courts had no appeal to the young Thomas – he was only fifteen when he commenced lawyer – and when in 1778 the Earl of Seaforth raised the Seaforth Highlanders (the 72nd Regiment), he obtained a commission. After three pleasant years in the Channel Islands, the regiment was sent to Madras to take part in the war against Tippoo Sahib.

In this campaign, Captain Thomas Maitland began to show his mettle. The army having laid siege to the fort of Palghatcherri, Maitland took advantage of rain to force entry into the first gateway and compelled the garrison to surrender. Those were stirring days in India, with much active service, and an officer like Maitland, with a flair for getting on with the job, soon distinguished himself. He was posted by Lord Cornwallis, the commander-in-chief, as brigade major of Madras before the Seaforth Highlanders marched into the Garden of Pearls at Seringapatam and induced Tippoo to surrender. When the Seaforths retired to Wallahabad, Major Maitland returned home.

He now joined his brother in politics. Returned to the House of Commons as Member for the Haddington Burghs, he made his maiden speech in February, 1791. It was a virulent attack on the management of India and the war against Tippoo Sahib, the commencement of a political career noted for its virulence. This, of course, was not simply due to the irascibility of Maitland. It was the age of immoderate oratory. Every speaker used the wildest exaggerations, ignored the facts, starred his speeches with unanswerable questions meant to suggest the very best or the very worst, made personal attacks so slanderous a character that it is difficult to see how any speech could have been listened to without disorder. In this sort of free-for-all assembly, Tom Maitland was a hard-hitting speaker.

But with the National Convention in France, the execution of Louis XVI and Marie Antoinette and the declaration of war against Great Britain, the attitude of Maitland changed. It changed much more quickly than that of his brother, in keeping with Thomas's more forthright and vigorous character. By 1797, he was past the slanging matches of politics and eager to do some practical work in a world where real things were happening. In that year, he was selected by the Pitt Government to go to San Domingo (now the island of Haiti), which was in the throes of civil war, with Toussaint L'Ouverture, the Black Napoleon, facing the French settlers, the mulatto mutineers and the British army of occupation. His task was to evacuate the British as cheaply and as safely as possible.

This Maitland did by sending an officer direct to Toussaint L'Ouverture, offering to leave the forts and the private property of resident undestroyed, if he would permit a peaceful evacuation and promise security for property. Thus at one stroke Maitland achieved his objective. But he returned home a sick man. He was no sooner home than he was sent to Philadelphia, to negotiate the acceptance by the United States of the commercial agreement he had with Toussaint L'Ouverture. In this he failed, for the United States has no intention of making any agreement.

Returning from this task, Maitland was next entrusted with the expedition to Bellisle, the island lying off the southern coast of Brittany, an expedition presumably based on the theory of attacking the "soft underbelly" of France. It was an enormous disaster, mismanaged from the first, in spite of Maitland's struggle to hold the thing together.

There followed a little over six months on the Board of Control of the East India Company and then, at the age of 46, he was appointed Governor of Ceylon. This was the real beginning of "King Tom's" career.

He was the second Governor of the Island, the huge interior in which was still under the control of the King of Kandy.

The previous Governor, Frederick North, had been defeated by the army of the King. He himself had disrupted the economy based on the village communities, by seizing and trying to rent communal lands which were held by village functionaries as service holdings.

Maitland immediately reversed this attempt to compel the Cingalese to work and pay rents. In his report to the Secretary of State, he showed that he had as good a grasp of economic and historical realities as his brother.

He wrote:

> "I think your Lordship will agree with me upon reflection that it would have been a most strange and unaccountable measure, supposing it possible when we were in this state of society, if one of the ancient barons had pulled out of his pocket Adam Smith, and said, I will apply to you vassals principles that you do not understand and that will not properly apply to your circumstances for another five hundred years."

In his forthright way, Maitland dealt with another problem.

There were still Dutch prisoners of war on the island,

adding to government costs. He sent to Batavia and asked if they could be taken away, and so got rid of a potential danger at no cost whatever. He dealt with other problems in the same common-sense way. Though his rough "Whig" ways sometimes caused offence. His ignoring of the English missionary enthusiasm brought complaints and the interference at home of William Wilberforce. His critics called him a pagan. Maitland retorted:

> "If showing proper respect for their feelings when I visit their temples is to be a pagan, I am one".

To-day that would be regarded as plain common sense and good governmental practice: in those days it was rank Jacobinism.

When measures of economy by the Governor of Madras brought about a mutiny of the English officers at Seringapatam, Maitland sent troops across the straits from Ceylon to help to quell it, but his comment to the Secretary of State was characteristic. Speaking of the Madras Governor, he wrote:

> "Barlow shows great personal courage, but he looks at nothing but measures, and never considers men."

Maitland himself never made that mistake and that was what made him a great and popular colonial administrator.

He brought about changes everywhere. The figures of smallpox in the island were brought to him and after one glance at them, he issued proclamation to persuade the population to be vaccinated and to provide facilities for this to be carried out. He was criticised for being too autocratic, to which he replied that the welfare of the people was his concern, their health his primary duty. As a result of his forceful methods the dreaded disease was extinguished in all British areas.

The soldier in Maitland demanded discipline, which he insisted on getting. His caustic tongue lashed the administrative departments on needless expenditure (for economy was the prime consideration at home) and if officialdom could not justify an expense, then it was ruthlessly cut. He has an orderly mind, the ability to assess a situation and the will to deal with it immediately and effectively.

He soon stamped his own efficiency on government servants. Before he left Ceylon, his typhoon policy showed good results: new roads were built, trade started to prosper, imports increased, with a corresponding lift in the general standard of living.

In 1810, he was seriously ill and was advised that he must not continue to work in hot climate. He asked to be relieved of the governorship at the end of his term and he returned home in the following year. As a reward, he was promoted Major-General.

He left Ceylon with a capable administration, a balanced budget and fast increasing in prosperity and independence. Unorthodox as always, he brought home with him the two sons of Mudilayar de Saram. Their destination was Trinity Hall, Cambridge. In this "King Tom" was certainly a man of vision. For these pioneer students, though at first their influence was negligible, were the first of a flow of British-trained students who were among the strongest agents in the social and political life of Ceylon, helping to mould the island's future.

The retired governor did not have a long respite, for in

1815, he was appointed Governor of Malta. The islands had been a British possession since 1800, one of many positions which Britain has established in the Mediterranean during the Napoleonic Wars in order to wrest control of the sea from the French. In the year 1813, Wellington was completing his victorious war in Spain and in the middle of October, Napoleon's army was defeated at Leipzig. Amid these tremendous events, Governor Maitland had landed at Valetta on October 3 to find that the plague was raging in Malta. For a whole year he was closely occupied in combatting the menace, for the system adopted by the doctors of having pest-houses here and there only succeeded in spreading the plague. Maitland flung himself into a crash programme to stamp it out, his main means being the establishment of quarantine islands to stop the spread of infection. When Napoleon abdicated on April 6, 1814, Maitland was able to say that the plague had been conquered.

Napoleon has seized long ago the Ionian Islands and the British Navy has taken them. Now, after Waterloo, in December, 1815, Maitland was made Lord High Commissioner of the Ionian Islands and Commander-In-Chief in the Mediterranean. Here were new islands to plough.

Sir Thomas now had two main problems on his hands.

The Corfiotes were enthusiastic and unscrupulous politicians: the Barbary Coast was still the home of venturesome pirates. To the Ionians he gave a constitution and made an agreement with the Bey of Algiers. He also persuaded the home Government to institute the Order of St Michael and St George, to be awarded to Maltese, Ionians and Corfiotes who gave loyal service to the British administration.

He pursued his policy of meeting every situation as he found it in his own free and easy way, oblivious to protocol. Despite his ability as an administrator and the success he obtained, his stormy tactics made him enemies. In the secluded corridors of power at Westminster umbrage was taken. Members opposed to Sir Thomas launched an attack upon him in Parliament. And the youthful critic of Warren Hastings and Pitt and Dundas now found himself the subject of heated recriminations. Critic after critic jumped to his feet to make accusations of his intolerable interference with the natural rights of abuse hurled at him over the benches, though this was a charge that could not be proved, for self-interest was certainly not one of Sir Thomas's faults.

After Vehement debate, he gained a satisfactory victory over his opponents by a vote of 97 to a meagre 27.

Vindicated, "King Tom" returned to Malta. But his seemingly tireless energy was running out. On the 17th January 1824, after completing his morning's work, he was seized with an apoplectic fit. Shortly after ten in the evening, to the stunned inhabitants of Valetta, came the news that the Governor was dead.

He was buried with great pomp. His body lay in state in the hall he was the first Grand Master. An aide-de-camp stood watch at the head of the coffin and at the foot were displayed the insignia of the three Orders with which he had been honoured. The funeral procession was accompanied by the crash of guns at one-minute intervals. An oration was pronounced over is grave by Count Spiridion Bulgaris, the representative of one of the noblest Corfiote families.

Finally, after all the pomp and glory, came the last simple tribute to a gallant soldier – three volleys of rifle fire.

To "King Tom" the King's Service was everything. No monarch ever acted with more freedom from respect to other men's views, when he thought the King's Service should be advanced. It was said of him that he was a rock – a rock on which one might be saved or dashed to pieces, but always a rock. Even those that called him a rough old despot had to admit that he had a high talent for command, which he always used to the advantage of his country. The benefits of his "reign" as Governor, both in Ceylon and in the Mediterranean, remained to prove his worth.

In Thirlestane Castle there is a fine portrait of Sir Thomas, painted by John Hoppner (1758-1810), the fashionable portrait painter of his days. It shows him in the uniform of a general and wearing the three Grand Crosses of the Orders to which he belonged. Although the Order of St Michael and St George was Sir Thomas's idea and he wore its star set in diamonds on official occasions, it was characteristic of him that in private he scorned such "baubles" as prizes for a man doing his duty. He tersely described it as "the most contemptible thing on earth!" The old Whig fire-eater remained unchanged beneath the orders dangling on his chest.

The Ionian Greeks erected a bronze bust of Sir Thomas on the island of Zakynthos in 1818. It was removed by the Italian army during the last war and probably destroyed, but its original model is to be seen in the Thorwaldsen Museum in Copenhagen devoted to the works of the sculptor, Bertel Thorwaldsen (1770-1844).

Sir Thomas died a bachelor.

25. NINTH TO ELEVENTH EARLS

Little is known about the life of James Maitland, who succeeded his famous father as ninth Earl of Lauderdale.

James was the quiet one of the family, who went about the ordinary business of Member of Parliament and landLord without creating the stir in the world which was the life and breath of his father, uncle cousins and younger brother. It was not in him to compete with a Peregrine, a Frederick Lewis or a Thomas. While Anthony, a year younger than himself, was fighting American privateers in the Atlantic and Barbary pirates in the Mediterranean, James was at home, either at Walthamstow or Thirlestane or Dunbar.

Born in May, 1784, it is likely that the infant James spent much of his boyhood in the old town of Dunbar, for his father had bought a house in the High Street of the seaside burgh in 1788. Surely it was here that the Countess of Lauderdale and her young family lived during Scottish summers and among the rocks of the Lothian coast and down in the antique harbour that the boy Anthony absorbed that liking for the sea which began his naval tradition in the Maitland family.

It was not until 1820 that the ninth Earl became a Member of Parliament, long after the storms of the French

Revolution and Napoleonic Wars. He sat as member for Appleby, the county town of Westmorland, until 1831, when Lord John Russell was closely defeated on his Bill for Parliamentary reform and was succeeded by Lord Grey, who carried through the famous Reform Act of 1832.

It was a time when local government was coming to life after generations of somnolence. The old town councils were being ushered out by the reforms made in the Municipal Corporation Act of 1835 and in Scotland the burghs were modernising themselves. Lauderdale House in Dunbar now became a focal point for interests of the ninth Earl, who was one of Dunbar's earliest provosts under the new dispensation. The was a sphere of public work which best fitted the character of Earl James, who died unmarried in 1860.

He was succeeded by his brother, Anthony, who by that time was Admiral of the Red.

Anthony was no stay at home boy nor was there to be any politics for him. The call of the sea took him into the Royal Navy. Born in June. 1785, as soon as he was old enough to do so, he joined His Majesty's ships as a midshipman on the frigate "Medusa". He soon showed his bold and daring character, when taking part in the close fighting in which the crew of the "Medusa" was engaged during Admiral Lord Nelson's attack on Boulogne flotilla in 1801. He was severely wounded in that engagement but was back on deck as soon as he was fit, for during the first years of war against Napoleon the British effort lay mainly in financing our continental allies against the French armies and in obtaining naval command of the seas.

By the end of the war, Anthony was Captain of the frigate "Pique" in the West Indies. By this time, the United

States of America had been drawn into the war, partly by the disruption of her shipping and partly by the privateering of the Yankees themselves. For both Napoleon and Pitt had blockaded each other, the one to close Europe to the British merchants, the other to close France to world trade. In this situation, the resource and ruth of the commanders of His Majesty's ships counted for most.

Captain Maitland's share in this war of ships is well illustrated by the despatch to the Lords of Admiralty from the Commander-in-Chief, Leeward Islands, dated the 21st June, 1814, which reads:

> "The Captain of H.M.S. "Pique" The Hon, Anthony Maitland, did on the 26th April 1814 capture the American privateer schooner 'Hawk' of four 6-pounders carriage gun, one long 12-pounder and 68 men. Also on January 13th the Swedish ship 'Bernat' laden with flour and a Swedish ship 'Margaret' in ballast on January 19th."

From the West Indies, Captain Maitland was sent by their Lordships of the Admiralty to help in cleaning up the Mediterranean. Already his uncle, Sir Thomas Maitland, was busy organising the civil and military administration of Malta and the Ionian Islands. The remains of the French fleet had turned pirate and were intent on continuing the war from the port of Algiers, where the arsenal established there and the friendship of the Bey / allowed them to rival the exploits of the pirates which had made the whole of the Barbary Coast notorious for generations. This menace to the peace and safety of shipping in the Mediterranean and of the new British bases being established in the inland sea had to be crushed once and for all.

Appointed in 1816 to command the "Glasgow" of 40

guns, Captain Maitland joined Admiral Pellew's squadron which was ordered to bombard and destroy the French fleet and arsenal at Algiers. For this exploit, Admiral Pellew was made Viscount Exmouth and Captain Maitland was made a military companion of the Order of the Bath.

He continued to serve in the Mediterranean until 1821. The year before he was made a Knight Commander of the Order of St Michael and St George, the order which his uncle has promoted to reward service in the creation of the colonies and empire. In later years came further promotion. In 1848, he was appointed Rear-Admiral of the Red, then Vice-Admiral and in 1858 full Admiral of the Red.

The rank of Admiral of the Red requires explanation, as it has been obsolete since 1864. In the Royal Navy of to-day there are four grades of admiral – Admiral of the Fleet, Admiral, Vice Admiral and Rear Admiral. In the days of sail there were only three grades, named from the colours of their flags – admiral of the red, admiral of the white and admiral of the blue – who, in engagements at sea, held the centre, van and rear respectively.

Admiral Maitland succeeded to the earldom in 1860, when he was 75 and long retired from active service. He survived his brother by only three years, dying on 22nd March 1863. Like his brother, he was unmarried, and with him the English title belonging to his father, the eighth Earl, became extinct. The earldom and Scottish titles went to his cousin Admiral Sir Thomas Maitland, eldest son of General William Mordaunt Maitland.

It would have seemed natural if the boy Thomas had decided to follow in his father's footsteps by joining the Army, in which General William Mordaunt had has a long and distinguished career. But perhaps his cousin's exploits in the Senior Service swung him to a life at sea. He joined the Royal Navy when he was thirteen years of age and soon showed that he intended to make his mark. The imperial designs of Napoleon had been defeated but there were still plenty of enterprises and dangers for the British Navy. There were the new colonies to protect and the trade routes to be guarded.

In May, 1823, Thomas was promoted Lieutenant and given command of the "Euryalus". Two years later he was appointed to the "Superb" guardship at Portsmouth and then transferred to the "Ganges", flagship of Admiral Sir Robert Otway, for service in the South American station. Promotion to commander came in 1827. In 1832 as Captain of the "Sparrowhawk" on the West Indian Station, he brought home safely to Britain a treasure freight of half a million dollars and 42 bales of cochineal.

Following this Captain Maitland was posted to the north coast of Spain during the civil war in that country. For his services to the Spanish King, he received the Cross of the Order of Charles III, which he was allowed to wear officially by the Lords of Admiralty.

In June, 1837, he took part in the first Afghan War under Admiral Sir Frederick Lewis Maitland, the veteran of Napoleonic Wars, who was to die on board his flagship off Bombay in November, 1839. After Afghanistan, Captain Maitland played an active part in operations in the Persian Gulf and in China during the First Chinese War of 1840-41.

In 1843, he was Knighted.

When, in 1857, he had risen to the rank of Rear-Admiral, home defence was very much in the minds of the government. Iron and coal, steel plate and steam-driven machinery were now making ironclads a possibility and forward-looking naval men already saw the days of sail would have to be numbered. A Royal Commission was set up to consider the defences of the United Kingdom and one of the men with practical expertise on naval matters who was called upon to be examined on his views was Rear-Admiral Maitland.

While industrial development was forging ahead in Britain and giving new possibilities in arms and ships, France and Germany and the United States were not lagging far behind.

While throughout the Empire there existed many forts and well-protected harbours, Britain itself had no fortified ports. And there was a school of defence which pointed to the great fortifications of Vauban and his imitators.

Maitland had given the whole question of defence and naval strategy much thought. Seizing upon the basic point of the revolutionary techniques that were taking place, he had built up his own strategy, which perhaps may be summed up in the modern times – mobility.

Accordingly, when called upon to give evidence before the Commission, he spoke his mind in forthright manner and argued effectively against the proposed building of fortifications on land, which could be pounded to pieces from ships at sea, if they were left free to do so. He insisted that the vast experience of money envisaged in land defences would be more efficiently employed in the building of modern ships equipped with the challenging dictum:

> "If you can secure being masters of the Channel, I do not see any absolute necessity, as far as security

goes, for fortifying Spithead".

He spoke not only in the spirit of Drake and Nelson, of the sailors who had gone before him, but also with the vision of sailors of the future. Our ports remain unfortified to the present day.

Perhaps Rear-Admiral Maitland was considered too outspoken and should be quietly sent as far away as possible or perhaps he was being rewarded for the soundness of his comments on behalf of the Navy – in any case, his next posting was as Commander-in-Chief Pacific! He had held this position for three years when, in March, 1863, he succeeded his cousin as eleventh Earl of Lauderdale.

In 1873, his naval services were recognised by the award of Knight Grand Cross of the Order of the Bath and he was made principal naval aide-de-camp to Queen Victoria. He became Admiral and in December 1877 was by special promotion advanced to Admiral of the Fleet on the retired list. He died on 1st September, 1878.

Admiral Maitland had married Amelia Young in 1828. Of their four children, only one survived childhood – Mary Jane, who married in January, 1868, Reginald Brabazon, the twelfth Earl of Meath. To commemorate their marriage, a monolithic stone originally brought from the Dye Water, deep in the Lammermuir Hills in the heart of Lauderdale and know in Lauder as the "Lang Stone", was erected by Dabb's Hood. The Brabazons have also paid tribute to the memory of Lady Mary Jane by continuing the use of Maitland as a Christian name in the family.

The title passed to a cousin, Charles Maitland.

26. LIGHTNING STRIKES

Charles Maitland was born on 29th September, 1822, the only son of the Rev. Charles Barclay Maitland, rector of Little Langford in Wiltshire. He was a great-grandson of Charles Maitland, second son of the sixth Earl, who had married a Miss Barclay of Towie.

The new Earl was understood by the family to be an irascible gentleman of nearly sixty years, unmarried and not likely to take kindly to anyone broaching the subject. The immediate succession had been legally settled but there was much speculation over the tea cups in family circles about the future. The twelfth Earl had succeeded by reason of his descent from the sixth Earl. The possible heir would also be a descendent of the sixth Earl but on this point there were serious differences of opinion in the family.

With the sudden death of the Earl on the moors on the opening day for grouse shooting in Scotland in 1884, the question passed from family gossip into a legal dispute for the Lauderdale title.

Charles Maitland was buried in the family vault in the Lauderdale Aisle at Haddington, the last Maitland to be buried there. There is a memorial tablet in bronze, mounted on grey marble and surmounted by the Lauderdale coat-of-arms, in his father's church at Hanging Longford. It reads:

"In Memory of Charles, 12th Earl of Lauderdale, killed by lightning on Braidshaw Rigg Moor, Berwickshire, on the 12th day of August, 1884, aged 62 years. He was the only son of the Rev. Charles Barclay Maitland, formerly Rector of this Parish. Interred in the Family Vault at Haddington Abbey, N.B. Erected by his niece, Harriet Louisa Dyer."

Harriet Dyer was a daughter of the Rev. James Hardwicke Dyer, Vicar of Great Waltham, Essex, who married the Earl's sister, Maria Anna Maitland.

Obsequies over, the law firms of the rivals claimants to the earldom prepared their depositions and began the long struggle in the courts.

The first contender was Major Frederick Henry Maitland, eldest son of Major-General Frederick Henry Maitland, eldest son of Major-General Frederick Colthurst Maitland, son of Patrick Maitland, the second son of Colonel Richard Maitland, fourth son of the sixth Earl.

The second was Sir James Ramsay Gibson Maitland, great-great-grandson in lineal descent of Sir Alexander Maitland, fifth son of the sixth Earl.

The title carried with it the ownership of the large entailed estates in Berwickshire and the legal battle came to be fought with a degree of bitterness that marred relationships between the various lines of the family.

It must be remembered that in the 80s of last century, the pride and prestige of aristocratic precedence was a powerful urge in society. An Earl of Lauderdale could walk with kings and on his own lands, he was himself a miniature royal figure. Actual wealth was enormously enhanced by the tradition of lineage and the social privileges of nobility.

Eventually the issue went before the Committee of Privileges of the House of Lords, which decided that Major Frederick Maitland had substantiated his claim to the earldom and that all the family honours and entailed estates devolved upon him.

His brother, Lieutenant-Colonel George Thomas Maitland, of the Bengal Staff Corps, was granted the rank and precedence of an Earl's son. He died, unmarried, in 1910.

Frederick Henry was born on 16th December, 1840, and according to the pattern established in his family, he entered the Army, as a cornet in the Second Dragoon Guards in February, 1861. On promotion to Lieutenant in 1867, he joined the 4th Hussars and two years later transferred to the Bengal Staff Corps, in which he rose to the rank of Major. Shortly after succeeding to the earldom, he retired from the Army with the rank of Lieutenant-Colonel.

In 1864, he had married Charlotte Sarah Sleigh, daughter of Lt-Col. B.W.A. Sleigh, of the Middlesex Regiment, and there were three sons of the marriage – Frederick Colin, Sydney George William and Alfred Henry.

The thirteenth Earl took his seat in the House of Lords in 1888, having been elected a Representative Peer for Scotland, and was continued in this office until 1918.

After death of Lady Lauderdale in 1879, the Earl married again in 1883 Miss Ada Twyford Simpson, daughter of the Rev. Henry Trail Simpson, Rector of Adel, Yorkshire. Their daughter, Lady Ada Marian Maitland, married Captain Sir Ralph Henry Wilmot, Bt,. of the

Coldstream Guards, who dies of wounds in January, 1918. Lady Wilmot remarried in 1921 Mr Arnold Nield, of Warrington, Lancs.

The thirteenth Earl died in 1924 at Lauriston, St Leonards-on Sea, Sussex. His Countess survived him until 1931.

Frederick Colin Maitland was born on 12th April, 1868, and went into the Army. He married in 1890 Miss Gwendoline Lucy Williams, daughter of Judge R. Vaughan Williams, of Bodlonfa, Flintshire.

He took part in the Boer War, in which his brother, several cousins and other relatives also fought. He served in the Imperial Yeomanry and was mentioned in despatches and received the South Africa Medal with four clasps. Between the Boer War and the Great War, he was assistant director for auxiliary forces on Headquarters Staff. During the first two years of the war and the Great War, he was Lt.Colonel of the 23rd Battalion the Royal Fusiliers and in 1916 was placed in command of the 3rd Garrison Battalion Northumberland Fusiliers.

He was a deputy-Lieutenant and justice of the peace for Berwickshire and was honoured by being appointed a member of the Honourable Corps of Gentleman at Arms. He died on 14th September, 1931, his wife have already died in January, 1929.

Ian Colin Maitland, the 14th Earl, was born on 30th January, 1891, and was educated at Eton. He served in the First World War with his father's regiment as a captain in the 3rd Battalion Queen's Own Cameron Highlanders. In 1916 he was appointed aide-de-camp to the Lord Lieutenant of Ireland and in the following year was promoted Staff Lieutenant. In 1918, he entered the Ministry of Shipping. Before the war, in 1912, he had married Ethel Mary Bell-Irving, the elder daughter of James Jardine Bell-Irving, of Makerstoun, Kelso.

The first of the 14th Earl's two brothers, Sydney George William Maitland, became a clergyman in the Church of England, and the second, Alfred Henry Maitland, joined the Army.

His active service began in the Cameron Highlanders in Lord Kitchener's army in Egypt, when the Camerons took part in the famous advance on Khartoum to rescue General Gordon, in April, 1898, and then in September in the battle of Omdurman, when the Madhi's army was finally defeated. He was awarded the Sudan Medal with two clasps and the Khedive's Bronze Star.

Alfred Maitland was with the Camerons in the Boer War, winning the South Africa Medal with five clasps, and as Major crossed the Channel with the British Expeditionary Force in August 1914. The Camerons went through the battle of Mons and the retreat which was checked at the Battle of the Marne, from which they flung the Germans back on the river Aisne. There the Germans and British began to dig themselves in and the long period of trench warfare began.

It was on the blood-soaked banks of the Aisne that Major Maitland was killed in action on 14th September, 1914. He was 41 years of age and unmarried.

Lady Nora Maitland, sister of the 14th Earl, married Sir William Fitzherbert. 7th baronet, of Tissington Hall, Ashbourne, Derbyshire.

There was one son, Ivor Colin James Maitland, by their marriage and one daughter, Lady Sylvia Gwendoline Eva Maitland, who married in June, 1937, William Francis Conolly-Carew, sixth Lord Carew, of Wexford, and left issue, being two sons and two daughters.

Ivor Colin, Viscount Maitland, was killed in action in North Africa, aged 27. He married, in 1936, aged 21, Helena Ruth Perrott the daughter of Sir Herbert Charles Perrott,. They had three daughters all raised to the rank, style and precedence of an Earl's daughter by Royal Warrant dated 28 October 1953, and published 24 November 1953 in the London Gazette.

The death of the 27-year old Ivor, Viscount Maitland in the North African Campaign was a severe blow to the family, who we return to in our final chapters.

First, the history of other branches of the Maitland's of Scotland.

27. THE MAITLANDS OF ABERDEENSHIRE

It was believed that the progenitor of the Maitlands in the North East was Robert Maitland, one of the Thirlestane family, who married Mary Gordon about the year 1417, heiress to the lands of Gight. In 1435, Robert Maitland of Netherdale witnessed a charter of James Dunbar of Frendraught, in which is he styled "Dominus de Schivas" – that is, Laird of Schivas.

The Maitlands of Balhalgardy maintain the tradition that their lands were held by Maitlands as far back as the Battle of Harlaw, which was fought over their ground, in 1411. It is reasonable to suppose that the migration of Robert Maitland to Aberdeenshire and his marriage into the Gordons was connected with the battle, for the army which marched out of Aberdeen to face the Wolf of Badenoch must have contained many young Southern Knights. It is also significant that Maitland of Schivas witnessed a Dunbar Charter, for the Maitlands had married into the Dunbars, another Border family which spread into the North East during this period.

Patrick Maitland, Robert's son, was heir to Schivas and Gight and married Margaret Innes, but the marriage produced no heir and the estates passed into the possession of George Gordon, Earl of Huntly.

269

The Poll Book of 1695 records Robert Maitland as being owner of Balhalgardy.

Adam Maitland, described as a manufacturer, of Insch married Janet Mearns, a daughter of the Rev. Alexander Mearns, who was minister of Insch from 1729 to 1789. Their son, Adam, farmed Balquhain, in the Chapel of Garioch, and married Janet Gray, a daughter of Thomas Gray and Mary Cuthbert, of Easterton, Fyvie. It is known that there were two sons of this marriage. Duncan Mearns Maitland, born in 1806, emigrated to Australia and became a surveyor. His eldest son, Duncan Mearns Maitland, was also a surveyor and did much to open up the back blocks of Australia. He married Emily Dalgetty and their two sons were Geoffrey and Herbert Lethington.

Herbert Lethington Maitland was born in November, 1868, and educated at Sydney University, where he graduated M.B., Ch.B., in 1892. He spent his whole life in the medical profession in Sydney, was Knighted in 1915, and became known as a master of surgical technique. He was one of the first surgeons to take out an appendix and during his career he performed 4,000 appendectomies without losing a single patient. He died in May, 1923. Both his sons entered the medical profession.

At the time of writing, Geoffrey Douglas Maitland is lecturer in physiotherapy at the University of Adelaide and is author of two standard manuals on the subject.

Andrew Gibb Maitland was born in Huddersfield in November, 1864, the only son of George Maitland. His grand-father was Andrew Maitland, bookseller, a native of Aberdeen. In his early twenties, Andrew carried out extensive geological field work in the coal districts of Yorkshire and at the age of 24, he went to Australia as assistant geologist on the Queensland. In 1891, he made a general Geological survey of British New Guinea.

When the Geological Surveys Department of Western Australia was established in 1896, Andrew Gibb Maitland was asked to be its first director, a post he held for thirty years.

He found that there was a tract extending along the coast for nearly three hundred miles south of the North West Cape which was suitable as a pastoral area but for the lack of water.

On his recommendation the Government put down a bore near Carnarvon to a depth of 3,011 feet and struck water, bringing up over half a million gallons a day. As a result, more than a hundred bores have been put down in the coastal parts of Western Australia.

Maitland's geological survey of the Pilbara goldfields, when he surveyed and mapped an area of over 30,000 square miles, was a remarkable pioneering achievement. His work had not only had great practical results but also scientific value. His discovery and study of the immensely old rock formations in Western Australia, which is named the nullagine series, places his name firmly in the history of geology. To commemorate his pioneer work, a rare compound of thorium and uranium first found at Wodgina has been names Maitlandite in his honour.

He capped his scientific and practical work by a splendid venture into the field of education. In the early days of broadcasting, his popular talks on geology had a big listening public.

His elder son is Dr G.B.G. Maitland, O.B.E., D.S.O., C.D.M., E.D., of Perth, Western Australia, and his younger son, Mr A.J.G. Maitland, M.B.E., is manager of the Distillers Agency Ltd for South Australia. His two daughters are Mrs E.C. Johnston, of Sandringham, Victoria, and Mrs M.U Hubbe, of Kojonup, Western Australia.

The record of the Maitlands in the field of medicine begins with Charles Maitland, of Methlick, Aberdeenshire, who was the pioneer of inoculation for smallpox. His father, Patrick Maitland, of Little Ardoch, Methlick, probably belonged to the Pitrichie branch of the family. Born in 1668, Charles was educated at Aberdeen University. Nothing is known about him until in 1717 he was appointed physician to the English Ambassador at Constantinople, Lord Edward Wortley Montagu.

In Turkish capital, Maitland (as he himself described)

> "had a fair opportunity fully to inform myself of what I had long heard, namely, the famous practice of transplanting or raising the smallpox by inoculation."

The almost universal prevalence of smallpox, its lethal results and the unsightly pockmarks which it left on those who recovered, made it a disease which was dreaded. The Ambassador's wife, Lady Mary Wortley Montagu, found that smallpox was widespread in Constantinople and instructed Dr Maitland to inoculate her four-year-old son. He was at first hesitant about carrying out the experiment but there was no resisting Lady Mary's belief in the virtue of the process and his ability to apply it successfully. The idea of a preventative measure of this sort fascinated Lady Mary and she became the first advocate of inoculation.

Writing from Constantinople to a friend, she declared that she intended to bring the "useful invention of ingrafting of the smallpox into fashion in England." When, on her return to England, she discovered that there was an epidemic of smallpox in the City, she had Dr Maitland inoculate her three-year-old daughter. Maitland called in three members of the college of Physicians on this case and one of them, Dr James Keith, was so impressed that he had Maitland inoculate his son, aged nearly six, who was the only son of his children who had not fallen ill of the disease. The inoculation was a complete success.

The Prince of Wales was an enthusiast of science and new inventions and under his patronage a public experiment was organised. Six prisoners at Newgate Prison were chosen to act as guinea-pigs, with the reward of a free pardon. In August, 1721, three male convicts and three women were inoculated by Maitland under the supervision of the royal physicians and before a gathering of surgeons, physicians and apothecaries. Three days later, because the incisions were not so inflamed as he wished, Maitland repeated the operation. The results were satisfactory and in September the six convicts were pardoned and released.

In 1722, he assisted the King's surgeon to inoculate Princesses Amelia and Caroline. He then published, "Mr Maitland's Account of Inoculating the Smallpox." This aroused strong opposition from the churches. But Maitland continued undeterred and by the end of the year had completed 57 inoculations. His case-work was meticulously recorded: his reports for 1728, written in his fine handwriting, are to be seen in the British Museum.

At that time, Maitland was the only doctor in Britain doing inoculations. The treatment was still in its experimental stage and it was finally made safe by the work of Dr Edward Jenner (1749-1823), who discovered the method of inoculating with cowpox. Charles Maitland died in Aberdeen in 1748, aged 80, and is remembered by a stone in the old kirkyard at Methlick and by the Maitland Trust for the poor of the parish, still being administered by the Kirk Session. An obituary in the "Aberdeen Journal" of February 7, 1748, wrote:

> "He is reckoned to have left £5,000 sterling, to a considerable portion of which his cousins, Alexander Bannerman of Frendraught, and Mr Charles Cheyne, Merchant, Edinburgh, have succeeded."

28. THE REVERENDS

The Royal Burgh of New Galloway is on the River Ken in the Glenkens of Kirkcudbright. Nestling on the hillside overlooking the little town is Kells Kirk, surrounded by weathered head-stones in the ancient graveyard. The Kirk stands four square in enclosed ground, unperturbed by the changes of time. Below the Ken winds its chuckling course through a rich carse that has filled the barns and stackyards of generation upon generation of prosperous farmers. To the south lies Loch Ken, on the west bank of which stands Kenmure, the ancestral seat of Gordons of Kenmure and Lochinvar. Farther afield are Barcaple, Valleyfield and Tongland. This at one time was all Maitland country, for in 1525, James Maitland, a scion of the Lauderdale family, came into possession of the lands of Eccles and his descendants spread south as far as Cumstoun and Dundrennan, Balgreggan, Freugh and Garthland in the Rhinns o' Galloway.

But the graves at the back of Kells Kirk are not of these Maitlands but of a family whose origins were rooted in the North East of Scotland. The principal stone reads:

> "To the Memory of the Rev. James Maitland, D.D., D.L., J.p., of the Stewartry of Kirkcudbright, 46 years Minister of this Parish. Born at Minigaff 18th October, 1797, ordained Minister at Kells, September 1826. Received the Degree of Doctor of

Divinity from Glasgow 1852. Moderator of the
General Assembly 1860. Died 21st September,
1872."

The Very Reverend Dr James Maitland was a true son of
the manse. His father was the Rev. John Garlies Maitland of
Fairgirth, a graduate of Glasgow University, who was
ordained in 1789 and became minister of the now ruined
Kirk in the old village of Minigaff. He must have been held
in high repute, for he was nominated to be Moderator of
the General Assembly, the highest honour the Kirk can
bestow, but for some unknown reason he declined. He died
in 1835.

His father was the Rev. James Maitland, minister of
Sorbie, Wigton, for 36 years. He graduated at Marischal
College, Aberdeen in 1729, was ordained in 1738 and died
in 1774 at the age of 62, so that whole ministry was spent at
Sorbie. The patron was the Earl of Galloway, whose family
resting place is in the ruins of the old Kirk at Sorbie. The
Earl is also Lord Garlies, and Galloway House, a little to the
south of Garlieston, Wigton, was once the family seat.

The father of the minister at Sorbie was the Rev. John
Maitland, minister of Banchory-Devenick, Kincardineshire.
He has a brother, Richard, who was also a minister, first of
Aberchirder and then of Inverkeithney. The Rev. Richard
Maitland had two sons, again both ministers: Richard,
minister of Nigg, Aberdeen, who was deposed in 1715 as a
Jacobite, and John (1634-1698) who followed his father as
minister of Inverkeithney, whose grandson, John, was
chaplain to Lord Strathallen, was chaplain to the Jacobite
Army at Culloden and went into exile in France.

So far as can be discovered, the originator of all these
ministers was Peter Maitland, advocate in Aberdeen, whose

grandfather was yet another minister, the Rev. Walter Maitland (1588-1612) of King Edward, Aberdeenshire, a descendant of Robert Maitland of Auchincrieve, one of the Pitrichie family.

From the family history it will be realised that the very Rev. James Maitland of Kells had a powerful ecclesiastical tradition in his blood. Little is known about his early years. He served as an assistant in one of the Edinburgh churches before his ordination in at Kells in 1826 but it was there that he spent the whole of his pastorship. He was both minister and Laird, for he owned considerable landed property in Wigton and Kirkcudbright. For many years he was president of the Glenkens Agricultural Society and was Deputy Lieutenant of the Stewartry. The crowning moment of his career came in 1860, when he was chosen to be Moderator of the General Assembly, the honour which had been declined by his father.

Dr Maitland was twice married, first in 1826 to Jessie Norval, daughter of Captain Corby Norval of Boghall, Linlithgowshire, and secondly, in 1837 to Louisa Gordon, eldest daughter and heiress of the Hon. Mrs Bellamy Gordon of Kenmure. The 8th Viscount Kenmure having died in 1847 without male issue, their daughter, Louisa, who had married Charles Bellamy, became known as Mrs Louisa Bellamy Gordon of Kenmure. Their daughter in her turn became known as Mrs Louisa Maitland Gordon of Kenmure (1817-1890).

The Doctor's sister, Mary, married Lieutenant-Colonel John Hobbs of the Royal Engineers, who was responsible for the construction of the roads in Kandy, Ceylon, so establishing a link with Sir Thomas Maitland, who was then Governor of the colony. Their elder daughter, Elizabeth White Hobbs, married Dr William Henry Maitland, the

medical officer in the East India Company in the service of
Nizam of Hyderabad. This joined the Kells family with the
Maitlands of Eccles.

29. THE MAITLANDS OF ECCLES

James Maitland, a descendant of the Sir Robert Maitland of Thirlestane (who was killed at the Battle of Neville's Cross in 1346), was in 1525, possession of the lands of Eccles and Penpoint in Dumfries-shire. From him branched the Maitlands of Barcaple and the Maitlands of Dundrennan.

At the end of the 17th century, the Rev. William Maitland, a son of Robert Maitland of Eccles, was minister of Beith, Ayrshire. He married three times, his third wife being Mary McMichan, joint heiress with her sister, Rachel, of her father's estate of Barcaple, Kirkcudbright. On her father's death, Mary Maitland settled two-thirds of her inheritance on her son, the Rev. Alexander Maitland, minister of Tongland, and one-third on her other son, John. At a later date, the Rev. Alexander Maitland purchased from his aunt, Rachel, her half of her father's property of Barcaple. He died in 1746 and his eldest son, David, acquired from the heirs of his Uncle John his part of Barcaple and thus become in full David Maitland of Barcaple. His younger brother, Alexander, was in possession of Nether Barcaple or Valleyfield.

David Maitland of Barcaple had four sons: David, who succeeded him in Barcaple: Alexander, who became owner of Chipperkyle: Adam, who married the heiress of Dundrennan, and Robert, who went to America and settled there.

Dr Charles Maitland of Eccles, who wrote the famous Leyden Thesis on Scurvy died in 1724 and was buried at Penpont. His son, Charles, left an only daughter, Grizel, who married John Bushby. He, in the customary fashion, took the name of Maitland. Their eldest son, John Bushby Maitland of Eccles was admitted to the Faculty of Advocates in Scotland in 1788 and was Sheriff of Wigton from 1794 until 1818. He sat as Member of Parliament for Camelford for two years before his death in 1822.

Their son, John (1792-1865), became a solicitor and for 25 years was connected with the Edinburgh firm of Walker and Melville before going to London as a parliamentary solicitor, setting up practice with a partner as Maitland and Graham. He was a solicitor for the General Assembly of the Church of Scotland and parliamentary agent for the City of Edinburgh and many other corporations. During the administration of Lord Derby, the firm were the Government's agents in all Scottish parliamentary business.

John's son, Kenmure, was apprenticed to the firm in Edinburgh with which his father was connected (now Walker, Richardson and Melville, W.S. While a conveyancing clerk, he was appointed by Sheriff Gordon to assist in taking the 1851 census and as a result entered the Sheriff-Clerk's office. In 1859 he became Sheriff-Clerk of Midlothian. In private life, he was a writer of humorous songs and ballads and was the author of the last two pantomimes produced by the Theatre Royal, Edinburgh, before his death.

His only son, John Gordon Maitland (1848-1884), was admitted advocate in 1873 and became produrator-fiscal for Berwickshire. He married Kate Wyndham, the daughter of

R.H. Wyndham, the agent of the Theatre Royal, Edinburgh, who survived him until her death in July, 1930.

The second David Maitland of Barcaple had one son, David. A son of the Rev. William Maitland of Beith, John, who had the estate of Tongland, was married three times. One son, Robert, went to London and commenced merchant, at Kings Arm Yard, Coleman Street. He prospered and two of his sons became active in the City of London. Ebenezer Maitland, of Clapham Common, became a director of the Bank of England. His son was Ebenezer Fuller-Maitland of Stansted, Essex.

Robert Maitland became a West India merchant in Basinghall Street, married Elizabeth Ridge, only child and heir of John Ridge, of Kingston, Sussex, and established Maitland House at Blue Stile, Greenwich. His eldest daughter, Mary Anne, married in July, 1792, Joseph Wilson, a younger son of Joseph Wilson of Highbury Hill Little Massingham, Norfolk, and Stowlangtoft, Suffolk.

Their son, Henry (1797-1866), married Mary Fuller-Maitland, daughter of Ebenezer Fuller-Maitland, and the family adopted the surname of Maitland-Wilson. Their eldest son, who married Agnes Caroline Kindersley, a second daughter of Sir Richard Torin Kindersley, had three sons, two of whom had brilliant military careers.

The eldest, Arthur (1857-1934), was captain in the Suffolk Regiment and High Sheriff of Suffolk. Henry Fuller Maitland-Wilson joined the Rifle Brigade in 1878 and after rising to become Colonel in command of the 2nd battalion, eventually became Lieutenant-General Sir Henry Fuller Maitland-Wilson.

He married Charlotte Elsie Gough, a daughter of the

celebrated cavalry commander, General Sir Hugh Henry Gough, V.C.

The two sons of Arthur Maitland-Wilson had brilliant careers in the Army. Henry (1881-1964) was a Lieutenant-General and in command of the Rifle Brigade in 1939, when the Second World War began. He was appointed to command the British Army in Egypt and led it to success in the initial advance in Libya, capturing Bardia, Tobruk and Benghazi. In February, 1941, he was placed in command of the short and ill-fated Greek campaign and was then appointed Commander-in-Chief, Palestine and Trans-Jordan, later being transferred to the Persia-Iraq Command.

In February, 1943, he assumed the Middle East Command and at the end of the year succeeded General Eisenhower as Commander-in-Chief of the Mediterranean. But there was still more important work to be done. The death of Field-Marshall Sir John Dill, head of the Inter-Service Mission in Washington, left a vacancy for an outstanding military diplomat. In appointing General Maitland-Wilson, Winston Churchill wrote to him:

> "I can find only one officer with the necessary credentials and qualities, namely yourself."

Maitland-Wilson was given Field-Marshall rank. After the war he was created Baron Wilson of Libya and Stowlang-toft.

His son, Patrick Maitland Wilson, 2nd Baron Wilson was born on 14 September 1915. He married Storeen Violet Campbell, daughter of Archibald James Hamilton Douglas-Campbell and Hon. Anna Leonora Beatrice Massey, on 12 January 1945.

30. THE MAITLANDS OF MONTROSE

The founder of this branch of the Maitlands was William Maitland, the 18th century historian. He is supposed to have been born in Brechin, Angus, about 1690. As a merchant he travelled in Sweden, Germany and Denmark and having made his fortune, settled down in London, 1730, and became an antiquarian writer, In 1733, he was elected a fellow of the Royal Society and two years later a fellow of the society of Antiquaries. In 1739 he published "The History of London" and followed this up in 1753 with "The History of Edinburgh," both full of curious information. By this time he had returned to Scotland and died in Montrose in July, 1757, and was buried in the old kirkyard. He left over 10,000, a considerable fortune for that time.

William Maitland was unmarried and the heir was his sister, Lilias Maitland, who married Robert Ramsay. Her daughter, Katherine, married to James Pyott, junior, a merchant and Baillie of Montrose, and on their inheriting the considerable part of Uncle William's fortune, Pyott took the name of Maitland, under the old Scottish custom when a wife inherited an entail.

This James Maitland had thirteen children by his wife

Katherine and another six by his second wife, Marjory Coupar. Not all these families have been traced and we will deal with the fortunes of two of the sons.

William Maitland settled in Exeter and had a family of five sons and three daughters. Elizabeth married Colonel William Jervois and their son became Sir William Francis Drummond Jervois, C.B., Governor of the Straits Settlement, Australia and New Zealand. His son, Thomas Henry Maitland entered the Church and one of his sons, Edward Jervois Maitland, founded and was headmaster of Banstead Hall School, Surrey, being succeeded as headmaster by his son, John Edward.

Another son, Robert Forsyth Maitland, had a son, Paul Fordyce Maitland, (1863-1909), who became well known as "the artist of Kensington Gardens."

Edward James Snow Maitland (1811-1864) was a wine importer, who travelled widely, but had a permanent residence in Montreal, where he became one of the city notables. A William Maitland was one of the shareholders of the Bank of Montreal and it is presumed that this was Snow Maitland's father. When King Edward VII as the Prince of Wales visited Canada in 1860, Snow Maitland acted as his host. He married in 1839, Mary Ann Bell, daughter of General Sir George Bell, and died in 1864 at Marseilles where he was buried.

His son, Captain William George Maitland (1840-1878), after service in India and China, became a tea planter at Dibroogar, Assam, and was buried in the English Cemetery in Shillong.

Edward Snow Maitland's daughter, Margaretta Marianne, married Arthur Gee, a barrister, of Shudy Camps

Park who assumed the name of Maitland in 1903.

Their eldest son, Brigadier-General Edward Maitland Maitland, C.M.G., D.S.O., A.F.C F.R.G.S. was an outstanding pioneer of aviation at a time when lighter-than-air craft were being developed. He became a second Lieutenant in the 2nd Battalion of the Essex Regiment and 1900 and in 1906 was made Adjutant of the 3rd Battalion.

Turning to the new sport of ballooning that was exciting the world, in 1908, when Major C.C Turner induced the "Daily Graphic" to sponsor a balloon flight, Edward Maitland was one of the three aviators who carried out the voyage of 1,117 miles to land in a snowstorm at Mateki Derevni, forty miles from Dvinsk in Russia.

In the following year he was appointed to the Balloon School, South Farnborough, and in 1910 to the Air Battalion. He was the first Army officer to build an aeroplane at his own expense. He subsequently sold it to the War Office. It was styled, "No. 1." and was the forerunner of the Royal Air Force. The Royal Flying Corps was formed in 1913 and Maitland was given the post of Commanding Officer No. 1 Squadron (Airships).

During the war he played a leading part in the use of kite balloons and parachutes for reconnaissance work and worked energetically for an airship building programme. On the formation of the Royal Air Force in 1918, he was promoted Brigadier-General and held the equivalent rank of Air-Commodore in the new force, holding pilot's certificates for aeroplanes, balloons and airships.

He took part in the epoch-making flight of the airship R34 to New York and back and later published his "Log of H.M, Airship R34." In August, 1921, the latest airship, R38, set off on her trials, with Maitland aboard.

Over the Humber she made a sudden turn, there was a tremendous explosion, the dirigible cracked in half and went up in a sheet of flame. There were only five survivors. General Maitland's career was ended in middle age, for he was only 41.

Of the other children: Henry Maitland Maitland was an author and soldier. Ethel Marion Maitland married Brigadier-General Frederick Gore Anley. Margaret Emma married Major George Whitaker of the Coldstream Guards. Major Whitaker was an enthusiastic yachtsman and built his own three-master schooners, one of which, the "Margherita", beat Kaiser's Meteor II." Kathleen married the Hon. Claude Maitland Patrick Brabazon, whose mother, the Countess of Neath, was Lady Mary Jane Maitland, only daughter of the 11th Earl of Lauderdale.

Snow Maitland's second son, Augustus Wetherall Maitland, married Amy Katherine Prescot, daughter of Col. Arthur Prescot of the Bombay Light Cavalry. Their eldest son, Arthur Edward, was Lieutenant-Colonel of the Essex Regiment and won the M.C. and D.S.O. in the First World War and was mentioned four times in despatches. Their daughter, Florence Isobel Maitland, is a well-known painter. She is probably the only exponent of portraits in the style of 16th century Limoges enamels. Their son, William George Bell-Maitland, is an authority on Kipling and was a librarian of the Kipling Society for thirty years.

31. THE CLAN CHIEFS

Turning back to the Earls and Clan Chiefs, the death previously described, in 1914, of the young Viscount Maitland in the Great War, North African Campaign, left as heir his cousin, the Rev. Alfred Sydney George William Maitland.

He was the elder son of Sydney George William Maitland, second son of the 13th Earl. Sydney Maitland, after serving as a Lieutenant in the Royal Scots Fusiliers, entered the Church of England and became Rector of Ingstre, Staffordshire who died in August 1946.

His elder son was born in 1904 and educated at Westminster School and Sydney Sussex College. He went to Cambridge to read theology and graduated B.A,. later taking his M.A.

For many years he was priest-in-charge at St John's West Worthing and in 1953 was appointed curate at All Saints, Woodham, Working. From 1957 until he retired because of ill-health in 1960, he was Rector of Catsfield, Sussex.

The Rev. Alfred Maitland's first wife, Norah Mary La Touche, whom he married in August, 1938, died in November of the same year. Two years later, he married Irene Alice May Shipton, daughter of the Rev. Charles Percy Shipton, of Halsham, Yorkshire. There was no issue.

When the Rev. Alfred Maitland became Earl of Lauderdale in 1953, his brother, Patrick Francis Maitland, was given the precedence of an Earl's son, with the title of Master of Lauderdale, and his sister, Ella Mary was given the precedence of an Earl's daughter. Lady Mary had married in September, 1932, Mr John Alder Cripps Blumer, formerly of the Education Department of Tanganyika, third son of Dr F.M. Blumer, of the Mount, Stafford.

It was largely owing to the interest and enthusiasm of the Master of Lauderdale for everything connected with the family of Maitland and the Lauderdale heritage that the Maitland's became officially recognised as a clan, that a Maitland tartan was devised and officially approved by the Lord Lyon King of Arms and that the Clan Maitland Society was inaugurated.

His brother, the Earl, was also enthusiastic but, unfortunately, his health did not allow him to be active and he delegated many of his official duties to his brother.

Patrick Francis Maitland, 17th Earl of Lauderdale succeeded his brother on November 27, 1968.

With the succession of, at the time of writing, the present Earl, the history of the family turned away from Navy, Army and Church, the spheres in which for so long it has played a notable part, to return to the old tradition of politics and the pen.

Born on 17th March, 1911, Patrick Maitland was educated at Lancing College and took his B.A. degree at Brasenose College, Oxford, in 1933. He entered the profession of journalism, by getting a job as an office boy for the Daily Mail's Vienna correspondent, returning to

Fleet Street as a sub-editor at the Mail.

Following a time in Rome, late in 1938 "The Times" sent him as their correspondent in the Balkans. A linguist with half a dozen languages, he was well equipped for a life as a foreign correspondent. A life of danger and adventure, commenced, graphically told in his book, "European Dateline."

He saw Czechoslovakia blow apart, Albania seized by the Italians, Poland invaded by Russians and Germans, Hungary, Romania and Bulgaria undermined, the Nazi assault on Greece and the fall of Yugoslavia.

He married Stanka, the eldest daughter of Professor Milivoye Losanitch of Belgrade, Yugoslavia in 1936. They had two daughters and two sons. Prior to the start of World War II, he sent his wife and family to New York before the impending invasion by Germany into Yugoslavia. He was a war correspondent during the second world war.

A special assignment for the "News Chronicle" sent him to Washington and then he was war correspondent for the same paper in the Pacific and Far East until 1943. On his return to London he was employed in the Foreign Office until 1945. In the same year he launched the Fleet Street Letter, a vehicle for his views and a springboard into politics.

In the 1951 General Election, he was returned as Conservative Member for Lanark and represented the constituency until 1959. During this period he published his second book, "Task for Giants," a thoughtful survey of the Commonwealth and its future.

After succeeding to the Earldom, he registered the Maitland tartan, and made a worldwide appeal for Maitlands to come forward to the clan.

The Earl restored the Lauderdale Aisle (built by the Earl of Lauderdale about 1635) to be used as a Chapel by the mainstream churches; it was consecrated by the Anglican Bishop of Edinburgh as the Shrine of Our Lady of Haddington, to be known as the Three Kings Chapel and the Shrine of Our Lady of Haddington. The Shrine is located in St. Mary's Parish Kirk in Haddington, Scotland. Each year a pilgrimage is held for all faiths to attend.

As the 17th holder of the Earldom, created in 1624, he is Chieftain of the Clan Maitland and the hereditary bearer of the national flag of Scotland, bestowed in 1790. His earnest spirit about the Maitlands can be seen from his words, in one of his annual messages for the Clan Maitland Newsletter (early 1970s):

> "I pray earnestly I may be a wise and worthy Chief to my Clan."

END.

ABOUT THE AUTHOR

Rognvald A. Livingstone wrote and edited the Clan Maitland Newsletter from 1963 to 1970 This book, which he intended to publish, is mainly drawn from the Clan Maitland newsletters, which he wrote and edited, and other research.

Born in 1902 in Kingston Jamaica, he is the youngest son of author and editor, William P. Livingstone. His family, on return to the United Kingdom in 1904, firstly lived in London and then in Edinburgh. Rognvald was educated at Alleyn College, Dulwich, London and George Watson's College in Edinburgh.

Rognvald A. Livingstone joined the Royal Bank of Scotland and was transferred, at the age of 22, to be bank manager of several Allahabad Banks in India. While manager of the Nagpur Branch he married Anne Maitland in 1934. They had one son Rognvald Maitland Livingstone, born 27th January 1935.

Returning to the UK in 1939 Rognvald A. Livingstone acted as a special constable during WW2 and joined the Marine Research Laboratory in Aberdeen, the home of his wife Anne Maitland of the Balhalgardy Maitland line. Always interested in family history, he became editor of the Clan Maitland Newsletter.

A lesser-known fact is that, as a result of a letter to the minister of Athelstaneford, East Lothian, Rognvald A. Livingstone became the instigator for a memorial and Saltire (Scottish Flag) now being flown there. The letter included the words:

> *"You will doubtless be aware of the legend of how the King of Scots [Achaius] prayed before battling with the Saxon King [Athelstane] and how, in answer to the prayer, a white cross in the form of the letter 'X' appeared in the blue sky and the Saxon King [Athelstane] was defeated. Ever after the Scots carried a blue flag with a white St. Andrew's cross on it and it is therefore our national flag."*

After Rognvald. A. Livingstone's death, at the age of 69 the completed manuscript of this book passed to his son R. Maitland Livingstone. This book is reproduced in 2015 faithfully in accordance with the editors notes and Rognvald. A. Livingstone's wishes, as noted in correspondence between the author and a gentleman called Frank Maitland.

Despite our efforts, we have thus far found out little about Frank Maitland whose correspondence to the author was in the file alongside the original manuscript. It is apparent from these letters that Frank Maitland conducted the editing of the manuscript in 1971 and his contribution is acknowledged. On the date of publication (2015) we have not yet managed to trace him (or his family), although we hope to do so.

Publication, in 2015, is in memory of Rognvald A. Livingstone, and on the occasion of his son Rognvald Maitland Livingstone's eightieth birthday.

The Maitlands of Lauderdale

Rognvald A. Livingstone

www.ingramcontent.com/pod-product-compliance
Lightning Source LLC
LaVergne TN
LVHW050044090426
835510LV00043B/2804